Canine Adventures

Canine Adventures

Fun Things to Do with Your Dog

CYNTHIA D. MILLER

Animalia Publishing Company
Yuba City, CA

Individual Sales. Animalia publications are available through most bookstores or can be ordered directly from Animalia Publishing at the address below.

Quantity Sales. Special discounts are available on quantity purchases by corporations, associations, and other organizations. For details, contact the "Special Sales Department" at the Animalia Publishing address below.

Animalia Publishing Company
P.O. Box 1390
Yuba City, CA 95992
(530) 755-1318 Fax: (530) 755-2695
Toll Free: (888) 755-1318
e-mail: animalia@jps.net

Library of Congress Cataloging-in-Publication Data

Miller, Cynthia D.
     Canine adventures: fun things to do with your dog/Cynthia D. Miller—1st ed.
          p. cm.
     Includes bibliographical references and index.
     ISBN 0-9649413-0-9
     1. Dogs. 2. Dog sports. 3. Dogs—shows. I. Title
     636.7MIL   98-96556

Interior design: Joel Friedlander, Marin Bookworks
Printed in the United States of America
10 9 8 7 6 5 4 3 2 1

Contents

• The Immune System and Stress • The Source of Stress
• The Signs of Too Much Stress • What You Can Do

• Good Manners • Loose Leash • Leashless—The
Unpredictable Dog • The Ultimate Safety Device—A
Reliable Recall

• Concrete • Asphalt • Gravel • Dirt • Grass

• Rain • Heat • Fog • Cold • Wind • Snow

To my family—Kyle, Alessandra, Rebekah, and Rachael—you mean the world to me.

To Snippy, Sheba, Shasta, Sierra, Retta, Mike, Cody, and Rex, the dogs in my life who have shown me unconditional, canine love.

Acknowledgments

It would be impossible to create a book I could be proud of if not for the support and expertise of Sharon Goldinger. Thanks again.

I am especially grateful to all the wonderful people in the "dog world" who took time out of their busy schedules to fill out questionnaires and talk to me. On the top of my list is Bob Levorsen who has capably dealt with any question I had and provided me with much information.

I must acknowledge all the impressive canine athletes that I have been fortunate enough to watch perform while researching this book. They have shown me the pure joy dogs express while partipating in fun activities with their owners.

And as for my own canine athletes, each has, in his or her own way, taught me many lessons. I am most indebted to Cody, who will try anything I ask and learns it seemingly in one try. Thanks, Cody, for being my guinea pig.

Introduction

Welcome to the exciting adventure of canine activities! You have begun a quest that will lead you to new experiences and expanded knowledge, introduce you to "microworlds" that you didn't even know existed, and get you involved and active in a new endeavor—and you get to do it all with your beloved canine.

What are some of the advantages of engaging your dog in an activity or sport?

Most importantly, you get to spend time with your dog. The hours you spend together will enhance your friendship and help you to appreciate all the wonderful talents and gifts—and love—that your dog offers you.

Engaging in exercise will also lessen the stress in your dog's life and help him better cope with the stress that does come his way. Your dog is continually asked to inhibit his natural flight/fight/freeze response in his home environment. This built-up anxiety is one of the leading causes of stress in our dogs. Exercise helps your dog release this anxiety and live more comfortably within your behavioral boundaries.

Beginning a fitness program with your dog will also alter his energy level. If he has been a couch potato, your dog will become spunky (or at least spunkier). You may even be able to convince him that a game of fetch is not an insult to his royal life of leisure. If your dog is the opposite—too energetic—a vigorous exercise regimen will burn off some of that extra energy and allow him to relax. Exercise will put his brain to work also. Otherwise, your dog may find something else to put his mind to—like how to get to the cat's litter box.

Your dog's health will benefit from regular physical activity. The aging process will slow down, and you will have your fit, smart dog around longer. Your dog's immune system will become stronger, and he will be able to fight off illness and disease better. Exercise stimulates a dog's metabolic and circulatory systems, helping his body remove wastes more thoroughly. Regular exercise also helps keep off excess fat and its accompanying problems, such as diabetes and heart disease.

To top off all these benefits, exercise increases the production of endorphins, and although we can't be absolutely sure, these hormones appear to affect our dogs in the same way they affect us, making them feel good. Doesn't your dog seem happier, more content, and calmer after a good run?

With all these good reasons to be active with your dog, do you sometimes wonder how to begin? That is the purpose of this book—to help you find an activity (or two or three) that both you and your dog will enjoy and to show you how to prepare your dog's mind and body for the activity's physical and mental demands. The sport you choose can be casual and uncomplicated or intense and increasingly challenging. You can start with a basic activity that has few requirements and then expand from there if you and your dog would like to. This book will explain the theory and techniques for increasing fitness in your dog, no matter what his present level of ability. It will also discuss performance-enhancement techniques so that if you decide to compete in your newfound adventure, you and your dog can get the most out of it.

Part II of this book—"Quick Peeks"—is devoted to providing information about many different activities and sports for the canine enthusiast. You can browse through it and enjoy the possibilities. See the introduction to part II to learn more about the quick peeks.

For convenience, when referring to your dog, I have alternated the pronouns *he* and *she* at each chapter. Of course, the advice in this book applies to dogs of both sexes.

My goal in writing this book was to give caring dog lovers knowledge, to stimulate their imaginations, and to convince them to get out and become active with their dogs. I urge you to try some of the activities discussed. Life holds many adventures, but could there be a more satisfying pursuit than a canine adventure?

Part I

The Adventure

A long time ago, at the beginning of creation, a great earthquake shook the world. A vast abyss began to separate the earth—humans on one side and the animals on the other. As the chasm grew more immense the animals escaped to the safety of the woods. All except the dog. The dog jumped the chasm in a moment of bravery and dedication, to separate from the world of the other animals and forever live with humans.

NATIVE AMERICAN FOLKTALE

CHAPTER ONE

So Many
Exciting Choices

A Bit of History

The story goes that 13,000 years ago, a primitive human made friends with a wolf. While we don't really know how the ancestors of humans and dogs came to live so closely together, what we do know is that this has been the closest, longest-lasting friendship between humans and another species. Dogs are devoted to us and have been by our sides through history. I firmly believe that without dogs, we humans would not have been able to accomplish what we have. We even might not have survived. Although dogs haven't always benefited from their devotion to us, they seem to retain the desire to make us happy. They are still very much our treasured friends in a turbulent world.

Through generations and generations of selective breeding, we humans were able to create companions who could herd, pull carts and sleds, stand guard, and hunt for us. What started out as friendly get-togethers to see whose dog could herd (or hunt, run, or pull) the best evolved into large organized events. The competitions gave breeders a chance to show off the talents of hard-working canines and to exhibit the prowess of a particular bloodline. The results helped the breeders, who also used these dogs for labor, to choose only the most talented of canine stars to breed.

Competitions of this kind were once the only activities besides work that dogs and humans could enjoy together. Today we dog lovers are fortunate to have a remarkable array of activities to choose from. It seems new sports or activities come into existence as fast as our imaginations can create them. And as fun pastimes with dogs evolve into organized sports, people find even more new and exciting things to do with their furry friends.

The Emergence of Canine Sports and Activities

I think the renewed interest in dog sports we see today has come about for several reasons. First, many new human activities are being introduced as technology keeps advancing, and when we find something new to hold our attention, we often include our dogs in our adventures.

Second, dogs are no longer only working hands living outside at night and working long, hard hours during the day. They are our close friends and confidants, living in our homes, their lives intwined with ours.

However, without work to perform for us, dogs are having problems. The same diseases of inactivity that people suffer from are claiming victims in the canine population. Our dogs need to exercise. Even conformation dogs (sometimes looked upon as canine beauty pageant contestants) should be fit and healthy. Inactivity affects our dogs' minds as well as their bodies. Working breeds, especially, suffer when they have nothing to do with their time. They want jobs. They want us to put their dedication, their intelligence, and their incredibly powerful bodies to use. We need to give them exercises for their brains and their bodies.

What does this mean to you and your pup who doesn't know what to do with her extra energy? By taking your dog's natural, bred-in instinct, her individual characteristics, your likes and dislikes, and both your personalities into consideration, you can find an activity that will be challenging yet fun—in short, an adventure.

Finding the "Perfect" Adventure

The goal of this section is to help you find the most appropriate adventure for both you and your dog. Finding a mutually satisfying adventure brings happiness. If you both have a "just for fun" attitude, you can try anything and experience enjoyment from it.

The first step in determining the activity that both you and your dog might enjoy is to take a survey of the personality, physical attributes, and limitations of both you and your dog. You will be analyzing your strengths and then your dog's separately. Because you will be a team, it is important to discover activities that suit both of you. I don't want you to think that this survey is some kind of magic formula; it is only a starting point. Before you select the "perfect" adventure, you may want to dabble in a couple of different activities and research several sports. Many activities are interrelated. Be adventurous and never say never. In time, you probably will find yourself spending much of your free time participating in one or two favorite adventures.

You may already know exactly what you enjoy doing with your spare time and may want to know only if your present canine buddy will enjoy it too. Or you may want to know what kind of dog you should adopt to fit your lifestyle. The same survey questions will help you in either case. If you have more than one dog, answer the questions separately for each.

Remember when evaluating your and your dog's possible interests that some dogs will naturally perform better in some areas than others because of individual body structure and natural inclinations. But don't let this stop you from exploring other possibilities. Just be aware that some activities will have to be done just for fun and undertaken with a light heart, and others are more apt to put you in serious contention for blue ribbons.

Answer the following survey questions as best you can and see if the light bulb above your head goes on. If it doesn't, don't despair. Use your imagination, browse through the quick peeks in the second part of this book, and just jump right in and try an adventure or two. Watch the sport or activity firsthand. Read suggested books and write to informed individuals or organizations for more information. Talk to as many people as possible who are involved in the activity so you will hear the broadest range of views about it.

As long as you are spending time with your dog and enjoying her company, you are meeting the goal of exercise. So get up and get moving!

Questions for Exploration

This section asks that you delve into the personalities and physical styles and attributes of you and your dog. The questions are posed to stimulate ideas for adventures that will fit your needs and desires and mesh with the inclinations of your canine friend. To begin the search for an appropriate adventure, it is important to realize the quirks and characteristics that make you and your dog individuals.

Before you skip this section, thinking you already know what activity you want to pursue, realize that the true answers to some of these questions may surprise you. Sometimes you must ponder the questions in order to arrive at the real answer. It may take extra effort on your part to look beyond what you wish were true and to be honest with yourself.

For example, perhaps you know the world of conformation showing is demanding, competitive, and expensive. You may think that you are willing to make all the necessary sacrifices. After further reflection, you may have to admit to yourself that you don't have the time or the money to pursue this dream or that your dog may not be of the caliber to be a major competitor. This insight may be disappointing to you. But it is better to realize this now than to wait until you have invested a lot of time and money and received only frustration as a payback.

The wonderful thing about introspection is that when one door closes, another opens. You may discover that what you'd really appreciate is a creative, fun but challenging, freestyle routine competition.

Here are the steps to finding the right activity for you and your dog:

1. Answer the following questions as honestly as you can and see where they lead you.

2. Jot down your answers.

3. Get the opinion of a trainer, competitor, or veterinarian if you are unsure how to answer any of the questions regarding your dog.

4. Browse through the quick peeks in part II to see what seems to fit you and your dog.

5. After that, you will have to do your own footwork and research.

Here we go on the first step of your marvelous adventure!

QUESTIONS ABOUT YOURSELF

Competitiveness

Are you a competitive person? Are you the type of person who likes to be the best at what you do? When you take up a new sport, do you lose interest if you can't excel in it? Are you the type of person who likes to get involved in sports just to have fun? Does it bother you if you are not a shining star or the best? Are you looking mainly for a good excuse to socialize with other dog-people?

Would you rather be alone? Do you like your quiet and solitude? Are you looking for some time alone for you and your dog? Do you need a lot of action and excitement?

Rewards

Do you enjoy trying activities that are different from or more difficult than anything else you have done? Are you looking for a challenge? Do you need tangible rewards to feel accomplishment—ribbons, trophies, or money? Do you need to be accepted by your peers? Do you crave prestige? Or are you more interested in self-satisfaction and the feeling of accomplishment? Is being with your dog your whole reward in this adventure?

How Many Rules Do You Want?

Are you the type who needs organization and rules to follow? Do you prefer to belong to a group and be with like-minded individuals? Do you need the assistance and support of other people? Do you need their enthusiasm to feed yours? Do you prefer to work closely with others, possibly in a team sport? Or do you prefer to work alone, just you and your dog? Do you like to make your own rules?

Level of Commitment

Do you have the time, energy, and resources to travel? Do you enjoy traveling? Would you like to explore the country, participating at the national level of a sport? Can you make the commitment to traveling every weekend during part of the year? How much time do you want to take away from your family life? Can your spouse and children be a part of the adventure? Do you have a busy life or plenty of spare time? Could you devote many hours to training?

Do you have the money to compete at higher levels? Or are your finances limited? How much are you willing to spend on your adventure? What sacrifices are you willing to make?

Activity Preferences

Are you the type of person who would much rather spend time outdoors than indoors? Are you tolerant of different kinds of weather? Are you comfortable in strange places? Do you like to spend time camping and hiking in the wilderness? Would you be more comfortable having a hot shower and a cozy bed? Would you rather be home? Do you spend most of your time inside or in your backyard? Would you rather spend time outside only when the weather is pleasant? Do you like to be out and about in the neighborhood? Would you like to spend time away from your home and explore other locales?

Physical Abilities

Do you regularly participate in sports and fitness activities? Are you a physically talented person who will try new activities willingly and with confidence? Are you limited physically? Are your limitations something you can change? Are your limitations permanent? What are you able to do? Do you have a positive attitude about your abilities? Are you willing to cooperate with a trainer in devising a good strategy for training and showing your dog?

QUESTIONS ABOUT YOUR DOG

Competitiveness

Is your dog competitive? Does she try to outrun, outjump, and out-tug other dogs? Is she the lazy variety, needing a push to get going? Does your dog live by a serious work ethic? Or is fun most important to her?

Trainability

Is your dog well disciplined and precise? Is she somewhat independent? Does your dog seem to learn quickly? Does she retain what she learns? Does it take a long time for your dog to learn something? Does she obey your commands consistently? What kinds of skills does your dog seem to learn quickly? What kinds of skills are more difficult for her? Does she prefer to be close to you, participating with you eagerly? Would she really rather be working on her own, checking in with you every once in a while? Is your dog good with people? Is she eager to please and responsive? Is she sluggish? Would she rather be left alone? Is she good with other dogs? Or is she intolerant of other dogs?

Personality

Does your dog need a lot of exercise before she can calm down? Does she have a thirst for excitement and novelty? Is she always getting into trouble? Does it seem that she just can't follow instructions? Does she always get a lot of attention whenever you two go anywhere together? Does she solicit and enjoy petting and attention? Must she be persuaded just to get off the couch?

Activity Preferences

Does your dog love to run, jump, climb, pull, herd, or show off? Does she stay calm when confronted with new surroundings? Is she explorative? Is she more comfortable in a familiar environment? Does she greet you calmly, if at all? Does she greet you by jumping on you, wagging her tail energetically, and licking you even if you had stepped out of the room for only a minute? Has your dog had any injuries that could affect her ability to participate in some activities?

HOW DOES PERSONALITY AFFECT A PERFORMANCE DOG?

Imagine two dogs and their handlers arriving at the grounds of an agility competition.

"Lady" and her owner arrive at the field in the misty early morning hours. The handler unloads their gear and sets up an exercise pen and shade covering. The activity is exciting to Lady. Dogs and their people mill about, setting up their equipment, checking the class schedule, and signing in. Lady knows the routine.

Lady eagerly takes in the surroundings. She looks forward to the fun. She focuses on her owner, eyes intently fixed on her every move. She doesn't want to miss out on anything they are going to do. She confidently walks to the measuring stick and stands still for measuring, waiting to hear "Good dog" from her beloved person.

Back at her exercise pen, she waits alone patiently. She knows her person will be back, so she is calm and confident. Even though some people actually bump into her pen and a couple of dogs bark at her, she stays relaxed. Lady is a pro, even though this is only her second show. She handles this busy environment well because she has a stable, controlled temperament. She is balanced, dedicated to listening to her handler, and trusting.

Now let's look at "Lucy." Lucy has been to numerous agility competitions, beginning with fun matches a couple of years ago. She has never fully adjusted to the trauma she is confronted with at competitions. She is nervous. Her handler feels like she must practically drag Lucy to the grounds. As the equipment is being set up, Lucy tangles herself around her handler and cringes at passersby. Her owner's patience begins to dwindle, and the setting up is barely done before measuring time. After refusing to walk up and stand still to be measured, Lucy must be physically placed under the measuring stick, where she trembles in fear while being measured.

Alone in her exercise pen, she becomes a nervous wreck, whining and barking for her absent handler. She is sure that her owner is never coming back and shakes with fear at the thought of never seeing her human again. She alternately defends herself or urinates submissively when strange dogs come too close to her area.

Which dog do you think will do better on the field? Which do you think will earn a higher score? More importantly, which dog do you think truly enjoys the adventure? Which handler do you think truly enjoys the adventure?

The best dog for high-pressure competitive events is one who is confident, trusting, attentive to her handler, and focused. If you are considering such events, you want a dog who can handle the stress of competition. Your canine buddy should be able to concentrate on the job at hand in the midst of many distractions. You can take a less-confident dog through less-competitive events, but a dog in constant fear is not going to find it pleasurable to participate in any type of competition. Many sensitive or fearful dogs respond well to gentle exposure to low-key activities and become more confident in their abilities, although they may never be ready for competitive events.

NOW WHAT?

As you read through the above explorative questions, did you write down your answers? If not, please read the questions once more and do so. Your responses will give you a clearer picture of your and your dog's adventure personalities.

You did consider the questions thoughtfully? Wonderful. "Now what?" you may ask. You can apply your answers from this insightful exercise to finding an exciting, yet appropriate, activity for you and your dog. Keeping in mind the responses you wrote down, you may wish to take some time now to thumb through part II, Quick Peeks, to explore a wide array of canine adventures and to find one (or more) that interests you. For example, if the above questions helped you to realize that you are definitely not a competitive person and you just want a fun but not too challenging activity for your mixed-breed pup, then browsing through the section called "Hanging Out" (see page 245) will assist you in finding an activity that's right for you.

If you still haven't developed, or recognized, your vision of an ideal activity, do some brainstorming and create a mind map as described below. To help you best understand the steps to discovery, I offer an example of one person's quest on page 17. Above all, remember to have fun and let your imagination soar.

Creative Brainstorming

An analysis of the answers to the previous questions should have helped you find an activity that matches your wants, needs, and dreams. But if you still haven't found an activity that interests you, you can use brainstorming to discover one. Brainstorming is the most effective method of evaluating your unique situation and making a good choice.

Brainstorming is powerful. Done correctly, it can increase your creativity, enhance your goal-making ability, and help you discover aspects of a problem or situation that you haven't thought of yet. The key to efficient brainstorming is to put down on paper as many ideas and inspirations as possible. Exploring your ideas, thoughts, and solutions and then organizing them will help you create the best plan for you and your dog's grand adventure.

THE MAGIC OF MIND MAPPING

Mind mapping is the clearest, most effective, and most successful form of brainstorming. I have used it for many situations—including producing a complicated business plan, planning a camping trip, outlining each chapter of this book, and scheduling training time for my dog. Mind mapping frees your brain to work in a nonlinear fashion, as it was meant to. Mind mapping is easy, free flowing, and fun. If you relax, your brain will impress you with a burst of creativity that feeds on itself. You'll have so many ideas you'll marvel at how brilliant you are.

HOW TO MIND MAP

To mind map most efficiently and most creatively, surround yourself with an environment that stimulates creativity. Use a big piece of paper when mind mapping. Selecting poster paper in a wild color and a marker in an equally wild color will spark your creativity. If you hang the paper on a wall, you will get added stimulation from standing up and moving around.

Begin at the paper's center. Place a sentence, word, or image that describes your focus in the middle of the page and circle it. It is important to place the focus objective in the center because a creative brain works from the center of a space.

Draw branches (lines) extending outward in any direction from this center circle. Each branch represents an idea, thought, or solution. Use one or two words, symbols, shorthand, abbreviations, or even short sentences to describe your idea. Continue building on the thought with sub-branches and sub-sub-branches, adding as many levels as you need. If a new idea relates to a previous idea, connect them with a sub-branch. You can add connections from one subject to another all over the sheet.

Do not pause to judge or critique your ideas or you will stop the creative process. Even if an idea seems fanciful, impossible, or out of this world, write it down. You can evaluate it later. Keep your hand moving and your ideas flowing.

If you aren't experiencing a rush of ideas and things seem to be moving slowly, use another-color pen, stand up, or change locations. If you find your flow of ideas coming to a standstill, then draw some blank lines. Your brain will find something to put on them.

After you have all your ideas on paper, organize your mind map by grouping related ideas together. Doing this should give you a clear picture of the type of adventure that will suit both you and your dog. An example of how one person used mind mapping to guide her in choosing an adventure is included in the following section.

One Person's Quest for the "Perfect" Adventure

The following story tells of Erin's search for an activity to share with her dog. It shows how she analyzed her and her dog's personalities, created and refined a mind map, and investigated several different activities before finding the right one for them.

THE INFORMATION GATHERED

Erin is the proud caretaker of a Shetland sheepdog she calls "Suzie Q." Erin realized how bored her two-year-old pooch was after Suzie Q shredded Erin's third bedspread in four months. Deciding it was time to do more with her canine buddy than play games in the backyard or take a walk around the neighborhood a couple of times a week, Erin began exploring the sporting activities in her area.

She started her quest by answering questions about herself and her dog. She compiled the following information:

I am competitive and like to be "one of the best" at everything I do. I set my goals high and feel confident that I have the ability to reach any goal I set for myself. I have plenty of friends, so I don't feel the need for my doggie activity to be a social event, yet I know that others' enthusiasm and support keep me motivated. I'm also impatient and must have early success in order to stay interested in an activity, which will need to be something my dog does well naturally. I would like to work with a trainer who can guide me through the early learning. I have a family and many responsibilities and cannot devote too many hours to training and traveling. Expenses won't pose a problem as long as they are not extraordinary. I am a good organizer and planner. I am physically fit and enjoy being outdoors as much as possible.

Suzie Q is bored easily (as demonstrated by her boredom-relieving technique of shredding bedspreads) and has lots of energy. She is agile and curious, and she greets everyone she meets with boundless jumping and spinning. She is a quick and eager learner but does not respond well to discipline, even when applied mildly. She likes to be busy, preferably doing something with me. She follows me throughout the day, never letting me get too far out of sight.

Erin then decided to create a mind map. A copy of what her mind map looked like follows. She pondered her answers to the personality questions, studied her mind map, and formed an idea of what her and Suzie Q's activity preferences might be. Erin had always wanted to compete in obedience competitions. She originally adopted Suzie Q for this reason but just never got started. Her personality profile and Suzie Q's seemed compatible with obedience, so Erin enrolled in a basic obedience class.

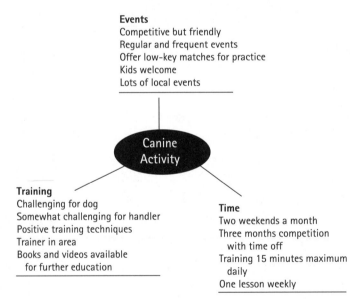

Events
Competitive but friendly
Regular and frequent events
Offer low-key matches for practice
Kids welcome
Lots of local events

Canine
Activity

Training
Challenging for dog
Somewhat challenging for handler
Positive training techniques
Trainer in area
Books and videos available
  for further education

Time
Two weekends a month
Three months competition
  with time off
Training 15 minutes maximum
  daily
One lesson weekly

INVESTIGATING OBEDIENCE

Although Suzie Q was a quick learner and briskly advanced to more-challenging work, Erin began to feel obedience was not the activity for her and her dog. Suzie Q was not the eyes-glued-on-her-owner dog that obedience competition requires. That in itself could have been corrected, but Erin didn't have much time to spend one on one with her dog; when she did, she liked their moments together to be extremely active and stimulating. She liked to come away from her time with her dog feeling exercised both mentally and physically. Erin tried to like obedience, and although she could see how some people would find it therapeutic, she wanted more excitement.

Erin brought out her personality questions and answers and her mind map again. By adding the new information from her experiences in obedience and reading through descriptions of various activities, she discovered what she thought might cure her problem—agility.

A NEW ACTIVITY TO EXPLORE

Erin considered other activities that she read about in the quick peeks, but one by one she eliminated them from her wish list. She was attracted to lure coursing; she pictured graceful, lithe hounds flying over the grass. But she had to admit to herself that Suzie Q didn't fit that image. Besides, few events were held, and Erin could locate only a couple in her area a year. With this limited competition schedule, her chance to participate would be slender. There were a lot of retriever trials in her area that she could easily participate in, but she wasn't interested, and Suzie Q wasn't the best dog for this activity. Flyball was an activity Erin knew they would both like. The problem was finding enough people to make a team. Erin didn't have any friends that were interested, and she wasn't sure she could make that kind of commitment to others at this point in her life.

Suzie Q loved to jump, and although many dog activities involve jumping, there seemed to be a good fit between agility and Suzie Q's and Erin's personalities. Because Erin was competitive, she felt her chosen adventure had to be a well-established sport in the canine world. Agility met this criterion too. She would need a trainer, and that suited Erin's and Suzie Q's learning style. Joining an agility club would also give Erin the support and enthusiasm she needed.

The closest agility trainer was a 30-minute drive away, but Erin thought that one night a week with the training club would be an acceptable amount of time away from her family. Agility competitions were held frequently during trial season within an hour's drive from her home. This meant she could find enough competitions without traveling great distances. Erin could compete only once or twice a month, and having many trials in her area would give her the opportunity to be flexible about her schedule. The atmosphere of the agility trials was friendly, so her family would enjoy the day as much as she. (She discovered this after attending a couple of trials to get a feel for the event.)

Since Erin wasn't going to be able to take Suzie Q to the trainer's facility more than once a week, she would need to purchase some training equipment. Because Erin's finances weren't restrictive, this would be possible.

Suzie Q was dog-friendly and reliable, so the presence of many excited dogs at training and the trials would not disturb her. Because Suzie Q seemed to have the natural personality for agility, there was an increased possibility that she would do well from the beginning, which would fuel Erin's confidence and motivation.

During their first training session, Erin observed that Suzie Q seemed to find agility fun and stimulating. As they developed a regular training program, Suzie Q began to relax more and was calmer at home (no more shredded bedding). Because Suzie Q was quick to learn, she and Erin became a good working team right away, and because agility is taught using only positive training methods, Suzie Q was encouraged with an upbeat attitude, and her sensitivity to discipline was a moot point.

Erin did make some sacrifices in choosing an adventure (nothing's ever perfect). Although she valued success and enjoyed the prestige of being best, Erin found that in order to move up as quickly as she wanted to through the different levels of competition, she would have to compete and train more often than her schedule allowed. She was therefore forced to lower her sights to more attainable goals. But because this activity was so perfectly matched to other aspects of her and Suzie Q's personalities, this was an acceptable sacrifice.

The training time could have overwhelmed her had she not lowered her goals. She trained Suzie Q in the morning for only a few minutes on a couple of pieces of equipment, and then she worked with Suzie Q again in the afternoon for closer to ten minutes. Because the equipment remained set up in Erin's yard and because Suzie Q was more than willing to "play" on the equipment, this training became part of Erin's fun time and did not intrude on her other responsibilities. Erin wanted the training to be challenging enough to keep her interest but not too overwhelming (she just didn't have the extra time). Agility training again fit the bill.

Erin needed the motivational support of fellow agility participants more than she first realized, but she did not live close to other handlers and did not have the time for much travel. She solved this problem by making contact with other agility enthusiasts through e-mail, regular mail, and the Internet (which she could do after her children were in bed or whenever she had a couple of spare minutes).

Enjoyable, exciting, physically active, and most of all, fun, agility was a good choice for this human-dog team.

If you answer the foregoing survey questions truthfully and create a mind map, you, too, will be able to find the "perfect" adventure for you and your dog.

Loving the One You're With

Perhaps you have spent the last five years attending one conformation show after another. Maybe you've proven your dog is a classy pooch who conforms to the breed standard, and you're ready for a change. Maybe you're tired of the pressure of competing at higher levels of obedience and want to add some fun and adventure to you and your dog's life. You know your dog deserves to participate in an activity that is close to her heart.

Perhaps you've realized that you just aren't as close to your house pet as you would like to be. Maybe you have found yourself overwhelmed by a dog that has more energy than a tornado in Kansas and the athletic prowess of an Olympic athlete. She simply is not content to laze around the house all day. Whatever your reasons for reading this book, it will help you find the right activity for you and your dog.

WHICH ADVENTURE SEEMS RIGHT FOR YOUR DOG?

You may want to include your dog in an adventure that you already participate in without her. For example, if you love to mountain bike, including your dog in the adventure may seem exciting. But what if your dog is not physically fit, is overweight, or has a structural fault that would increase her risk of injury during this demanding activity? What if, upon spotting a rabbit, she loses her sense of her place in the world— namely, by your side? What if her hair is long and difficult to keep clean, brushed, and tick-free? These attributes can make mountain biking with your dog a taxing or dangerous experience.

Some of the above problems can be remedied. You can, for instance, shave your canine friend. You can put her on a weight-loss program and gently and slowly build up her strength and endurance at home. But other problems cannot be overcome. You may have to mountain bike on your own and find another activity for you and your dog to do together.

If your dog seems to have magnets in her teeth that catch a flying disc no matter how terrible the throw, if she has boundless energy and the agility of a ballet dancer, then maybe you have a disc-catching competitor on your hands. If competition doesn't interest you, play just for fun. Pick up a book or video on Frisbee catching. Search out someone in your area who competes and is willing to give you and your dog some lessons. This may prove to be a great adventure.

Earlier in this chapter, you were asked to answer a myriad of questions regarding the personalities and physical conditions of you and your dog. This was the beginning of your exploration. With an idea of which activities may best suit the two of you, you can look, for inspiration, at the possibilities presented in the second part of this book. Be ready to experiment while finding the right pursuit for you and your canine companion. Challenge yourself and your dog. The search for adventure is a reward in itself.

YOUR CHOICE OF ADVENTURE VERSUS YOUR DOG'S ABILITIES

Perhaps you enrolled in a basic obedience course just to give your bulldog some manners and teach her some ground rules, and you discovered competitive obedience. What a thrill! The challenge energizes you, the training motivates you, and you want to go to the top. But while some bulldogs may be able to perform at the top level in competitive obedience, yours really lacks the spark and physical prowess. You live in a hot, humid climate, and during the summer your dog cannot even go outdoors to do her duty without having to rest in the air conditioning for 30 minutes afterward. This is not the ideal start for an enthusiastic obedience hopeful. What do you do? What are your options?

Do It Just for Fun

Lessening your aspirations is your first alternative. Maybe competing for and winning the top obedience awards at a national level isn't going to be an attainable goal. You can compete just for fun.

Why not concentrate on the training? Make a hobby out of seeing how much fun you can have with your snorting love bug while getting her to perform maneuvers that seem almost impossible.

Consider competing in local dog shows only when the weather is comfortable for your dog. If you stay close to home, you can cancel if she just doesn't seem up to competing, and you won't lose money on an unused motel room and travel arrangements.

You may not walk away from an obedience ring with the highest score in the class, but you will have fun. If you lessen your competitive drive, you will realize the joy in the activity itself and reduce the stress on you and your dog.

Try Another Activity

That same bulldog of yours that may not be the epitome of physical agility and enthusiasm may just turn out to be a true example of her breed in conformation. Why not work on earning her beginning title in obedience and her championship in conformation?

Maybe another activity altogether would be better suited to your dog's style. With so many activities to choose from, you will never have time to try them all. If you approach the process with an open mind, trying activities you may never have thought you or your dog would enjoy, you will surely find something to concentrate your energies on.

Dipping into a number of different activities is especially beneficial for those people and dogs who don't have a thirst for high-level competition, who want to keep things simple, or who don't have hours to train.

If you haven't done so yet, browse through the second part of this book and ponder the possibilities. Forget any limits you may have placed

TURNING TO OTHERS FOR IDEAS

When you seem to run out of ideas or just don't know where to begin looking for a fun thing to do with your dog, turn to others. Keep your eyes, ears, and most importantly, your mind open for inspiration. Here are some possible sources for ideas:

➤ Your dog's breeder

➤ Another enthusiast of your dog's breed

➤ Your veterinarian

➤ A good trainer

➤ Dog magazines and other publications

➤ The World Wide Web

➤ Dog shows or events

on yourself or your dog. Let your imagination soar. If you don't, you may miss out on something that would be truly entertaining for you and your dog. In the meantime, spend time playing with, walking, caring for, and loving your dog.

What about Another Dog?

Suppose your aspirations in a particular sport or activity are very high. You read about the topic, rehearse success in your mind, think about it endlessly, and attend any and all events you can. You possess a vivid, unwavering dream. You have the other necessary resources to accomplish your goal (time, money, family support, and commitment). You love your dog dearly, but she just isn't capable of reaching your goals.

Giving up on your dream may cause you to resent your dog. Suppressed frustration may break to the surface in undesirable ways. Getting another dog may be a good solution—*but only on two conditions*:

- ❧ Condition #1—You have the extra resources for another dog, including time, money, energy, patience, family support, tolerance, room, and love.

- ❧ Condition #2—You will never forsake your first true love. Your current dog will always come first and will always be treated to the same love and attention she is accustomed to.

"Can't I just get rid of my dog and get another?" The answer is No! If your lifestyle doesn't allow you to care for more than one dog, you must adapt to the one you already have.

STAYING COMMITTED TO YOUR CANINE FRIEND

Your dog is a valuable, unique individual who deserves to be respected for who she is. Although her abilities may fall short of your hopes, you cannot hold this against her. You already know what makes your dog special, and that is what you need to concentrate on. Your dog will not understand if you turn against her. She would love nothing more than to make you the happiest person in the world, but when your expectations and your dog's talents are in conflict, it is up to you to redefine your expectations. Accept your dog as a special friend, regardless of her shortcomings, and appreciate fully the wonderful qualities she brings to your life.

There's no replacing a true companion. Your dog may not be able to accomplish the lofty goals you have placed before her, but she will always remain loyal to you. Remember, these aren't her goals anyway; they are yours. Her goal is simply to make you happy. You will never be able to replace the friendship that she freely gives you. Treasure that, no matter what you decide to do about your dreams of competition.

CHAPTER TWO

Before Beginning
Your Adventure

If you have selected an activity that really strikes your fancy, eagerness to get your canine buddy to participate is probably foremost in your mind. In all the excitement you may forget, or cast aside as unimportant, the necessary preliminary preparations. Think again. There are important details that you should consider and that require energy and time before you begin your adventure.

Remember the scouting motto Be Prepared? Planning is the surest way to be successful and to have the most fun. This chapter is meant to remind you of the considerations that need your attention before you engage in your chosen activity or sport. If you already understand the importance of doing your homework first, this chapter will help you build the most optimal foundation for fun.

Are You Ready?

Imagine this scenario: You slip into your shiny, new pair of in-line skates and adjust the laces just so. You don the cool, new sunglasses that identically match the luminescent purple of your skates. You adjust your newest skating garb and tie your dog's matching bandanna cleverly around his well-groomed neck. You check the mirror one last time. No helmet or pads spoil your image. You grab a leash and your pooch and you're off!

But once out the door you're suddenly in trouble. Before you can get your balance, your dog starts trotting. You yell, "Stop! No, Spot! No!" as you're dragged down the driveway at what feels like at least 30 miles per hour. Off into the neighborhood you go.

The trees seem to rush by at a staggering rate, and your life passes before your eyes. (You don't remember those quad skates you had as a child being this fast or hard to control. Of course, this time you are benefiting from advanced technology and rambunctious canine power.) Your dog, meanwhile, just keeps running—faster and faster. You can't get him to slow down. Pulling on the leash just makes him pull harder. You cling madly to the leash, afraid to let go.

Visions of your brand new skates and skating garb ripped to shreds enter your mind, along with images of your scraped knees, your bruised face, or worse. Your sense of balance seems to have left you at the front door of your house, and as you try to maintain an upright position, your weight shifts violently from front to back. You flail about like a slapstick comic desperate to keep your balance.

If you can just hold on for another couple of minutes, maybe your dog will get tired. If only you can stay upright on those wobbling ankles.

Then it happens. Your dog spots the neighbor's cat, and before you can say the first words of your chosen prayer, your dog takes a sharp leap to the left. As for you, it's all over in a split second. Your skates crash into the curb. You make a spectacular dive onto the sidewalk, sliding belly first into the neighbor's well-manicured evergreen bush. The force of the jolt blasts your new sunglasses from your face, crushing them into the concrete. Ouch! As stars fill your vision, you think maybe a helmet would have been a good idea. You only hope no one was around to see any of the disaster. And you wonder how you'll get your aching body home. And by the way, where is that clever little dog of yours?

You lie on the ground, contemplating your scrapes and bruises, curious if your wrist is shattered. You decide that this adventure-with-your-canine-buddy stuff is for the "lunatic fringe." You vow to keep your dog out of your recreational life and to find a more gentle activity for yourself. You wonder how much a pair of once-worn, slightly mangled skates can be sold for.

What's wrong with this adventure? Everything. There was no preparation, no planning, and no thinking ahead. The situation could have been even worse, ending with multiple broken bones or the dog running into traffic. If the fun in your activity is lessened by a lack of preparation, the possibility that you or your dog will give up becomes greater. You'll lose the enthusiasm that otherwise would keep you active with your canine. Your dog will be relegated to a boring life without much inter-action, and you will wonder why you and your dog aren't as bonded as you had hoped to be.

Thinking ahead will make your adventures more pleasant in the beginning and more successful and enjoyable as you continue.

YOUR PROFICIENCY

The above example of good intentions gone awry demonstrates the importance of being proficient in your chosen activity before including your canine friend. Some canine activities and sports do not require active physical participation on your part, but for most activities, prepar-ing yourself will increase your enjoyment.

Each of the quick peeks in part II of this book includes suggestions to help you evaluate your own proficiency in an activity before you include your dog. Having 60 pounds of muscle at the end of a leash is not the easiest way to learn how to in-line skate, bike, run, skateboard, ski, or pursue any of the other activities that you may like. If, for example, you decide to try mountain-bike riding with your dog, then you should be able to ride your mountain bike in wilderness terrain proficiently before taking along your canine buddy.

Proficiency on your part also makes it easier for your dog to learn his part. Frisbee competition is a good example of this lesson. If you can't control a Frisbee with confidence, then expecting your dog to learn to catch one is unfair. You don't have to be a master of your chosen activ-ity, but you should have some experience with it prior to engaging your dog. In this way, you will both avoid mishaps.

Sometimes, as in the case of skijoring (having your dog pull you while cross-country skiing), you may need to take human-only lessons in the beginning. In order to safely incorporate your canine into skijoring, you should be able to cross-country ski at an intermediate level. This may require a winter season of training on your part.

Most skijoring instructors will insist that you demonstrate your ability to ski at the necessary level before accepting you as a student. Once you add your dog, you should be able to concentrate on working together as a team. Having to instruct you on the basics of cross-country skiing will frustrate your instructor and sidetrack the learning program, and if you are in a class, no one will appreciate your slowing the group down.

Sometimes, just increasing your level of overall physical fitness may be required. If you want to train your dog for search and rescue or field trials, for example, you should have the physical conditioning needed to keep up with your athlete. Canine freestyle (dancing to a musical number with your dog), on the other hand, requires that you have a sense of rhythm, musical interpretation, and coordination. Research the activities and sports that are interesting to you to discover if you should start by improving your abilities in specific movements.

PROTECTIVE GEAR

The skating story demonstrates the importance of protective gear for many sports and activities. Protect yourself with the recommended safety equipment for whichever sport you choose. Participating in activities on the street means being fully aware of the potential for accidents.

When engaging in a water adventure, a life jacket is a must for each of you. Although you and your dog may be strong swimmers, an accident in which one of you is rendered unconscious could be disastrous without life jackets.

When you include your dog in your recreational pursuits, you must realize that you are dealing with another living, feeling creature who can, in an unguarded instant, decide to go against the will of his human buddy. A cat, squirrel, interesting smell, or enticing rustling in the bushes can distract even the most obedient animal. The right protective gear can help prevent injuries when you face unexpected circumstances.

A Well-Mannered Dog

A dog who will listen to your commands is an important ingredient in the quest for a gratifying canine adventure, but every aspect of your relationship, including day-to-day life, will be improved if your dog knows basic obedience. In order for you and your best friend to live harmoniously together, he will have to know the rules of good behavior. Your part of the bargain is showing him in a kind and respectful way what you expect. Dogs must be given direction. For centuries, dogs have been bred to crave this direction, and if you don't offer it to your four-legged friend, you are letting him down.

BASIC OBEDIENCE

If your dog has not mastered his social graces, train him right away. You may need to start at the beginning, with a basic obedience class. Even if your dog knows most of the basic manners you want him to know, he needs to be exposed to the various stimuli and other dogs that a group class offers. If you are having any behavioral problems with your dog, especially aggression, you may need to seek the advice of a trainer or a behaviorist before you can pursue your chosen adventure. You will need to know how your dog reacts to other dogs and the high energy of a group setting if your plans include shows or competitions.

My Australian shepherd taught me that lesson. In my backyard, he was almost obedience-ring ready. I was proud of him and not a bit worried about taking the control test for an agility class. The night of the test, however, he became a different dog—one of the most out-of-control dogs there. My frustration and embarrassment just fueled his excitement. He had been exposed to other dogs, of course, but not 10 dogs in one yard. He just couldn't calm himself, and because I wasn't composed enough to help him, it was a difficult night. The team of evaluators passed us (although we were put on probation), but I think we passed because I had been part of the agility group for a number of years, and the staff had confidence that I could help this dog control himself next time.

You will probably need to enroll in a training program specific to your chosen activity. Taking a training class is another chance to spend time with your dog. The communication and shared effort required when teaching a dog are beneficial to your relationship, if you use respectful methods of training. Chapter 7 will assist you in finding an instructor or training club that will provide the most value to you and your dog.

The obvious commands to teach your dog for almost any activity include control commands such as heel, stay, and come (the recall command). It is extremely important that your dog respond immediately when you call him. Your dog will require further, specialized training once you have chosen an activity and have begun participating, but every dog should look to his handler for guidance from the start.

A basic obedience class can lead to all sorts of discoveries. The other caretakers and the teachers may have suggestions, references, and information on dog-related activities. A group obedience class is a great excuse to "talk dog" with like-minded people.

Leash Manners

Leash manners are a must for many pursuits. Pulling, lagging, and fighting with the leash are all problems that you can't ignore. Your dog should be respectful, receptive, and eager when on a leash. Your leash training should involve positive reinforcements for good behavior and limit the amount of corrections and coercion. A willing, happy dog is the kind of creature who makes for exciting recreational pursuits.

On the other hand, a distrustful or angry dog on the end of a leash is trouble. A simple walk with such a dog can turn into a battle of wills, with you as the discouraged loser. If you don't have enough control of your pet, he may decide to suddenly cut across your path while you are bike riding or running. This can be dangerous for both of you.

While you are out, your dog can and should be on a loose leash—sniffing hundreds of interesting smells, looking here and there, and simply having an opportunity to move around. This freedom does not mean he can direct your movement. Unlike formal heeling, this is a less precise and more relaxed mode of traveling on lead. Often preceded by the command "let's go," free-heeling is less rigid and more accepting of the natural curiosity of your canine friend.

Although the informal "let's go" command is more commonly appropriate, a formal, finely tuned heel is useful and sometimes necessary. This control command is a vital means of regaining faltering attention and averting possible disobedience. If a doggy magnet appears on your peaceful jogging venture, you can use the heel command to gain control, to remind your dog who is in charge, and to engage your dog's mind in a more noble pursuit—listening to you. It is also useful when approaching other people. You can ask for a formal heel, reassuring strangers in your path that you have a friendly, obedient dog who will stay out of their way. Many people are frightened of dogs, and your dog's heeling will demonstrate that you have control of the situation. You can also train your dog to formally walk on your right side and thereby avoid having the dog between you and passersby. My dogs, and many of my friends' dogs, are trained to walk on the right side with a "side" command. I use this form of placement control more often than "heel." (There is more on neighborly conduct while out with your dog in chapter 5.)

A formal heel is also useful in high-traffic areas because you will know exactly where your pooch is, and you can require him to stay there. This can be very reassuring if a convoy of trucks whisks past you unexpectedly on the street or if strangers bump into your dog and cut across his path on busy sidewalks.

The Death-Grip Trip

The free-heel is also a way to make sure that you are not holding on too tightly to the leash. A tight leash makes a dog anxious and causes more misbehavior than it cures. It tells him "Something is wrong. Stay very close to me." Of course, your dog has no idea what is wrong, so he is wary of everything.

The tightness around his neck can also cause him to be more aggressive. Constantly pulling against the neck of your dog will cause him to be alert for any problem and quick to react when he perceives one. And what he perceives as a danger may be quite different from what you would. You want to engage in a fun activity with your dog concentrating on you and on his job. The free-heel gives you and your canine athlete permission to relax while you are enjoying yourselves.

At the beginning of each venture, if your dog is overly enthusiastic and ignores your requests, you can ask for a more controlled heel. As he begins to tire and is less excited, you can allow a looser lead. Remember that even if he seems too tired to chase a fleeing squirrel, he may have one more burst of energy available, so be attentive to his body language even toward the end of your outing.

A Stable Temperament

Having a dog with a stable temperament makes preparing for and participating in a new adventure more enjoyable. If your dog does not adjust well to changes; is nervous around strange people, dogs, or places; or is aggressive or fearful, you will have to make some improvements. Sometimes just the added attention from you, the training, and the increased confidence built by participating in an activity will encourage your troubled canine to find a means to deal with differing circumstances.

Help from an animal behaviorist or trainer may be in order if the problem is serious or deeply entrenched. You cannot be worrying about whether your dog is going to bite someone or lose control of his emotions while you are learning a new canine hobby. Many organized clubs will not accept a dog who shows any sign of emotional instability. Even a quiet walk around the neighborhood can become disastrous with such a dog, so ask for help.

SOCIALIZATION

How do some of the above-mentioned problems develop anyway? What can you do to prevent them from happening to your dog? Providing your dog with early socialization is the answer.

The process of socialization is extremely important for any puppy but absolutely essential for the puppy who is expected to be confident, trustworthy, adventurous, stable, attentive, and friendly—exactly the characteristics you want in your canine athlete. The process of socialization gives your dog practice and confidence in accepting and adjusting to new and unexpected people, places, and things.

If you are raising a puppy, you are starting with a relatively clean slate (provided you got your pup from a knowledgeable breeder). You will be able to mold acceptable doggy behavior from the start. This is a large responsibility—one I find both challenging and terrifying. Being accountable for the mental development of your dog can be a weighty obligation.

If you are beginning with an older dog who is lacking in the social graces, you will have to be gentle, persuasive, and attentive to his reactions and adaptations. Be patient with the older dog. Go slowly, one step at a time, and get help from a professional if necessary.

If your dog happens to have the hereditary material that tends to make him shy, aggressive, or oversensitive and he hasn't been socialized, you may not be able to make much headway in changing his personality enough to engage in an activity that includes groups of people and dogs. A dog with this sort of personality and a crowd of strange people and dogs could present a disastrous combination.

Even a dog that comes from a confident, outgoing, mentally stable bloodline can, without socialization, become neurotic and unpredictable. Without positive experiences and social interaction with humans during the first few months of life, especially during the fear-imprint period, a dog will not trust and may not tolerate humans throughout the rest of his life. This lack of trust may manifest itself in aggression, shyness, or the inability to relate to people.

Socializing your puppy can be fun, but it will require some dedication from you. You must be willing to take advantage of situations that expand your pooch's universe. If you make your puppy or dog an inti-

KEY SOCIALIZATION POINTS

➤ Be sure your puppy's first social encounter is positive. Have control of the situation when making first impressions on your puppy.

➤ When making introductions to new stimuli, allow your puppy to make the first move. Allowing him to go at his own pace helps him feel more in control and confident.

➤ Introduce puppies to people who like dogs. Someone who is frightened of dogs will send confusing messages to your puppy.

➤ Give strangers treats to offer your puppy, especially if he seems nervous and uncertain around them.

➤ Make sure your pup's first introductions to children are to well-behaved youngsters only.

➤ Never introduce your puppy to children without first getting their parents' permission.

➤ Before you introduce your puppy to another dog, ask for the dog owner's permission.

➤ Never force acceptance of novel situations or objects on your pup.

➤ Praise your puppy enthusiastically when he welcomes something new.

➤ Don't use baby talk or coddle your frightened dog. Act matter-of-fact, and your positive, confident attitude will rub off on him.

➤ Offer many variations of the same experience to allow your dog to make generalizations.

➤ Introduce your puppy to as many new experiences as possible. Provide him with a stimulating environment.

➤ Do as much socialization as you possibly can before your puppy is four months old, but don't stop there: Make your dog a part of your life. Give him periodic reminders that the world is a safe, comfortable place.

mate part of your life, socializing will be a natural extension of this closeness and will require no extra effort on your part. Exposing your dog to the wonders of the outside world will have long-lasting and far-reaching effects on your dog's life and your relationship with him.

Know the Sport

Once you have decided what activity you would like to try, learn as much about it as possible. While doing your initial investigation, you should have attended at least one event so you get an idea of what the "game" is like. If the sport is an organized one, you will need a clear understanding of at least the most important rules.

Request a rules and regulations guide from the organization that governs the event. You will learn most of the ins and outs of the rules while participating, but you should not go in blind. Some sports have specific guidelines on the commands and techniques that you may use. If you have trained your dog differently, you may find you need to start from scratch.

If you seek the assistance of a trainer in this venture, then the trainer will help you understand the regulations you need to know to get started. Joining a club, as discussed in chapter 7, is beneficial in many ways, one of which is giving you a better understanding of the mechanics of your chosen pursuit.

Even if your recreation is not an organized activity, there are still guidelines you should follow. Rules of the road or trail are important for getting along with others who share these places with you and your dog. If you are venturing into the wilderness, there are regulations and restrictions that you will have to investigate and adhere to. For instance, your dog may have to be leashed at all times, may be restricted from traveling in certain areas, and may not be able to stay in a campsite. You need to know such rules ahead of time.

In addition, you will need to know what to do in an emergency situation and how to meet your dog's basic physical needs. An understanding of canine nutrition, physiology, performance criteria, and movement is critical.

As you begin participating in activities with your dog and exploring the unending opportunities for fun and challenging hobbies, you will increase your knowledge. You will find yourself unable to quench your thirst for a deeper understanding, and you will soon realize that you can never know too much.

When Travel Is Part of the Adventure

Many activities will lead you outside your home and beyond your neighborhood—at least to a nearby training area. If your instructor or club isn't within a few blocks, you will probably be using your car to get to training sessions or meetings. Even if you only need a change of scenery and want to go somewhere different to throw the ball around for your doggie buddy, he must be able to travel comfortably and safely.

CAR TRAVEL

Most dogs love car rides, and you probably won't have a problem convincing yours to jump right in for a cruise. Some dogs may need to be shown that riding in a vehicle is not so terrible. If your dog is not familiar with the sensations of a moving car, you must help him get comfortable with the unusual sights and motion. Take short rides with him, letting him adjust slowly to the vehicle's movement.

Your dog needs to be protected and safe while traveling. The best way for a dog to travel is in a crate: he'll be out of your way, he won't be jumping from seat to seat, he'll be safe in the event of an accident, and you won't have to worry about whether the sound you're hearing is your dog chewing on the arm rest. (See the section on page 43 for more information regarding the use of crates.) But if your dog is large and your car is small, a crate may not work for you. In this situation, you can use one of the many belting devices specially designed for pet travel. You may also place your pet in a halter-style collar and leash and attach the leash to a seat belt. This method is great for restraining but may not offer protection in an accident.

Traveling with your dog is like traveling with children—the more you do it, the easier it becomes. It will soon feel like second nature. The

THE DANGERS OF LEAVING YOUR DOG IN THE CAR

Leaving your dog in your car, even for a moment, can be dangerous. The number one cause of danger is heat (which is discussed on page 41), but there are other issues to consider:

➤ Anyone stealing your car would also have your dog. What would a thief do with him? Don't count on your dog protecting your car. A determined thief may hurt your dog in order to get your vehicle.

➤ A thief may actually want your dog and dognap him.

➤ Children or adults may tease your dog through the windows, trying to rile him. If your dog was to defend himself or his territory (your car) and hurt someone, you could be sued.

➤ Children or adults may try to pet your dog. Again, if he protects himself or his territory, you could be in trouble. Don't assume that because your dog is friendly with strangers when you are around the same holds true when he is alone in the vehicle. He may see it as his job to protect your possessions and interpret the people as a threat. Dogs tend to be more protective when their space is small and they are in strange surroundings. Unfortunately, many people don't teach their children that no one should ever attempt to pet a dog left in a car or tied up without asking permission from the owner first.

➤ Well-intentioned children or adults may let your dog out of the car. They may want to play with him, or they may think they are rescuing him from certain harm.

➤ Vandals may throw firecrackers, rocks, trash, and poisonous food into the open window of your car and injure your dog.

➤ You may be cited by your local animal control department if a complaint is made about you leaving your dog in your car too long.

sidebar on page 42 lists the items you will want to bring with you when you travel. This list is a starting point; experience will tell you what to add or delete. Remember, though, the only time you *don't* bring something will be the time that you need it!

If the first few times traveling with your dog seem rough, take heart and know that with time, traveling will become easy for both you and your dog.

Heat Dangers

The risk to your dog in a hot car is real. A dog can easily fall victim to high temperatures. Your dog's ability to dissipate heat is far inferior to your own. If you are warm, your dog is hot. For this reason, leaving your dog in a car even briefly should occur only in cool temperatures.

An outdoor temperature of 85 degrees Fahrenheit will heat your car to 100 degrees in 10 minutes and to 120 degrees in 30 minutes. It is too dangerous to leave your dog in the car alone for longer than a few minutes. Even if you leave the air conditioner on, trouble could strike if the engine or air conditioner stops. You could return to your car to find a terrible nightmare. (See chapter 4 for information on how to identify and treat heatstroke.)

You must also take your dog's comfort into consideration while driving. Running your air conditioner is one way to keep the inside temperature of your car cool while traveling in hot weather. If you are not running your air conditioner or don't have one, then you will probably have the windows open. If your dog likes to hang his head out the window, you will have to protect him from himself. Using a restraint system is the best solution. You can also put accordion gates in the open windows. You can purchase these gates through catalogs and dog specialty stores.

Paperwork

If you will be traveling across state lines or over the border to Canada or Mexico, you will need to ask your veterinarian what paperwork is needed. No matter where you are planning to travel, you should have a copy of a current health certificate, immunization records, and rabies certificate for your dog. Rabies tags are not always proof enough. Each state has differing rules on what is considered a "current" health certificate, so inquire about the rules for each state where you will be stopping.

MOTEL STAYS

When traveling to a show or an event, you may need to stay in a motel. More motels will accept dogs today than in the past, but such

WHAT TO BRING WHEN YOU TRAVEL

Pet first-aid kit

Identification

Health certificate

Rabies certificate

Food and water bowls

Jug of water from home (to avoid stomach upsets)

Flashlight

Grooming necessities

Crate

Bedding

Pre-moistened towelettes

Necessary medications

3" x 5" emergency phone card

Food

Collar and leash

Retractable leash

Pooper scooper

Paper towels

Treats

Toys

Written reservations

Photos for identification purposes

Spray bottle with water (for cooling dogs who are hot)

places are still few and far between. This is where advanced planning will really pay off. If the motel you choose has a rule against accepting dogs, talk to the manager, explaining your level of responsibility. If you keep your dog crated, this can increase your odds of finding a motel that will accept your pooch.

When you make reservations and again when you check in, question the manager about any recent chemical use. A motel room that has been freshly treated with insecticides could make your canine sick. It could even be fatal. The possibility of fresh paint, new carpet, outdoor pesticides, and other chemicals should also be investigated.

Alone in the Room

Some motels have rules regarding leaving pets unattended in a room. You surely cannot blame them; many doors, carpets, and furniture have been ruined by nervous, stressed pets left in their motel rooms by their caretakers.

If you do leave your dog in your room, make sure that he is well secured in his crate or cage. He should have plenty of toys to keep him occupied. Leave your dog only for short periods. Return soon so he does not become nervous and start misbehaving.

It is a good idea while you are away to hang a Do Not Disturb sign on your door. This will eliminate the possibility of the maid coming in when you are not there. Pick up your own clean linen at the front desk to avoid having someone disturb you or your dog. Leave the television on to keep your dog company and to make the room seem occupied.

Motel patrons and personnel do not want whining or barking, lonely animals who disturb all the other guests. It takes only one bad experience for the motel to change its rules. Making sure that all goes well during your stay will assist the next person who wants to stay there with his or her pet.

Cleanliness

Keep your dog off the furniture to limit the amount of hair left behind. If your canine normally sleeps on your bed, bring your own blanket or bedding from home.

Set a good example and help increase the acceptance of pets in the hospitality business by cleaning up your motel room and leaving no obvious signs that an animal has been there. Bring your favorite hair-collection tool and get rid of most of the shed hair. And, of course, always clean up after your dog relieves himself on the motel grounds.

A DEN AWAY FROM HOME—THE CRATE

Some animal lovers see a crate as a torture device. Those who have used them know how useful and versatile crates can be. More importantly, they know how much their dogs come to love their crates. For the canine athlete on the go, the crate is a portable den. Some basic rules guide good human conduct when using a crate; these are listed in the sidebar called "The Do's and Don'ts of Crate Use" (see page 46). Here I want to focus exclusively on the benefits of crate use for your active canine traveler.

When you and your dog are traveling in a car, a crate is a good safety device. Keeping your dog out of harm's way and out of your way lowers the risk of accidents and mishaps. If secured by a seatbelt, a crate can help prevent injury in an automobile accident. If you are in an accident and your crate is sturdy and properly closed, your frightened, upset dog will not be able to run madly about. Some dogs will guard their beloved caretakers, making it difficult for emergency personnel to help them. Sometimes paramedics must destroy an animal to save the person he is "protecting." If your dog is safely enclosed in his crate, you will avoid this trouble.

In a car, the crate should not be placed on the floor because of the danger of carbon monoxide poisoning and because of fluctuations in temperature. The crate should be placed out of direct sunlight and shaded with a light-colored towel or blanket. The towel or blanket will do double duty by calming excitable animals.

An active dog who must travel regularly will come to view his crate as his home away from home. While traveling, waiting on the show-grounds, or sleeping in never-before-seen surroundings, your dog will feel more secure and comfortable in his familiar den. At shows, events, and trials, your dog must be contained in a safe area during different periods of the day—a crate suits this purpose very well. Attend just one dog show and you will see how indispensable a crate can be. Affixed with wheels and decked out with packs holding doggie essentials, crates of all sizes filled with all sorts of dogs are pulled around the grounds with ease.

If your dog becomes a globe-trotting canine, or even one who ventures long distances in our own country, you must have a crate for plane rides. Airlines have particular requirements that must be considered. When choosing what crate to purchase, you should take into account any air travel your furry friend may have to do. (See page 47 for more on airline regulations.)

Tips for Choosing a Crate for Your Traveling Canine

Size—Your dog should be able to stand up, lie down, and turn around in the crate. The crate's manufacturer will probably offer a size guideline by breed of dog.

Ease of Cleaning—If you are going to be using your crate often, it is important that the crate be easy to clean. Otherwise, you may be tempted to let it stay dirty. Crates with smooth edges and ones that disassemble easily make cleaning less trouble.

Vinyl Coated versus Wire Sided—Vinyl finishes come in different colors, resist rust and scratches, and are easier to clean than wire. They may be less durable, though, in the long run.

Weight—Wire crates are heavier than plastic (vinyl) crates. Having a lightweight crate can really make a difference after a long day of active participation in your event. If you must move your crate around often at home and move it in and out of the car numerous times, weight could be important to you.

Latches—A strong, sturdy latch will keep your dog secure in his crate while traveling in the event something happens as traumatic as an accident or as irritating as a big bump. You can add an extra lock on the crate's door for another level of security. The latch should be easy to open and close.

Ease of Assembly—You may be taking your dog's crate apart and putting it back together often throughout its lifetime. If it must be moved frequently or stored away when not used, you should look for a crate that is simple to set up and take down. Many wire crates are designed to fold down to an easily stored size.

Your Dog's Tolerance to Temperature Fluctuations—If your dog has a thin coat or wispy build, a plastic carrier will offer more protection from the elements. If your dog is heavy coated or heat intolerant, a wire crate with more ventilation may be preferred. You can always throw a towel or blanket over a wire crate when necessary.

THE DO'S AND DON'TS OF CRATE USE

Do use the crate as a training tool.

Don't use the crate as a substitute for training.

Do use the crate to prevent your dog from getting into trouble when you cannot keep an eye on him or when he is under foot or bothering others.

Don't keep your dog in his crate for longer than two hours for a puppy and four hours for an adult dog.

Do allow your dog to be with you when you are home to interact with him and guide his behavior.

Don't place your dog in the crate as punishment or because you are frustrated with him.

Do offer treats to your dog when you are introducing the crate and keep him closed in only for short sessions (10 minutes to start) until he is accustomed to it.

Don't let your dog out of the crate if he is whining or barking—wait until he is quiet.

Do make the crate comfy and homey with a blanket or mattress.

Don't place your dog in a crate for long periods if he hasn't been exercised and allowed to relieve himself.

Do leave the door open so that your dog can use his crate as he wants throughout the day.

Don't use the crate as a substitute for your attention.

Your Dog's Tolerance to Outside Stimulation—If your dog is a bit excitable when traveling or at events, a plastic crate offers more "protection" from the world. This sense of security may be all it takes to keep your dog calm in otherwise overstimulating environments. Then again, you can also cover a wire crate when necessary.

Other Conveniences to Consider—Some crates come with doors on the side or the top. Many come with a combination of the traditional front door and a door at the side or top. Some crates are slanted so that they will fit in the back of a station wagon or hatchback. If you have more than one dog and are limited on space, you may need crates that can stack on top of each other. Plastic crates have easy-to-remove doors or tops and can serve as comfy beds for deserving canine athletes.

THE FLYING DOG

Your adventure may take you far away. You are then faced with a long car ride and motel stays or with flying. Which should you choose? This depends on you and your dog. Opinions differ as to the safety of airline travel for dogs. Many dog fanciers have been flying their dogs around the country and the world with nary a problem; others can relate terrible stories that ended in heartbreak. Fortunately, animal lovers have pressured airlines for more stringent regulations, and most airlines are now doing their best to make flying as safe and stressfree as possible for our canine friends.

If you are traveling by plane, you will have to meet specific requirements and plan far in advance. You must have reservations in writing to take your pet along. Find out from the airline all its requirements for health certifications and carrier specifications, and then meet them.

Freight Compartment versus Cabin

Most often when you fly, your dog will travel via the freight compartment—not the most desirable way for an animal to travel. If you make reservations well in advance and ask for a written confirmation, you may be able to take your dog in the cabin. Most airlines will allow a predetermined number of animals per flight in each cabin. Your dog will have to be small because he must fit in a carrier placed under the seat. Call the individual airlines to get exact space measurements.

If your pet is too large to fit under a cabin seat, he will have to fly in the freight compartment. Tell the airline that you are shipping a live animal, and again, make sure that you fully understand all the regulations and follow them exactly. To be certain that your animal is completely healthy, a visit to your veterinarian is in order. Your veterinarian can supply you with a statement of your dog's good health.

What to Look For

When you have no option but to fly and your canine athlete must be in the freight compartment, you will want to investigate the conditions of the flight to be sure your companion will be safe.

The plane's cargo area must be pressurized; smaller planes and commuter planes can't be used. Generally, the larger the plane, the safer the hold.

Temperature fluctuations can present a grave danger to your dog. The plane's cargo area must have temperature controls regulating air conditioning and heat. Above 10,000 feet in altitude, the air is very cold. Another serious threat is ground temperature. While waiting for takeoff, your pet may have to wait in the cargo bay for some time. During this period, the cargo area is not cooled and can become much hotter than the outside temperature. Depending on the length of time the plane is delayed, the temperature in the cargo area can escalate as much as 20 degrees Fahrenheit above the outside temperature—a dangerous situation at warmer times of the day or year. The United States Department of Agriculture prohibits animals from traveling by air if the temperature is above 85 degrees or below 45 degrees Fahrenheit.

Ask how and where your dog will be taken off the plane, and arrange for your companion to be carried off and not released onto the luggage carousel. Request that your dog fly "counter to counter."

When to Travel

To make flying easier on your dog, choose to travel during slow or off-peak periods. Arrange a flight during the week, and avoid the rush hours of late afternoon and early evening. An uncrowded flight will lower the amount of luggage crowding your pooch in the cargo hold and increase the likelihood of his receiving more personal attention.

Do your best to reserve a nonstop flight, remembering that the most compromising time for your dog is during clearance waits, takeoffs, and landings. If you have no choice but to stop, find out if you have to change planes, which can be a risky and difficult process for your dog. If your dog must change flights, verify that he has been moved to the new plane before takeoff.

If the weather is warm, schedule your flight for when it is cooler: early morning, late evening, or night. Midday flights are best for very cold weather. Remember, even though the freight compartment is supposed to be climate controlled, mishaps do happen, although rarely. You take this risk when your dog flies in the freight compartment.

The Crate

Your dog will have to travel in a crate. Be sure he is accustomed to his crate well before he must travel alone in a cargo hold. His crate should feel like a refuge—safe and comfortable in a strange environment.

Each airline has its own requirements regarding the carrier design, so check with the airline you plan to use most often before purchasing a crate. You can also check with several airlines and then try to find a crate that will fit all their requirements.

Dogs who fly will need a sturdy, well-built plastic crate. Don't scrimp here. The crate should be big enough for your dog to stand up, lie down, and turn around inside. A water dish should be attached. Choose a light color for the crate to keep the temperature inside at a more comfortable level. The crate's bottom should be solid and furnished with a comfortable and absorbent lining. Good ventilation is important.

A strong, sturdy lock is an absolute necessity. If your crate is made of two sections held together with nuts and bolts, use locking washers under the nuts for more trustworthy construction. Securing the locked door with a strap or bungee cord running completely around the crate is a good extra safety precaution.

If your dog is small and you are taking him in the cabin, you may use a soft-sided carrier. It must fit under the plane's seats, be sturdy, and offer security as well as a view.

Identification and care instructions should be attached to the crate where they can be easily located. Label your crate with a Live Animal sticker, and off you go!

Using Tranquilizers

Some dogs are naturally high-strung and nervous. If yours is one of these and you have no choice but to send him by air freight, you may want to talk to your veterinarian regarding tranquilizers. Tranquilizers depress breathing and slow the animal's heart rate, so make sure your dog is healthy before using them. The cargo area of a plane may have little air circulation if takeoff is delayed, taxing the already inhibited respiratory system of a tranquilized dog.

Testing the tranquilizer and how it affects your companion before you take off is a good precaution, but the effect a tranquilizer has on your pooch while on the ground may not reflect what will happen when the plane is cruising at a high altitude. Your animal's reactions to tranquilizers while in flight are unpredictable, so use a tranquilizer with caution, only under the supervision of a veterinarian, and only if it is absolutely necessary.

CHAPTER THREE

From Couch Potato to Super-Dog: Conditioning Your Canine for Activity

Is Your Dog Ready?

How do you know if your dog is ready to begin an athletic fitness program? Is she too young or too old? Will her bowlegs or her chronic arthritis limit or exclude certain activities? How will her being a little overweight affect her abilities and the development and progress of her conditioning program?

Some people may not even ask these questions, opting for the jump-right-into-it approach. But by knowing the answers to them, you can better handle your dog's special circumstances, adjusting the physical and mental requirements of your chosen activity to the condition of your dog. Giving your dog a solid foundation, by beginning at her current level, offers her the best opportunity for success combined with good health throughout her life.

HOW AGE INFLUENCES CONDITIONING

As with humans, each stage in a dog's life brings with it particular joys and problems. Recognizing these stages and understanding their significant peculiarities will help you handle and train your dog with more acceptance and thoughtfulness.

Below I discuss puppyhood, adolescence, and old age. You may experience unique problems and situations during these stages, but knowing what to expect will allow you to better deal with them. Adulthood is the prime of your dog's life. During this period, you and your dog can fine-tune her athletic performance and skill knowledge. Your sporting time with your adult canine athlete (barring injury or other unforeseen problems) should be the most predictable, harmonious, and successful of your adventurous life together. By having a deeper understanding of the other, more difficult stages, you will reduce frustration and be able to take joy in the entire process of your growing and maturing canine companion.

Puppyhood

You've just brought home your carefully researched, painstakingly chosen canine athlete star-to-be, and you are ready to put her on the path to greatness. This cute little butterball is going to be the new champion in the family. Before you start training, however, you should first understand some facts about puppies.

Generally, if your dog is under 12 to 14 months old, she is considered a puppy. Puppies have special physical and psychological needs. Emotionally, your pooch is still quite immature. A puppy's attention span is short and directed more toward play than serious work. Puppies learn their lessons of acceptable behavior through play, and through play, you can introduce your puppy to your chosen adventure.

As mentioned in chapter 2, the importance of socialization cannot be overemphasized. Take every opportunity to let your little canine sponge soak up the many wonders of the world. Have fun while you introduce her to all sorts of interesting objects and experiences. See Jean Donaldson's *Culture Clash* for some exceptional suggestions for socializing.

Your puppy's bones are soft and immature, and her growth plates will not close until she leaves puppyhood. Too much strain and hard work while her bones are developing can irreparably damage them.

You're eager though—when can you start working with your dog? Dogs mature at different rates, depending on what their adult size will be. In general, dogs weighing less than 25 pounds when mature will be able to participate in vigorous exercise when they are around 8 months old. Dogs who will reach 45 to 95 pounds should be closer to 12 months of age. Those large beasts of 100 or more pounds at maturity should be at least 18 months old. These estimates should be used as guidelines— they are not set in stone. Much will depend on what activity you are considering, how vigorous your training plan is, what genetic components are working for or against your dog, and how good your puppy's general health is. To get an estimate based on your individual dog, talk to your veterinarian and your dog's breeder.

You can begin some light conditioning before your pup's ready for a full workout. For example, you can play easy fetch or ball-chasing games. Puppies lack coordination (don't worry, she won't always trip over those gigantic paws), and they are at greater risk of becoming injured. You can minimize the risk of injuries by keeping the games under control, by paying close attention to the terrain and your puppy's attitude (is she getting too assertive?), and by stopping the games if she becomes tired. As your puppy grows, you can gradually work up to moderate activity—a slow, short-distance run, for instance. When your pup finally reaches one of the aforementioned age milestones, you can start expecting more from her.

In the meantime, feel free to work on some basic obedience in a playful and casual manner, and by all means let that little rascal know what you expect of her behaviorally. But a three-month-old puppy should not be scrambling up a regulation-height A-frame, and a five-month-old should not be expected to perform a precision heel. Let your pup have fun for a while; there is plenty of time for work later.

Adolescence

Oh, adolescence. Is there a more trying time? If you have a puppy or an adolescent dog, you need a copy of Carol Lea Benjamin's book *Surviving Your Dog's Adolescence*. Even if you are in the company of an adult dog, this book is still good reading.

Adolescent dogs need to be treated differently from puppies. With puppies, everything should be fun, but you'll probably have to be firmer with your canine teenager—not meaner, just firmer. Your adolescent dog is going to test your authority, so be prepared to enforce your rules. She has a lot on her mind, and most often she's not thinking about what you want from her. Maintain your position of authority by expecting, and then rewarding, compliance.

In addition to the emotional upheaval during the adolescent period, your dog is experiencing physical difficulties. Now tall and lanky, she may not look quite like you thought she would—yet she's not that cute little puppy anymore either. While you are wondering about her outward appearance, she is desperately trying to figure out how to make her unfamiliar body move the way she wants it to. Just like teenage humans, adolescent dogs are uncomfortable in their awkward bodies.

Your teenage canine is working out the physical difficulties of doing what you are asking of her while fighting her instincts to assert her independence. Give her some leeway. Know when an activity or exercise is just too difficult for her, either because of her gangly body or because of her lack of coordination. Take skill training one day at a time—take one little baby step before going on to the next. For a while, it may feel as if she takes one step forward for every three steps backward, but one day your dog will understand what you want and be able to do it. Be patient with her.

You may be one of the few lucky ones. Your dog may breeze through adolescence with nary a complaint or problem. If so, count your blessings. But if your dog's adolescence seems like your worst nightmare come true, the good news is that it is a temporary stage. Your dog will soon pass into adulthood. You will come through this trying period with your sanity intact if you keep everything in perspective.

Old Age

You made it through puppyhood (only your carpet reminds you of the strain) and even adolescence. And for a few years, you had a dog who would listen to you (because you raised and trained her right), who could really perform in competition, and who could shine in any conditioning program you designed. Those were the glory years. They may have lasted a decade or more if you chose a long-lived breed or individual. With preventative veterinary care and your good coaching sense, your dog made it through her adult years healthy and fit.

And now comes another stage—old age, a period of well-deserved rest for your faithful canine athlete from the mental and physical requirements of performance and competition. By the time your dog reaches 7 to 10 years of age, you'll need to cut back on your demands, but stopping altogether is not usually necessary. With some extra precautions, your older dog can still be part of your active, adventurous lifestyle.

If you allow your older dog to retire completely and cease all exercise, she may become overweight, depressed, and less flexible. Many of the health benefits of having been active will be lost. If her health is still good, then she can, and should, continue with lower-intensity exercise. Moderate exercise can even help alleviate some of the problems associated with old age, such as arthritis. Talk to your veterinarian to be sure that no chronic conditions or illnesses should keep her sidelined.

Pay close attention to your older dog while she is involved in physical recreation. As you did during her competitive years, know her normal manner of moving and attitude and be aware of any changes. Any change should be reported to your veterinarian. Offer your dog plenty of rest breaks and never push her too hard. The best time to exercise your more sensitive, older dog is when the temperature is comfortable. Avoid any weather extremes.

If you are new to canine athleticism and your dog is older, then a pre-exercise check with your veterinarian is critical. You can start an older dog on a conditioning routine, but start off slowly (with short walks, for instance) and gradually increase her fitness. What you and she can achieve will depend upon your dog's age and health and your commitment, but she will never perform like a younger dog. Exercise with her anyway. Healthy twilight years are a wonderful gift to give your long-time buddy.

HEALTH RISKS

Structural Difficulties

People's opinions of what makes a dog functional or attractive differ greatly. For instance, the bulldog and the borzoi are two incredibly different dogs structurally that people have spent hundreds of years selectively breeding. Many times, this painstaking breeding produces dogs who are prone to physical problems. These dogs are undeniably good-looking (after all, that's what the breeders were working for), but they can have special limitations when it comes to physical activity.

Proper body alignment and a balanced body structure produce a dog who is capable of balanced movement. Breeding that exaggerates one or more body parts over others creates an imbalance. This imbalance results in greater stress on individual structural components, which increases the risk of injury.

To produce dogs who can perform an intended job superbly, each breed's physical structure became specialized. For instance, webbed feet are ideal for dogs who will spend considerable time in the snow or water, compact (cat-like) feet are optimum for endurance activities, and oval feet allow a dog to have greater initial speed and assist in jumping. No foot shape is "wrong"; each was developed by breeders with an objective in mind. Nevertheless, it will be easier for your dog if her foot shape is conducive to your chosen activity.

Particular conformation qualities can make activity difficult for some dog breeds. Almost every breed has at least one orthopedic problem that is inherent in the breed's structure, and many breeds have astonishingly long lists of possible problems. The problems associated with a particular breed are only possibilities; any dog of any breed, as well as mixed-breed dogs can be a victim of orthopedic disabilities and injuries. In addition, a predisposition for a problem does not guarantee your dog will succumb to it. However, if you understand the orthopedic problems that may affect your particular dog, you can keep a keen eye out for problems, have your dog tested if appropriate, and know what could possibly sideline your canine adventure.

All dog coaches should have a basic understanding of canine structure and movement and should know how to recognize possible problems. To help with your research, the appendix lists many good books and videos. You can also learn from experienced competitors and your veterinarian. Let them know you are interested in understanding more about canine structure.

The most common orthopedic problems are hip and elbow dysplasia and problems associated with the shoulder joint. Dogs with hip dysplasia and patellar luxation should be exercised only moderately. If your dog has only a mild case of these physical problems, you can take extra precautions by withdrawing from a competition if the ground is uneven. Staying attentive to signs of tiredness or pain—even subtle signs such as a grimace and stopping her participation if necessary—will decrease the likelihood of damage to your dog.

Any kind of physical activity will have to be modified for a dog who suffers from dysplasia. The type and amount of activity a dog can participate in will depend on the individual dog and how badly she is affected by her dysplasia. Some dogs with this type of problem can lead relatively normal lives, with only periodic bouts of discomfort, while others are in constant, intense pain and are seriously debilitated. Certain structural conditions can result in secondary degenerative joint disease (osteoarthritis).

Physical Liabilities

Physical conditions other than structural difficulties can affect a dog's ability to participate in recreational and competitive activities. Deafness, vision problems, and chronic illness, for example, can influence what adventures you pursue and at what intensity.

You probably already have an idea whether your dog is suffering from any of these conditions, and an examination by your veterinarian will assist in ruling out any problems you have not identified. You can work with and around many of these situations with the help of your veterinarian and breeder. Some organizations and sports bar dogs who suffer from specific physical limitations. If your dog has any of the conditions listed above, make sure she can participate in the sport or activity you are interested in.

One problem that will influence your dog's athletic ability is arthritis. This degenerative joint disease is more common in older dogs but can occur in younger dogs, especially ones who have had an injury to a joint area or who suffer from dysplasia or other conditions affecting the efficiency of an area of the body. My five-year-old Bouvier has arthritis in her spine, seemingly from an old injury. Arthritis gets worse the more the joints are weakened by overuse or fatigue.

Following a complete workup with x-rays, dogs with arthritis should be worked gently and only under the supervision of your veterinarian. A conditioning program must minimize the stress placed on the affected joints. Some dogs with mild arthritis can participate more fully using a mild pain killer. Others may not be able to do much more than go for an easy walk. Talk over your situation with your veterinarian.

An example of a physical trait that makes it difficult for a dog to participate in intense activity is a brachycephalic head. This head structure is characterized by a flat, upturned face such as those in pugs and bulldogs. A brachycephalic head makes proper breathing difficult. Dogs with this trait tire quickly, must exercise at a more moderate pace, and cannot tolerate heat as well as other dogs.

Short-legged dogs are also at a disadvantage because of the manner in which their weight is carried. They often have back problems. They also have a difficult time at the more advanced levels of some events because they may not be able to jump as well as other dogs. You will need to start short-legged dogs slowly, giving them more time to adapt to the conditioning program before moving on.

Some breeds and physical types will be able to do more, and some will be capable of less. The activity you wish to participate in will dictate which type of dog you choose, or if you already have a dog, her structure will influence the activity you choose. Beyond all the possible physical liabilities, your dog's attitude is the major influence in her success. You can introduce any activity to your dog if you take her willingness and capabilities into consideration.

Obesity

You probably know if your dog is obese, whether you want to admit it or not. A dog is considered obese if she is 30 percent or more above her normal weight. Of course, if she has been this way for long, you may not remember her normal weight. You can feel if your dog is overweight with the hands-on tests described below.

Just in front of her shoulder blades, pinch the sides of her neck with your thumb and forefinger. Pull up gently, letting the fat slide through your fingers. There should be only a small amount of fat. Place your thumbs on either side of her spine and run your fingers over her ribs. You should be able to feel the bumps of her ribs without pressing. One more place to feel her fat is on her hips. Run your hands over her croup and feel, without pressing, the bumps of her pelvic bones on either side of her spine.

You may have decided to read this book because your dog is a little thick around the middle and you want to find an activity to take care of this problem. Great! But if this is the case, you are going to have to take it easy on her. By engaging your dog in moderate exercise and implementing a calorie-reducing diet, with your veterinarian's help, you can take the weight off your hefty canine.

Elite canine athletes are lean, efficient machines (with a thinking mind and feeling soul, of course). In fact, many handlers prefer their charges to be so lean that to an outsider they may look too skinny. That's because extra weight hampers a dog's physical abilities and performance. Added weight stresses muscles, bones, and joints. Lung capacity and heart function are compromised and heat tolerance is minimized. Conditioned canine athletes are active enough that they are bound to stay at a fit, healthy weight, but you must start your overweight dog at the beginning with a low- to moderate-intensity program.

Pay particular attention to the wear and tear you are placing on your dog. Rough terrain, excessively long distances, and extended durations of exercise, as well as jumping and climbing anything but the lowest heights, can all add to the risk of injury. If you push your chunky dog too far too fast, even if she survives intact physically, you are going to sour her attitude. Relax. She'll be able to participate in a more vigorous training and conditioning schedule shortly, as long as you make the commitment to help her along the way to become the healthiest and leanest possible version of herself.

Heart and Respiratory Conditions

Heart and respiratory conditions can greatly alter the course of your training program. A dog with these problems should start slowly and increase activity gradually. Brachycephalic breeds have a tendency to suffer from these kinds of problems. Continual contact with your veterinarian is in order for these dogs. If heart and respiratory problems are a secondary reaction to another illness, such as heartworm disease, then the primary condition must be dealt with before your dog starts any activity. Your veterinarian will be able to discern the condition's origin and the best course of action.

When you take your dog in for her initial preconditioning exam, your veterinarian will listen for a murmur and an irregular heart rate. If a problem is suspected, the vet will probably recommend x-rays and possibly an electrocardiogram (EKG) to diagnose the specific affliction you are dealing with. If a heart or respiratory problem is not diagnosed before you begin a vigorous training program, your dog can suffer serious injury or even die.

YOUR VETERINARIAN'S ROLE

Your veterinarian is an important member of your training team. You both have the same goal—allowing your dog to participate in an activity with minimum risk of injury and discomfort. You both want your dog to realize her full health potential, and to do this you will rely on each other for input and knowledge. The relationship requires two-way communication that must be as straightforward and informative as possible.

During the pretraining exam, your vet will complete a thorough medical workup of the inside and outside of your canine athlete. An exam will provide you with baseline information about your dog's health. If a problem arises later during conditioning or competing, you can compare the new information to your baseline.

Discuss your conditioning program with your veterinarian. He or she will be able to make an accurate assessment and informed recommendations when your planned activity and level of intensity are clear.

The first order of business is to verify that your dog's vaccinations are current, especially if you will be traveling to doggie areas. If your dog isn't currently on a heartworm preventative program, you will want to start one now. Your dog's weight will be checked, and if necessary you and your vet can discuss weight control options. Your veterinarian will also examine your dog's toenails and pads and make recommendations involving their care.

Your veterinarian should assess your dog's structure and movement. If he or she specializes in athletic canines, this assessment may be very detailed. If any signs of lameness are present, then further diagnosis will be warranted. If your dog's breed is susceptible to any orthopedic problems, you and your vet may decide to have the prone area or areas x-rayed just to be safe, whether or not any complications are evident. These areas may include hips, elbows, and shoulders. During exercise, your dog's musculoskeletal system must tolerate an increased load. Exercise will strengthen her body and increase her fitness, but if your dog has even minute problems, she is at greater risk of injury. The constant imbalance and overworking of some areas can eventually cause a chronic condition or injury.

Even minor problems can distract and irritate your dog, making it challenging to train her and putting her at a disadvantage when competing. In some precision sports, a badly timed scratch can get your dog disqualified. A check for and treatment of worms, fleas, and other parasites therefore must be a part of your pretraining exam. Aside from being irritating and distracting, these pests can weaken your dog's bodily systems and increase her risk of illness, injury, or damage. Other skin problems should be diagnosed and addressed as well.

How is your dog's health on the inside? Internal organs, as well as the musculoskeletal system, can take a beating. As mentioned earlier, your vet will listen for a heart murmur and an irregular heart rate. As well as assessing your dog's joints, muscles, and tendons, your vet will check the health of her lungs, kidneys, and liver. Also, your vet may want to rule out urinary bladder infections. He or she may run a number of tests to get the "all clear." Your dog's mouth should be checked for broken, missing, and sensitive teeth. Her teeth may need to be cleaned. Her eyes will also be examined for infections, indications of possible degenerative conditions, and conjunctivitis.

Another concern to discuss with your veterinarian is nutrition. Your dog's nutrient needs will change as her fitness level increases. Discuss what food your dog is presently eating, how much work she is currently doing, what activities she'll be taking up, and whether or not her current food is adequate. If not, ask for some ideas on devising a better nutrition plan.

The importance of a pretraining exam should not be underestimated. Such an exam is a small investment to ensure that your canine athlete can have fun participating in an activity risk free for years to come.

Your dog can be so devoted to you that she may push her body harder than she should just because you ask her to. If you have an assessment performed by your veterinarian, you will have a much clearer picture of what to expect from your dog and of where to begin her conditioning program.

Conditioning the Active Dog

Embarking on a conditioning program with your dog should be exciting to you. Your enthusiasm will keep both you and your dog motivated, allowing you to follow through on your plans and reap the benefits of participating in your chosen adventure. The progression of steps outlined below will guide you in the development of your dog's program. By following these simple, logical steps, you can help your dog become a better athlete. As you gain more experience, you can adjust and refine your program. But for now, read the following information and get your dog busy!

PLANNING A TRAINING PROGRAM

Getting your dog into optimum physical condition takes commitment. How much commitment is required to help your dog reach the needed fitness level depends on your chosen adventure and your level of participation. No matter what you choose to do with your dog, if it involves physical activity you must educate yourself and proceed only after you have accumulated a basic understanding of how your dog's body works.

In order to design an efficient conditioning program, you must have a clear idea of your goals. Do you want to participate at high levels of competition? If so, your obligation to your dog's fitness program will be greater. Do you just want to have fun on the weekends hiking in the mountains? If so, your commitment will be to do some conditioning during the week. If your hiking expeditions are going to be an easygoing walk through the woods, then your fitness routine will consist of fun, low-intensity conditioning. If you have a more rigorous hike planned for you and your dog, then you will have to create a more vigorous conditioning program.

The program that you set up for your individual dog will be influenced by many factors. Some of these factors include

- your commitment
- your chosen activity
- your dog's current level of fitness
- your dog's energy level
- your dog's structure
- your dog's existing physical problems
- your and your dog's present skill levels

Each dog and human combination is unique. Your training and conditioning schedule must be balanced yet flexible. Your program can vary depending on many factors, such as the time of year or changes in your goal or lifestyle.

Once you have decided to participate in a physical venture with your dog, you become a team—a partnership. But you have more than one hat to wear. You are team member, training partner, buddy, decision maker, and most importantly, the coach. You have the responsibility to know what you want to achieve, how to reach your goal, and how to take care of yourself and your dog in the process. Your dog relies on you for direction. She will do what you ask, so be sure of what you are asking. Expand your knowledge and keep apprised of current information. Know your sport or activity.

Don't be intimidated. You can change your dog from a couch-potato canine to a fit, healthy athlete. If you keep in mind that you are getting active with your canine buddy to have fun, you *will* have fun. The emphasis, no matter what your goal, should be on enjoying the companionship of your dog while participating in fun and challenging adventures. This should be your motto: Keep it fun! Write it in big letters and post it by your training equipment, next to the leash, on the bathroom mirror, or on the dashboard of your car as a reminder.

WHAT IS CONDITIONING?

When all bodily systems of your dog are in a balanced, healthy relationship, then your dog is "in condition." These systems include the musculoskeletal, cardiovascular, and nervous systems (which I will discuss more fully later). Physical fitness encompasses strength, endurance, coordination, and agility. Enhancing fitness should be approached holistically, balancing all the above attributes in an ideal combination. This approach should emphasize your chosen activity, your dog's current fitness level, and her present weaknesses and strengths. Even if your dog's structure is ideal for your activity, conditioning will help your dog

THE BENEFITS OF CONDITIONING YOUR DOG

Proper conditioning of your dog does the following:

➤ Prepares your dog for specific events

➤ Develops strength, endurance, coordination, flexibility, and agility

➤ Improves the condition of bodily systems, including digestive, respiratory, circulatory, and cardiovascular

➤ Reduces obesity and its accompanying problems

➤ Helps to reduce complications and discomfort of other diseases, such as arthritis

➤ Releases endorphins (the brain neurotransmitters that make you feel good)

➤ Burns energy and helps an excitable dog relax

➤ Exercises your dog's body as well as her mind and helps to prevent many destructive and annoying habits that a bored dog engages in

➤ Gives you and your dog time together that will enhance your bond

➤ Keeps your dog more youthful in both mind and body

➤ Improves your dog's quality of life

maximize her potential. Training can also help overcome some structural limitations.

THE COMPONENTS OF A CONDITIONING PROGRAM

Warmup and Cool Down

Can you take your dog from her bed, hook her up to your bicycle, cruise down the road with her at a training pace, come home without first cooling down, and then leave her by the television without causing any physical damage or without creating a sour attitude? Not likely.

A warmup for the body lubricates the joints, raises the heart rate, and prepares the body for the more taxing work yet to come, thus lessening the risk of injury and soreness. A warmup for the mind puts your dog in a working attitude, starts her listening to you, establishes your intentions, and wakes her up if she's been snoozing. Warming up your dog also warms you up, getting you both focused and ready for a challenge.

A good warmup should last at least 5 minutes and include activities that your dog enjoys and finds rewarding. For example, if you are skijoring with your dog, travel at a relaxed pace on easy terrain for the first 5 to 10 minutes. If you are practicing agility obstacles, play an easygoing Frisbee game for 5 minutes. If you are working on obedience exercises, start with the commands your dog knows and performs reliably so that she can experience success. Starting at a relaxed pace with a skill that she can demonstrate successfully without much difficulty will increase her confidence. A confident dog will attempt more difficult requests with a good attitude and is more likely to succeed.

Warming up should include the specific components of your training program. For example, when you practice jumping, start with the jump heights set low and then progress to higher jumps when your dog is ready. Each activity will have slightly different physical demands and should be introduced in the same step-by-step progression in each practice session. When changing to another piece of equipment—for example, contact obstacles in agility or the flyball box in flyball—warm up for the specific skill required for that equipment. A few extra run-throughs will prepare your and your dog's minds and bodies for that particular activity.

A cool down is also important. If you are engaging in endurance activities, finish by lowering the intensity for 5 to 10 minutes, depending on the session's level of difficulty. The cool down should also consist of stretches such as the ones discussed in the section on flexibility. You should finish off an intense training session with an activity to calm you both down. A fun game, a vigorous grooming, or just some petting will all be appreciated by your dog and will bridge the extremes of hard work and relaxation.

Strength Conditioning

Strength conditioning is the work involved in making the musculoskeletal system stronger. Muscle strength is required to overcome inertia and to control the movement of your dog's body. It is especially important for activities requiring agility. An increase in musculoskeletal strength increases joint stability, protecting your dog from injuries and decreasing the possibility of joint diseases such as osteoarthritis. Muscle strength is also required for rapid acceleration and speed when running, jumping, and climbing.

Your dog won't be lifting weights, of course, but you can still engage your pooch in activities that build strong muscles. Some of these activities include wind sprints, hill or stair work, weight pulling, vigorous play, jumping, swimming, and hiking. Involving your dog in any physical activity strengthens and tones her musculoskeletal system, but variety is the key to a well-rounded conditioning program.

When creating a program with balance in mind, you will find that some activities require more work from particular muscle groups. Cross-training, discussed later, is important to ensure that your dog uses a wide variety of muscles. Some canine adventures require an intense use of particular muscle groups, which should be addressed in your conditioning program. Regularly engaging in activities that focus on these muscles will give your dog an added edge in competition and performance.

Every dog's muscles are made up of a combination of slow- and fast-twitch muscle fibers. Slow-twitch muscle fibers are the ones used to sustain activity, such as running long distances. Fast-twitch muscle fibers are the ones responsible for short bursts of intense movement, such as clearing a jump. Each dog has a unique blend of muscle types, making some dogs more naturally inclined to use brute strength and some more inclined to pursue endurance activities. Use your dog's strengths to your advantage, but don't forget to improve upon her weaker areas.

It is a good idea to begin your fitness program by checking your dog's current muscle tone. While another person holds up your dog's front legs, feel the animal's hind legs as she puts her weight on them. If one leg has more muscle tone than the other, the weaker side needs extra conditioning. Make a note of your observations in a journal so that you can address the situation in your next workout. After you have finished with your dog's hind legs, repeat the procedure by having her stand on her front legs so that you can observe those muscles working too.

Noticeably asymmetrical limbs may mean that your dog has a physical problem. She may have been injured or have a chronic low-grade structural defect or weakness. If you suspect such a problem, a visit to the vet is in order.

Endurance Conditioning

Endurance fitness is the ability to perform a particular activity for an extended length of time. Endurance conditioning is the use of sustained activity to increase your dog's cardiovascular and respiratory fitness. In many sports and activities—such as field trials, sledding, and skijoring—having excellent endurance is paramount. In other activities, you and your dog may have an extra advantage if she possesses excellent stamina.

Some dogs and some breeds are naturally able to work harder for longer periods of time because endurance was needed for the job the dog was bred to perform. Through conditioning, you can enhance the natural-born tendencies of a dog as well as build more endurance in a dog that lacks natural ability. If your dog has little endurance to begin with, you can increase it, but remember that a large, muscle-bound, boxy dog won't be able to successfully compete against a slender, sinewy, flexible breed in endurance sports. Deep chests, flexible backs, and many other physical attributes give some dogs an advantage.

Having a big dog is not an excuse to skip endurance work. Slow, sustained endurance training can be especially helpful as an outlet for excess energy. Also, endurance exercise will keep your dog at her optimum fitness level when she needs a break from competition training. Finally, endurance conditioning burns many calories, helping in a weight-reduction or maintenance routine, and it releases the endorphins that make your pup feel more content and relaxed.

Some people have a hard time performing endurance activities themselves and so deprive their dogs of this important training. If you are one of those people, try breaking up a long distance into shorter, easier-to-achieve sections. Instead of dreading that you have three more miles to run, concentrate on reaching the next corner or the next tree. Once you have reached the first milestone, work toward the next. Your workout will go by surprisingly quicker if you look at a long distance as a series of short increments.

Flexibility

Flexibility exercises act on the muscles, ligaments, and joints. Having a flexible musculoskeletal system helps maintain joint mobility, increases range of motion, and keeps ligaments and tendons relaxed for better performance and overall health.

Stretching exercises should involve all major muscle groups and joints. Perform some light stretching before any physical activity and save the bulk of the stretching for afterward.

One good stretch everyone should teach his or her dog is the play bow. You'll recognize this as the movement your dog uses to communicate "Come on! Let's play!" Your dog already naturally stretches this way when awakening from a nap. Add a command to this movement, and you'll soon have a stretch on command. For another valuable and dog-pleasing stretch, train your dog to put her front paws on your shoulders or chest (or a small dog can place her paws on your legs, or you can support them on your hands). You can then increase the stretch by taking a step back. Stretch your dog's sides by holding her haunches between your legs and enticing her to bend to either side around your leg. Teaching your dog to back up, crawl, and sit up increases both her flexibility and her strength.

Skill Training

When most people think about preparing a dog for a specific activity, what usually comes to mind is skill training. This type of training is more repetitive and more demanding of your dog's brain than the other components of your conditioning program. Still, skill training can and should be viewed as a fun part of the overall training and conditioning program. As the name indicates, this training involves teaching your dog the specific skills needed to perform your sport or activity correctly. Because each activity and sport in this book has a different series of skills that a dog will need to be taught, you'll have to research the specific skills necessary.

The discussion of each adventure in the second part of this book offers leads to get you started on your quest for training information but does not offer specific training advice. This book concentrates only on overall conditioning and preparation for your chosen sport or activity.

Skill training is an important part of your overall plan. It is the part of the conditioning program that asks your dog to think and remember. Without focused training in the specific skills needed in your activity, you will not be able to participate with much success. You and your dog will be extremely frustrated if you put too little effort into skill training.

But skill training doesn't have to be a miserable military-style procedure. It should not be the infamous hours of "heeling drills" that were once popular. Skill training is fun! Or at least it can be, with the right attitude. As important as it is, don't let skill training completely absorb your training time, leaving no time for conditioning. A balanced program creates a balanced dog.

What follows is general information regarding skill training to help you make the best use of your time and get the most out of your training session.

- Learn as much as you can about your chosen activity. A training club, an independent trainer, or books and videos can all be part of your education. If you attend actual events frequently, you will notice what successful teams have in common. Socialize with the handlers and their dogs to learn proven techniques.

- Keep skill-training sessions short (less than an hour), but have them at least three times a week. The good news for busy people like me who have only small increments of time available during the day is that the sessions can be as short as 5 to 10 minutes several times a day. Once your training gets more intense, you may extend the sessions to 20 minutes twice a day.

* For most sports or activities, you should not have to invest more than two or three hours a week in skill training. Some ventures, however, require larger blocks of time. Examples are field trials, for which you will probably have to travel a distance to practice in a natural setting, or skijoring, for which just getting to your training site could take an hour or more. But such training sessions are not daily requirements, and many activities have alternative means of training that can be done in your own neighborhood. For example, a wheeled cart for the road can supplement skijoring and sled-dog training.

* Stop a session before you lose patience, your dog gets bored, or either of you loses your concentration. End each skill-training session with your dog wanting more. In the beginning, when the training is new or your dog is young, the sessions will seem almost too short, but staying within the tolerance zone of your dog makes for a happy dog. If her body and mind become overwhelmed, she may simply ignore you and stop learning.

* Be creative with your training. For example, you may want to try incorporating one or more skills within the course of your day-to-day life. As your training progresses, you will want to train around more and more distractions to confirm your dog's focus in a myriad of environments. A change of venue can also help if your dog is stuck on a particular skill or is frightened of something. Dogs will often associate specific places with events that happened in the past. If your dog has had a bad experience in the far corner of your backyard, for example, she may not be able to concentrate when entering this area during training. Keep an open mind during skill training (and all training or conditioning, for that matter). Try different techniques or approaches to the same lesson or problem.

Your dog may respond well with one approach and not at all with another.

☙ Trust your instincts. If one of you is having a problem with a particular aspect of training, the problem may lie in the training method. Just because almost everyone in the sport trains one way doesn't make it the right way for your team. To discover what works best for your dog, listen to your inner voice. The same is true of your dog's health. Use your sixth sense to pick up the subtle language of your dog. When you know your dog well and use acute observation, you will be able to trust your instincts and follow through on them.

☙ Don't train if you are having a bad day. If one of you is in an "off" mood, skip skill training that day. Instead, make it a conditioning day. Take your dog for a walk, run, swim, or whatever helps you escape your world for a while. Skill training takes concentrated, focused energy, and if you don't have it, a training session will be ineffective. Small mistakes will slip by unnoticed and you'll get angry over the large ones. You'll miss opportunities to praise your dog for her correct responses and possibly reward incorrect responses. Train only when you are both relaxed, focused, and receptive.

☙ Keep a journal or record book. If you keep a record of your training sessions, you will be able to rely upon it to analyze your progress and to keep track of what may or may not be working, as shown in the example on page 77. Use it to keep notes on what exercises you have taught and what reactions your training techniques elicit in your dog.

☙ Plan each session, but be flexible. You and your dog are both individuals with good and bad days. Take advantage of the days when everything seems to flow smoothly and learning is quick and effortless. Know what step comes next in your training so that if your dog is learning quickly, you can make the most of the session. If your dog is having a particularly difficult time on a specific skill, it may be best to forgo learning for the day. Be willing to readjust your schedule as necessary.

☙ Begin and end on a positive note. Start each training session with something your dog knows to build confidence in both of you. You can then progress into more difficult commands or start teaching new ones. If you are teaching a new skill and your dog performs it well, stop there. A good response to a new skill should end the session. Continuing in the hope of perfecting your dog's responses will lead to frustration and fatigue. Finish the training session with something that your dog enjoys. Play a game with her. Make her stay while you toss a ball, release her to fetch it, and then request a skill on her return. Each subsequent time you toss the ball, eliminate one command. This process will relax your dog slowly and leave her ready to sleep or play for the rest of the day. It will prevent her attitude from souring and keep her looking forward to her training sessions.

☙ Train one step at a time. Break down complex movements into smaller steps that build upon one another. Wait until your dog has mastered a small portion of a complete skill before moving on. Never be afraid to go back a step if necessary. The more energy you spend on teaching a skill one step at a time, the more ingrained and reliable the skill will be.

☙ Allow learning to "bake" for at least 24 hours. After teaching a new skill, wait a day before asking your dog to respond to the command again. If your dog is having difficulty while learning a new skill, then stop the lesson and give her at least a day for the information to sink in. When you come back to the lesson, you may be surprised to find that your dog understands more clearly. This technique can be a remarkably useful one in your teaching.

🐾 If, as described above, your dog performs a new skill well and you stop the lesson, you may see improvement after a day. Your dog will be more relaxed because she already knows the skill so her response may be better than the previous time.

🐾 Be prepared for the learning curve. Oftentimes while learning, your dog will experience a period where the ability to perform a behavior or skill disappears. She may seem to have forgotten what she once knew so well. This is common, so stay patient. Your dog's concentration on new skills may get in the way of older skills. You can bring back an older skill, usually in one session, by starting from the very beginning and again teaching the skill one step at a time, rewarding each step. In a week or two, you may have forgotten all about this little lapse.

🐾 Whenever you change the rules, give the behavior a new name. For example, if your dog understands the "heel" command and you now want to add a command to walk on your right side, introduce another name. The new term will assist your dog in learning more quickly because it lessens confusion.

🐾 Videotape your training sessions. Usually, it's the pet owners who are to blame for repeated mistakes or learning difficulties in their dogs. One way to see what you may be doing wrong is to have someone videotape your training session (or better yet, several training sessions). When watching the video, pay particular attention to the subtle ways you interrelate with your canine friend. Are you crowding her slightly by leaning over her? How is your timing? Are your commands coming too late or too early? Are you using your posture and body language to your best advantage? Does your dog appear apprehensive about a particular request? Maybe she is suffering from a problem you have missed. Sometimes your intense concentration may prevent you from seeing everything that is happening during a training session. Videos are a valuable tool in analyzing your teamwork and recording your progress. Just imagine how much fun it will be a year from now to review the video of your first month working with your dog.

🐾 You don't have to train at competition levels every session. If your dog can jump a regulation-height hurdle, that does not mean you must train at that height in every session. The same is true for length, duration, and intensity. You should practice occasionally at high levels, but continuing to push your dog during regular training sessions will overwork her and possibly cause her to resist the chore at hand. Her performance will suffer.

🐾 Keep it fun. A good attitude is worth a fistful of first-place wins by an unhappy dog. If you keep the sessions upbeat and positive, your dog will remain that way too. Work without joy will dampen your dog's good feelings toward you and the activity. Never lose sight of the fact that preparing for an activity or event is supposed to help you and your dog remain friends, keep you both busy and fit with a fun adventure, and help you get more joy out of life. A stressed or forced dog may come home with ribbons, but at what cost? You will break the spirit of your dog. Your dog wants to do what you ask and she will strive to do her best. Appreciate this and *enjoy* training her and spending time with her.

🐾 Each training session should resemble a party rather than an exercise in submission or a competition in precise and quick work. If you keep the training sessions relaxed, then the competitions will remain relaxed for your dog. A relaxed dog who enjoys what she does will always do better in the long run.

HOW DOES IT WORK?

Although designing a well-balanced training program may appear involved and difficult, it will be easy if you follow the simple guidelines presented in this book. The main thing to remember is that your dog is

Session Focus ___heeling , finish~~front~~___
  Date___3-16___ Time___9:00am___ Length of Session___10 min.___

Dog's Attentiveness   Dog's Willingness   Your Focus   Working Rapport
      [2]   [2]   [3]   [2]

Comments, Feelings and Thoughts
  He wasn't paying attention. Very distracted. No
finishes w/o food enticement. Quit on a sour note
but then played fetch to relax both of us.
  Breezy.   Heeling in disarray.

Session Focus ___heeling, finish___
  Date___3-16___ Time___2:30pm___ Length of Session___15 min.___

Dog's Attentiveness   Dog's Willingness   Your Focus   Working Rapport
      [3]   [4]   [4]   [3]

Comments, Feelings and Thoughts
  Better. He tried harder. I was calmer.
The wind died down. Two finishes done well
but slow. Heeling also better, went wide.
Maybe he was afraid to get too close. I stayed
calm this time.

Session Focus ___heeling front___
  Date___3-17___ Time___10:30 am___ Length of Session___15 min.___

Dog's Attentiveness   Dog's Willingness   Your Focus   Working Rapport
      [4]   [4]   [5]   [4]

Comments, Feelings and Thoughts
  Yeah! Good heeling. He's still confused about
finishes, but was faster. One perfect finish and
we quit there. He'll get it soon.

Example of a Training Log

10 WAYS TO FIND 10 MINUTES TO TRAIN YOUR DOG

1. Make training your dog a priority. By placing a high value on training, you are saying that the time you and your dog spend together is important. In order to reach your goals and have a well-behaved dog, you must make time for training. Saying "I *will* train my dog today" will strengthen your commitment.

2. Put training your dog on your "to do" list. You will feel satisfaction when you complete the training session and cross it off your list. If you have a schedule book or day planner, make an appointment to train your dog, and treat that appointment as important as any of your other appointments.

3. Make training a part of your everyday life. If you are teaching your dog tricks, for example, have her run through a quick training session before you feed or pet her. When guests arrive, use the opportunity to teach your dog control exercises. Perhaps have her sit to greet the guests and then ask her to lie down and stay. Many day-to-day activities can involve directive commands such as "left" and "right." For instance, you can place your dog's dinner to her right and then command her to go right. You can also hide her snacks around the house and have her find them by using her nose.

4. Realize that 10 minutes isn't that long. You will create a mental barrier for yourself if you dwell on the idea that "I *have* to train my dog." A Herculean effort isn't necessary. In fact, most dogs appreciate short, quick, and exciting training sessions rather than long, tedious ones. Once you realize how quickly 10 minutes goes while training your dog, you can eliminate this mental block.

5. Take advantage of those times when you have a spare minute or two, for example, during commercials or while dinner is cooking. A couple of minutes here and there will add up and will make a difference in your dog's training. A friend of mine turns on the coffee maker in the morning and then goes outside and runs her dog through a set of weave poles while the coffee brews. Socializing and exploring also teach your dog important lessons, so take her with you when you run errands.

6. Get up earlier in the morning and take advantage of the quiet time to train your dog. If you are not a morning person, you may have a little difficulty concentrating at first, but since 10 minutes isn't that much earlier, you will get used to it in time. If you are more of a night owl, stay up an additional 10 minutes and train your dog before you retire for the night.

7. If your home is close to your workplace, train your dog for 10 minutes during your lunch hour. You'll still have time to eat and relax. Your dog would appreciate the break in her lonely day, and what better way to prepare you for an afternoon of work than by spending some time with your canine buddy.

8. You can find more than 10 minutes for training if you skip your least favorite television show. In the evening, instead of planting yourself on the couch to watch another rerun that you'll forget all about in the morning, take your eager dog outside and train and play with her.

9. Have your training equipment ready. If all you have to do is grab a handy leash or go outside to equipment that is already set up, you will be more enthusiastic about training. For some activities, just setting up for training takes more than 10 minutes. When you have everything handy, you only have to think about your dog and what you want to work on for 10 minutes.

10. Take advantage of your children's play time. I often have my dog practice on agility equipment while my children and their friends play on the swingset in our backyard. The children think it is great! They cheer and encourage my dog, and they always want me to set the jumps higher and go faster. If your dog is already familiar with her training equipment and commands, having children playing nearby will help her get used to distractions. It will reinforce your dog's ability to listen to you and work when a lot of other exciting things are happening around her.

Bonus Tip: Make up your mind that you will work on at least one skill each session. If you are feeling pressed for time or unenthusiastic, do a small portion of your training rather than none. If you are working on agility equipment, for example, decide to run your dog through the weave poles twice and then stop. If you are working on heeling exercises, make a commitment to heel around the perimeter of your yard with four right-angle turns. Once you start a training session, you may find it difficult to finish in the few minutes you have allotted yourself and will actually spend *more* time.

Now that you have seen how easy it is to find 10 minutes to train your dog, you may be able to add multiple 10-minute sessions to your day. Make sure to vary the sessions so you don't bore your dog with too much repetition. Try new and fun things to work on, or just enjoy a game once in a while. After you have made regular training sessions a part of your daily life, you will be rewarded with a well-behaved and talented pooch.

not a machine and should not be treated as one. She is an individual, unlike any other dog or yourself. She needs a flexible training regimen that works for her. Be sensitive to her areas of difficulty (taking it easy and slow), use her areas of strength to her benefit, and keep her psychological condition in mind as you work toward your goals. With a well-thought-out plan and the ability to be flexible, you and your dog will have fun, and she will remain healthy as you explore your adventure together.

Musculoskeletal System

The musculoskeletal system is composed of your dog's muscles, joints, ligaments, and bones. When the nervous system sends a message for your dog to perform a particular action, the muscles contract, thereby moving the bones at the joints and causing motion.

A well-rounded conditioning program increases the musculoskeletal system's fitness level. This fitness, in turn, allows your dog to perform the skills necessary for your specific activity with precision, strength, endurance, flexibility, finesse, and confidence. If your program is balanced, your dog will experience the added benefits of a generally stronger structural system, stronger bones, better muscle tone, and increased strength for daily activities.

For muscles to become stronger, you must apply the principle of overload: working the muscles to the normal activity would tax them and then continuing beyond that level. The muscles adapt to the added stress by becoming stronger. You can increase the demands on your dog's muscles by using the F.I.T.T. guidelines explained below.

Cardiovascular System

Cardiovascular (also called cardiorespiratory) conditioning is achieved by overloading the heart, lungs, and circulatory system. When an activity involving the cardiovascular system is performed, your dog's oxygen-exchange systems are asked to work harder.

Oxygen is needed to fuel the muscles for movement. When your dog places increased demands on the oxygen-exchange system, her heart and lungs must increase their efficiency and the cardiovascular system gets stronger. This conditioning is evident not only when your dog is working but also at rest and during normal daily activities.

In order for you to better understand the importance of cardiovascular fitness, a brief explanation of the cardiovascular system follows. The heart pumps oxygen-rich blood from the lungs through the body and receives the blood that is returning to be enriched with oxygen and nutrients. The circulatory system distributes the oxygen- and nutrient-fortified blood to the muscles being worked. The oxygen is then used to break down stored fat in the muscles so the calories can be used as fuel. Thus, the more efficient the cardiovascular system, the quicker your dog's muscles get the fuel they need to perform optimally.

Nervous System

The nervous system is the communication center of your dog's body. The cells that make up the nervous system carry messages (nerve impulses) that control movement. Some cells are also sensitive to temperature, pain, pressure, and changes in body position. These nerve cells are referred to as receptors and are located throughout your dog's body. The messages from nerve cells originate either in the receptors or the central nervous system.

The central nervous system, consisting of the brain and the spinal cord, is the nervous system's command center. It receives and integrates the information from the peripheral nervous system (the nerves that connect the body's extremities and the receptors).

When your dog is performing an activity, the central and peripheral nervous systems work together to initiate, guide, and monitor the activity. The impulses from the nervous system activate a contraction in your dog's muscles, the muscle contraction moves her bones, and there is movement. In order for your dog to learn, adjust, and perform simple or complex movements, there must be communication between the central and peripheral nervous systems.

How the Body Systems Work Together

A dog's ability to understand her handler's requests and execute them with finesse and expertise is the result of the handler's hard work and the dog's body systems' effectiveness. The nervous system delivers the brain impulses correctly, the musculoskeletal system moves your dog's body, and the heart and lungs provide the oxygen and other nutrients needed to produce fuel for her muscles. Each system must do its job efficiently for your dog's performance to be successful.

The various systems in the canine body, like those in our own, work in a circulatory pattern during physical activity. Each system relies on the other systems to work properly in synchronicity. How spectacular the body's movements are is dependent on how strong and healthy each system is, and the health and strength of the systems are the result of conditioning, training, and nature.

Heart and Respiratory Rates

Knowing your dog's heart and respiratory rates is important in understanding your dog's health. If you discover they are out of her normal range, either higher or lower, you will be alerted to possible problems.

In an emergency situation, comparing your dog's heart and respiratory rates to her normal rates will be extremely helpful in assessing your dog's condition and will assist your veterinarian in his or her evaluation. You can also use these figures to assess your training. If you are working your dog and you get a very high rate, you will know you have pushed too hard and it is time to slow down. When your dog becomes more fit and conditioned, her elevated heart rate (from exercise) will more quickly return to normal.

With a bit of practice you will be able to check your dog's heart and respiratory rates quickly and accurately. Like people, dogs have their own normal heart rates. Some are naturally more elevated or lower, and a more fit dog will have a slightly lower heart rate because of her more efficient cardiovascular system. To find your dog's normal rate, take her heart rate first thing in the morning for two weeks and average these results.

To feel your dog's pulse, place your flat hand on either side of her chest just behind her shoulder blade. Count how many beats you feel for 15 seconds and then multiply this number by four. The beats per minute (bpm) should fall between 80 and 120, which is the normal range for a resting dog. If your dog has been exercising or is excited, the pulse will be slightly elevated.

To read your dog's respiratory rate, watch and count how many times your dog's chest rises and falls in one minute. The normal rate is between 20 and 24 times per minute.

If you have read a fitness or beauty magazine, watched late-night infomercials, or explored fitness for yourself, you have undoubtedly heard about the "training zone," the heart rate target zone that you should stay in in order to gain the most benefit from exercise. As of yet, a training heart rate zone has not been established for canines. Although we may not know the best range, it is clear that no dog's heart rate should ever exceed 160 bpm, no matter what the activity.

When participating in a conditioning session, especially in the beginning or when you make a substantial increase in your demands, periodically check your dog's heart rate. If there is a larger than 10 to 20 percent increase in her heart rate over her normal rate, take a break and let her rest. If you check your dog's heart rate and find it at 160 or above, stop the activity immediately. Check to make sure that your dog has not become overheated and take measures to cool her if she has. Report this situation to your veterinarian as soon as possible as a high heart rate can be caused by disease, infection, or other medical problems. If your dog has a low reading, she could be slipping into shock. This situation requires immediate emergency care (see chapter 4).

The F.I.T.T. Formula

Frequency—Frequency is how many times a week you engage your dog in a training session. This frequency is dependent on your dog's experience and current condition, as well as your goals and experience. When planning the frequency of sessions, remember to include recovery periods and rest days. A balance of work and rest will result in optimal fitness. Your dog will be stronger, have more endurance, stay healthy, and be enthusiastic. Remember, however, that what is more important than a particular number of workouts a week is the quality of workouts your dog has.

Training frequency may be either increased or decreased to adjust your dog's program as needed. Decreasing the frequency may be necessary to give your dog time off after an injury, during the off-season, or when she needs a mental break. If your dog has hit a plateau in performance, a decrease also can shock her bodily systems into better performance.

Intensity—Intensity refers to the amount of energy it takes to complete an exercise or exercise session. You can increase or decrease intensity as necessary to make a workout more difficult or easier. There should be enough exertion to stress your dog's body, forcing it to adapt (the overload principle), without pushing it too far. After an event when your dog has exerted extra effort, she deserves a day of rest followed by an easy day before you increase the intensity again.

Time (duration)—How long should you work your dog during each individual conditioning period? Again, you have to take into consideration the many factors that influence your dog's present condition and what you would like to accomplish. If you don't, you may push your dog beyond safe levels. Her devotion and willingness to do as you ask may make her work longer than she should. By the time you notice a subtle change in her demeanor, she may have overexerted herself.

If you are working on difficult or new skills, you may want to keep the sessions shorter than if you are working on endurance or activities your dog really enjoys. If you increase another component of conditioning, such as intensity, you may want to lessen the duration of your workouts until your dog has adapted to the increased demands.

Type (of activity)—Remember, variation is important for you and for your dog. Challenge your dog's body by trying new things. Prevent boredom and monotony as well as overadaptation. Cross-training (page 91) accounts for a more balanced conditioning program. When

HOW HEIGHT-TO-WEIGHT RATIO AFFECTS PHYSICAL ABILITY

By manipulating naturally occurring differences in dogs, humans have been able to create such structurally diverse breeds as the Yorkshire terrier and the Great Dane. Each structural difference enhances the breed's ability to perform its traditional duties with precision.

Some breeds, like the greyhound and Saluki, are thin and lithe with deep chests for sustained energy output. Others are more stocky and heavy boned such as the St. Bernard and the mastiff. Most dog breeds fit somewhere in between, being of medium build and moderate bone weight.

In sports or activities where jumping and other agile and powerful physical movement is required, dogs who exhibit lower weight-to-height ratios (the relationship between a dog's weight and her height) are more apt to succeed. If a heavy dog is also a shorter dog, she is at a disadvantage in these activities as her musculoskeletal system must bear more stress while performing. To find the weight-to-height ratio of your dog, measure her height in inches at her withers and get an accurate weight in pounds (you can slip into your veterinarian's office and weigh your dog on the scale), then divide her weight by her height. Christine Zink, D.V.M., co-author of *Jumping from A to Z*, suggests that a ratio of 4 or greater puts your dog at risk of injury and permanent damage when participating in physically demanding activities, especially those requiring jumping.

This problem is especially evident in sports that require fixed jump heights. Such jump heights are established by measuring the height of a dog and do not take her weight into consideration. A heavier dog is put in a difficult position—having to jump heights that are more difficult on her than on lighter competitors of the same height.

Weight-to-height ratio is one convincing argument for keeping your dog's weight stable and light. It also enforces the importance of choosing the right dog for your adventure or choosing the right adventure for your dog. As always, but especially if your dog has a high weight-to-height ratio, keep your conditioning program balanced and incorporate strength-building activities to help your dog cope with the added stress.

choosing an activity, consider the kind of fitness you are striving to improve such as endurance, strength, agility or flexibility, or skills. As coach, you are responsible for deciding on the best types of exercises to condition the areas your dog is weakest in and to build on her stronger attributes.

Increasing Fitness Levels for Competition and Challenge

When you first lure your dog off the couch, you should start off slowly and steadily. After the first four weeks or so of your program, you should see an improvement in her performance and a difference in her muscle tone. As you gradually build your dog's endurance, strength, and agility, you lay the groundwork for more intense and sport-specific work. Remember that there are no hard and fast rules for increasing training levels. Your plan should always take your dog's mental and physical well-being into consideration. In order to improve her performance and ability, you need to push your dog, increasing the difficulty of your requests as your dog handles them. By asking for too much too soon, you risk paying the price in having an unhappy or unhealthy dog.

How much increase should you expect? Follow the 10 percent rule—increase your requests by 10 percent each week or as your dog is able to handle the increases. Calculating a 10 percent increase in distance and time is easy, but when it comes to intensity or skills, the increase is more subjective. By using acute observation, you will get to know your dog's normal reactions to exercise and will recognize any problems that may come up.

Keep the F.I.T.T. principles in mind as you increase the fitness training level. If you decide your dog needs additional endurance training, you can increase the length of time you expect her to sustain an activity. While your dog is working up to this new time, decrease the intensity of the exercise. As she becomes accustomed to the increase in duration, you can increase the intensity back up to the previous level.

Remember that the higher you set your goals, the more work you will have to do to reach them. If your objective is to participate in a national competition by next summer and your dog is at a beginning level, you'll have to ask quite a bit from your companion in the months to come. If you are sure she will be able to handle the pressure physically and mentally, you should devise a plan that allows for the maximum increase in fitness in the time allotted. You will have to know the dates of qualifying events and what level of performance will be expected of you and your dog by those dates. This type of accelerated training should be done by an experienced dog trainer. If you are inexperienced, it will be easy for you to miss symptoms of overwork or make mistakes in your training that will cost you time and possibly the health of your canine athlete.

Competing in an event entails some special planning. Before competition season begins, gradually increase the intensity, frequency, and duration of workouts for peak performance. Give your dog a day or two of rest before a competition. The highest-intensity training should occur a few days before the event. When there are breaks in the competition season, allow your dog periods of decreased intensity and duration.

Watch for boredom or fatigue in your dog. If you see signs of either problem, follow the tips in the sections on overwork and cross-training.

OFF-SEASON

Whew! It's the off-season. The hectic schedule of show after show, event after event, is over—for a while. You get a break and your dog deserves one—but how much of a break? While you don't want to maintain the intensity of your competition training schedule, you don't want to let your dog change back into the couch potato of the past either.

The key is balance. Stay involved in a moderate exercise regimen. Decrease the pace a little, but continue your endurance and strength conditioning program. You aren't looking for improvement at this point, only a sustained fitness level.

Put skill training on a maintenance status; do just enough so your dog won't forget. Since dogs have excellent memories, you won't have to train very often—once a month is adequate for many skills. Another reason it's important to continue regular skill training work is so you won't get rusty in your training techniques. If you aren't able to continue training in your chosen activity, the off-season may be a good time to teach your dog those tricks that greatly impress your friends. Practice will keep your training skills honed, keep your dog's mind exercised, and keep you both having fun together.

We can assume that dogs have what humans possess—muscle memory. Muscle memory is the muscles' ability to respond to an increase in conditioning after a lay off period by rapidly recovering their previous abilities. The shorter the lay off period, the faster the recovery. I venture to guess that a dog's muscle memory is even better than a human's, although I have seen no studies on this phenomenon in dogs. If your dog has been setting specific speeds consistently at flyball and is then forced to take a break, then after the break your dog's muscles, flexibility, and coordination will reach top condition quicker than when your dog was first striving to achieve those physical abilities. Muscle memory means you don't have to start from the beginning after time off.

During the off-season, you can focus on having fun. Play is the best way to keep your dog physically fit while letting her kick up her heels. If you have children and have demonstrated to them acceptable ways to play, then let them play with your dog while you relax and supervise. Visiting dog parks or a friend who has canines is a good excuse to let your dog just be a dog. If your dog has gotten somewhat out of shape, watch for overexertion or soreness.

During the off-season, your dog will be getting less exercise, so her nutrition requirements may change. Feed her less to compensate for the decline in caloric expenditure. Discuss with your veterinarian whether you should change the nutrient makeup of your dog's diet. You may have placed your dog on a high-protein diet while she was competing, but during the off-season, this extra protein may only cause problems. Switching her to a maintenance diet may be healthier.

If you continue a moderate exercise routine, renew your dog's skills once in a while, and watch your pet's diet, your off-season will truly be an enjoyable one.

YOUR DOG'S PERSONALITY

When it comes to which training style works best with your dog in any given situation, knowing your dog is all important. And of course, working with your dog is going to help you to get to know her better. As you discover what personality traits govern your dog's behavior, you can apply that knowledge to your training style.

Some dogs are so fearful of new situations that they may have diarrhea during an obedience class. Other dogs are so brave that they try to take over the entire obedience class—bullying the other dogs and not taking direction from the people. Whatever your dog's personality, you have to respond to her unique way of looking at the world and her style of learning. A good trainer can help you better understand the training style that will work best with your dog, but the truth is that you probably know your dog best. If you enroll in a training class or with an instructor and you feel the manner of teaching is not helping your dog, ask for an alternative. If you meet with resistance and are told that this is *the* method to use, find another teacher. A good instructor will have many alternatives to pull out of his or her bag of tricks. If your instructor cannot offer options, then another instructor may be better for you and your dog.

If your dog is fearful, you will have to make her feel comfortable and accepted. You should never give her reason to fear you or your training. Avoid encouraging her fear with your own behavior. For example, if your dog is quietly fearful, don't sit quietly yourself; you may be able to encourage her bravery by getting excited. If you increase your level of excitement and it seems to stress your dog, then stop and take a calmer approach.

You can encourage her bravery by allowing her as much success as possible. Ignore her wrong responses; there is no sense in correcting or punishing an already fearful dog. Stay confident yourself and do not baby your dog. If you coo at your pup, trying to make her brave by your loving words and attention, you are only increasing the likelihood that her behavior will continue, possibly long past the time that she is fearful. This kind of babying rewards the fearful behavior and usually makes an already fearful dog more unsure and anxious. Be matter of fact and relaxed, and your dog will copy your attitude.

If your dog is the wild type, you can help her concentrate and learn better. If she has a lot of energy, stay calm. Instead of working on increasing her speed, concentrate on gaining control. Reinforce your dog's willingness to accurately and quickly respond to your commands. Occasionally call your dog to you and ask for an energy-harnessing behavior such as a down-stay. With such a command, you can stop her and ask her to engage her mind once again.

Some dogs are naturally more sensitive than others. If your dog reacts to any type of correction by losing her concentration, you need to use a more gentle method, perhaps encouraging your dog with treats or using clicker training. Clicker training is the use of a small clicker that reinforces the desired behaviors by acting as a "bridge" between the correct response and a reward (such as food, praise, or petting). If you have a stubborn, strong-willed dog, you may have to be more firm. Certain dogs who understand what they are being asked to do may respond with a devil-may-care attitude, moving slowly to test your commitment. You may need to be a bit more forceful with this type also.

Many dogs seem to have a strong work ethic while others seem to have a stronger play ethic. Which outlook governs your dog? These orientations can change from time to time. Some dogs will always be playful or serious, with only occasional lapses; other dogs will vacillate between the two extremes, depending on their moods.

A dog who is work oriented may seem like a dream come true if you are a goal-minded handler, but the truth is that a dog who is all seriousness is missing out on the best part of being with you. You can use her seriousness to your advantage, especially if you are striving for a lofty goal, but you should also concentrate on having fun once in a while. Find activities your dog enjoys doing and add them to your weekly training schedule.

On the other hand, a play-oriented dog can be a joy to work with—most of the time. If you have this type of dog, you may find it hard to keep your dog's enthusiasm yet not contribute to her excitement so much that she loses her concentration. She is like the wild dog described above, except that her wildness is directed toward play (and often toward you). If you reward her with too much enthusiasm, she may think it is playtime, jump up on you, and break away from your control. You will soon learn, if you are observant, how much and what kind of praise works best for this kind of dog.

Whether your dog likes to work close to you or farther away from you will affect how you train her and what conditioning program will work best. Your dog may be from a breed that has been programmed to work away from their handlers, making decisions and doing their jobs on their own. These particular dogs are going to have a more difficult time working in an activity that requires close teamwork with their human handlers. Other dogs are intensely aware of the wishes of their handlers and must be directed and guided to feel useful.

CROSS-TRAINING

What Is Cross-Training and Why Is It Important?

If your dog repeatedly participates in the same activity, your training program lacks balance which is an essential component of fitness. As her coach and teammate, you should make cross-training a part of your plan.

If your dog performs the exact same actions continuously, the joints she uses most can wear down, making her more vulnerable to injuries. No matter how perfectly suited your dog is for your chosen adventure, she has weaker areas in her structure. While the strong areas work hard to compensate, the weaker ones are exposed over and over again to extreme amounts of stress. By changing activities, you vary the amount of stress on the diverse areas of her body. Different muscles are recruited for different movements and the strain is shared among all the joints, which creates more balanced fitness. Using different muscles at each joint will make the joints stronger and more flexible and help prevent injuries.

There is another physical advantage when you cross-train your dog. As your dog performs her normal conditioning routine, she will gradually begin to tolerate the workouts. She will progress until she is at an advanced level of fitness, then her progress will seem to stop as she reaches a "plateau." At this point, her body needs to be "shocked" into awareness. It has mastered the tasks that have been requested, and it is too comfortable.

Cross-training forces different muscle groups to work. These newly recruited muscles will be stressed and have to adapt to the unfamiliar workload in a different way. When you find your dog's fitness program stalling, add a new exercise. Your dog will be forced to work at the next higher level by performing activities she is unaccustomed to.

But why wait until your dog's fitness is at a plateau? If you make cross-training an integral part of your conditioning program, your dog will have the advantage of a more balanced body and a more complete routine right from the start.

Variety is another reason to cross-train. Variety is the spice of life for both you and your dog. When your dog works only on her sport, she may become bored and her performance will suffer. Your once shining star may put in a stale, lackluster performance. Your once eager, cooperative pooch may exhibit a bad attitude or a lack of interest in her work. If you find your dog is experiencing setbacks, she may have lost interest as a result of boredom.

How to Add Variety

When you use your imagination and trust your ideas, you will find endless ways to add variety to your program. You can vary your dog's routine within your given activity. You can increase or decrease work in any of the F.I.T.T. categories. You can even add interval training—short bursts of more intense energy output into an activity's prescribed time. For example, if you are doing roadwork, you can add a two- to three-minute high-interval burst by running during a walk or running faster during a run. When skill training, you can add variety by performing the exercises in different orders. That is, if you usually proceed through a skill-training session by working on A, B, and C, in that order, then next time change the order to C, A, and B. Play with the training. It will put the spark back in a possibly dull training experience. Your dog will pay closer attention to you because she won't know what is coming next. You will also discover where possible trouble spots may be hiding. You will see where your dog understands the commands and where she relies on other stimuli to remember how to perform.

True cross-training is the mixing of activities. If your primary activity with your dog is water-rescue tests, consider taking your dog hiking one day every month and playing Frisbee once a week. These activities will use different muscles than swimming alone—thereby helping your dog to be more balanced physically—and will vary her routine enough that she will revel in the activities. For fun, try mixing in swimming, flyball, Frisbee, biking, jogging, or agility obstacles. The list of possibilities is endless. Use the second part of this book to find something interesting to add to your routine.

The two most important and beneficial components of cross-training are play and rest. By interspersing these in your training, you will find that your dog remains healthy in both mind and body. You can add these two components to each training session or as separate phases of the entire program. You can stop skill training for a quick game of fetch to reward your dog when she is doing exceptionally well or to reinvigorate your dog when she is distracted, bored, or frustrated. Rest periods achieve the same results, and they have the added advantage of allowing your dog to rest her body. Rest periods will be discussed later, but you should know that they are a part of cross-training also.

Most dogs relish the play time they get with their caretakers. To these dogs, play is the best part of their lives. But some dogs don't know how to play or aren't that interested in playing. Remember the discussion on work-oriented dogs? You will have to coax your dog into playing if she is one of these. Having another dog around who is frisky and playful helps. My Bouvier, Retta, was not much of a playful pup. I couldn't get her interested in any toys. She remained serious—until Cody the Australian shepherd came to live with us. Retta's style of play is now to chase Cody and wrestle him to the ground. They both love it. She still won't play with toys and she won't fetch anything. But she will chase Cody around after he has fetched something.

If you don't have two dogs, you might want to find someone who has a dog that your dog could play with, or find a dog park in your area. It is therapeutic for dogs to play with each other. Unless your dog is aggressive toward other dogs (which makes competing or showing difficult), then this may be one of the best ways of letting your dog unwind and enjoy herself and still get some of the best exercise around. Playing with other dogs can actually prevent her from being aggressive if introduced early enough.

BREAKS AND REST

Breaks and rest periods are just as important as working days in an effective conditioning program. If you and your dog have had a hard day of exercise, it's wise to take it easy the next day. If you've had an *especially* hard day, take a day of rest. You and your dog need to build energy reserves and let your muscles rebuild and be strong for your next venture.

For both of your sakes, avoid the "weekend warrior" trap. If you are going to be involved in a physically demanding pursuit and you want to involve your dog, engage in the activity regularly, not just on weekends. An overworked and tired dog is more likely to be injured. Her muscles will be fatigued and depleted. Read the section on overwork to get a clear picture of why rest is crucial.

SETTING GOALS

The fundamental key to success—in any of life's ventures—is goal setting. By setting goals, you will have direction in your work. You can plan your conditioning and training program realistically and efficiently.

Some people find that setting goals causes them added stress. "What if I don't reach my goals?" "What if my dog isn't good enough?" "What if I'm not good enough?" First, you're the only person who has to know what your goals are (although most people find it more fruitful to share their goals with someone understanding). Second, your goals are not written in stone. You can change them as often as necessary.

Unforeseen situations often crop up, and you must be flexible in handling them. Maybe you can't spend as much time as you thought you could, or perhaps you cannot afford the equipment you need. In my own life, a surprise baby put many of my goals on hold for about a year. Readjusting and changing dates set me free to concentrate on my beautiful baby girl without an ounce of pressure regarding doggie goals.

The goals you set should be realistic yet challenging and exciting. They should stimulate you into action, not paralyze you with fear of failure. You should feel proud and happy when you accomplish your goals. Your goals should be meaningful, which does not mean they must be elaborate. If you and your dog have both been sedentary, your goal may be to work up to walking three miles five times a week. Be proud of that goal, write it down to demonstrate your commitment, and strive to accomplish it.

Goals should be worded in the positive. "I will not miss the next three training sessions" is not as powerful as "I will train three times this week." The best method I have used to set goals is the mind mapping tool described in chapter 1. This method can make goal setting quick and painless.

You should have both long- and short-term goals. Long-term goals are those that influence your dog's career. They are usually set yearly, but you can have goals that stretch over five years or more. You can also set intermediate goals, which extend about six months into the future. Short-term goals are those that get you to your long-term goals one step at a time. Those steps may be taken weekly or monthly, depending on how difficult it is to reach your long-term goals.

Daily goals (or daily tasks) help you and your dog reach your intermediate and long-term goals. Writing down the daily goals in advance for the following week will give you a wider view of what lies ahead. But if you are like me, you will need more flexibility in your schedule. I sit down the night before and create the next day's goals. You can also decide on each day's goals that morning.

Your goals must be written down if you are to take them seriously. It's a good idea to keep them in a training journal. Reread your goals on a regular basis, possibly once a month. If they need adapting, change them. If you are accomplishing more than you planned, readjust your goals so that your training program remains exciting and stimulating to you. If your original goals were set too high, lower them to reflect your true situation—without being bothered by it.

Remember, these are *your* goals, not your dog's. Your role as coach, instructor, and caretaker demands that you consider first and foremost your dog's physical and mental health. If you keep this obligation firmly in mind, your dog will continue to be your teammate and most loyal friend for many years to come.

THE DOG WHO DOES TOO MUCH

"A dog will do whatever you ask, even if it pushes the limits of her physical ability." This is a common lament. If you have a dog who isn't this dedicated, you may wonder what all the fuss is about. You may be thinking you'd be lucky if you could request that your dog get off the couch and have her do so, much less trek with you through the woods on a strenuous hike.

However, some of us do have this kind of dog—the kind that will run alongside her owner even though her paw pads are bleeding from the wear. Having a dog who will quit when the going gets tough makes it easier for you to know when to slow down or stop. As soon as my dog Retta gets winded on our runs, she lags behind me, and I immediately slow to her pace. She lets me know what is comfortable for her. My dog Cody, on the other hand, *never* slows down. I have to be an astute observer to tell if I am pushing him too hard. It is difficult to distinguish whether he can handle what I am asking because he is in great condition or whether he is pushing himself just to keep up with me.

If you have a dog who doesn't easily give up and will push herself, then you must learn to read her signals as discussed throughout this book. When you see that you have asked for too much, follow the suggestions discussed below.

Beginning at Your Dog's Level

If you have been riding your bike 15 miles five nights a week for six months, you shouldn't take your bonbon-eating dog out on your next scheduled ride. Your dog would probably try to keep up with you, being as devoted and hungry for stimulation as she is, but that wouldn't be safe or healthy.

When adding your dog to your already established exercise regimen, you must make adjustments in your routine to match your dog's level of fitness. For example, if you've decided to add your couch-potato canine to your five-mile-a-day running program, you will have to decrease your intensity for a while. Dogs get fit fast and will catch up to your training level quickly. Give your pet at least one week—two if she is really out of shape—to adapt before increasing the speed or distance.

Signs of Overwork

Out-of-shape dogs or dogs just beginning to learn an activity are not the only possible victims of overwork. Doing too much and not taking enough time off can also affect well-conditioned dogs. If you are asking your dog to work too hard and too intensely for too long, trouble is waiting right around the corner.

With some dogs, less is more. Many dogs are more efficient when they are allowed plenty of time for rest and play. Other dogs thrive on work and never seem to get enough. Take your dog's personality into consideration when planning a conditioning and training program. As long as you can recognize the signs of overwork and are acutely observant, proceed with your program. But remember, enjoy the process, not just the results.

After a difficult workout, your dog needs adequate time to rest. It is vital to allow her muscles to recover. They must have time to repair themselves and grow stronger from the stress of the work (that is, adapt). Your dog must also have time to replenish the depleted energy stores of her muscles and bodily systems. Without this recovery time, your dog will tire easily, and eventually her overworked muscles will not be able to respond to the demands placed upon them.

How will you know if your dog is doing too much? Don't judge how hard she is working by her panting. A dog pants to dissipate heat, like people sweat. Your dog may pant, with her tongue hanging out, when she is exerting herself even a little. She might even pant in anticipation as you are putting on your running shoes or gathering up the leash or equipment. If her panting is extremely heavy, you may have pushed too hard, but exhaustion is usually accompanied by other signs.

Watch your dog for these signs of fatigue: stumbling, anxiousness, and excessive panting. With some dogs you may be able to see a swelling of blood vessels on the face. If your dog slows down and lags behind when doing endurance work, rest awhile and give her a drink of water. If after a rest you cannot get her to enthusiastically begin again, you have pushed her too hard and you need to stop the session. Take off the rest of the day and the following day also. Give your dog a break while you watch closely for signs that she may have been injured, such as favoring one leg.

Stop also if your pet shows signs of lameness or heatstroke. If you notice her limping, stop immediately and check between her toes for stones or thorns. After you remove any foreign objects, your dog may be fine to carry on. Check the pads of her feet for abrasions or cuts. If she has damaged her pads, you need to take her home and let her feet heal. Dog feet bleed a lot, so don't panic. Get your dog home slowly, carrying her if necessary, and call your vet. The signs of heatstroke are described in chapter 4.

If you continually overwork your dog, you may produce boredom, staleness, and a decrease in performance by your dog. Or worse, your canine friend may suffer an injury. Remember, you want to get your pet in healthy condition and build your relationship; you are not out to break world records of canine performance at the expense of your dog's health.

Injuries

The keys to injury prevention are having a clear understanding of what is normal in your dog, being able to read the subtle signs of trouble, being patient with conditioning and training, and practicing a holistic approach toward your dog's health.

Signs of injury and specific treatment protocols are discussed thoroughly in the following chapter. Injuries are mentioned here because they are often the result of overwork.

The telltale signs of overwork mentioned above are a warning to protect your dog from injury. Your dog can become sore and stiff or injured from working too long and too hard. Fatigue, excessive repetition, and a lack of cross-training all contribute to overwork injuries.

Training the Mind

You cannot have a talk with your dog about positive thinking, visualization, and motivation, but your actions and thoughts greatly influence your canine friend. She will follow your lead and respond to training and competition as you do. When you remain calm and confident under the pressure of competition, your dog's performance and attitude will improve.

WANTING IT

Is winning ribbons, trophies, or honors your only source of motivation? Is it your most prominent motivation? This way of thinking can leave you frustrated. Winning or losing is often based on someone's personal opinion—it's subjective. In most competitions, the winner is chosen because of subtle differences perceived by one judge who, like all of us, has opinions, prejudices, bad days, and good days. The vast majority of judges are honest and do their best to be fair and unbiased, but they are still human. You may win first place under one judge one day and win nothing under another judge another day, even though your performances were the same.

This is true in any competitive venture, even outside the doggie realm. This time the spotlight may be on you; next time it may be on someone else. Instead of focusing on winning, concentrate on doing the best you can and improving your performance each time you compete.

Another danger of overemphasizing winning is that your attitude may become "win at any cost." Even if you don't mean to, you can lose the balance in your training program. You may find that your training and conditioning focus on how fast or how precise your dog can be, no matter what the effect on your dog or your partnership.

MOTIVATION

In order to stay committed to your adventure goals, you need the right motivation. Often, no matter how badly you want something, life gets in the way. You are busy and tired, and other things need your attention. But if you arm yourself with motivational strategies, you will find that you can maintain the excitement of your chosen adventure. If you're having problems finding your motivation, try the following ideas.

Surround yourself with upbeat handlers and dogs. Nothing will sap your enthusiasm faster than having to work with difficult people and dogs. No matter how extensive a trainer's experience, it will not help you if you dread going to class or have such a sour attitude you find it hard to concentrate on your training.

If you are working with your dog alone all the time, you may want to find other like-minded individuals, at least once in awhile, and play or train together. Make sure these people are fun to be around. Spending time with someone with a good sense of humor can really make a difference in your attitude. For the sake of compatibility, the others should have the same level of commitment as you.

Find the right balance of work and rest. If you have set realistic goals but are continually missing them, then you may need to increase your training—if your dog can handle the added work. The rewards that come from doing more will feed your desire to consistently do more. Then again, you may need to add more rest and variety to your schedule.

Put your goals in writing and refer to them regularly. Some people read them every day. You may want to read them before a training session or on some regular schedule, such as once a month. If you haven't set goals yet, read the sections on mind mapping (page 15) and goal-setting (page 95) once again. Setting goals will help give purpose to your work with your dog.

Start your practice sessions slowly. Take a few minutes to ease into the conditioning or training session and get your dog's mind and body in gear.

A good attitude will make a big difference in your training and conditioning sessions as well as your dog's performance. When training gets difficult, stop and check your attitude. You may need some time off to rediscover the meaning in your work with your dog.

If you find yourself becoming angry, frustrated, or sad during a session, you can change your attitude by changing your body posture. Stand up straight, smile, pick up your pace, swing your arms, speak distinctly. If you do these things, you may find your attitude changing for the better.

Create a regular routine that starts your training sessions. Consistent chores and actions help trigger your unconscious mind to prepare for the training ahead. The ritual you create is a powerful tool to get both you and your dog in the right frame of mind. You may want to have different rituals for different tasks—one for a training session and another for participating in an event, for example.

Keep a training journal. You can use the journal to determine what when wrong when you have a particularly frustrating training session. If you know what is causing you and your dog difficulty, you can either work on it, confront it and deal with it, or decide to ignore it.

With a training journal, you will have a record of your progress. Nothing is more motivating than to see how much you and your dog have improved. When you are close to a situation and entrenched in a relationship, you can be blind to your progress. When you look back on what you were doing not so long ago compared to what you are doing now, you will be pleasantly surprised and encouraged to continue.

Another reason the training journal is a great motivator is that you (if you are like me) will feel terribly guilty if you leave too many blank pages in a row. Maybe this need to record something that shows you're working toward your goals will motivate you to train at least a few minutes every day. I once took a class that required the handlers to turn in homework sheets from every day's training session. I don't think I missed one single day of training in eight weeks, simply because I didn't want to hand in a blank page of homework.

The best advice is to get out and do what you need to do. More times than not, once you start your training or conditioning regimen, you will quickly forget all those excuses you had to skip your session. Make room for your training program in your daily schedule and give it the priority it deserves.

WHEN YOUR MOTIVATION NEEDS A BOOST, TRY THESE IDEAS

➤ Take the pressure off. Lower your expectations awhile until you are mentally ready to get serious again.

➤ Change scenery. Train or play somewhere else a time or two. It is amazing what this can do for your motivation.

➤ Train every other day for a while. Sometimes when the mind loses its motivation, it is because the body needs a rest. Take a few days or even a week off. Don't take off more than three weeks or you may fall out of the training habit.

➤ Add more sessions to your schedule, at least for a week or two. Your motivation problem may lie in the fact that you are not working enough.

➤ If adding more sessions doesn't bring improvement, go back to the frequency you find most comfortable and advantageous for you and your canine.

➤ Start your practice sessions especially slowly. Of course, you should always start your dog's workouts with a good warmup, but for now, try starting slowly and keeping the whole session at a slow, easy pace.

INSPIRATION

Inspiration is the fuel for your fire. When you accept the challenge of committing to a goal, inspiration is what gets you through the tough times. Inspiration, like motivation, primarily concerns your mental status. And as with motivation, your attitude and emotions will easily, quickly, and naturally be picked up by your dog and incorporated into her psyche.

Inspiration can take many forms. The accompanying box lists different ways you can seek inspiration when facing challenges. Listening to yourself, paying attention to where your thoughts lead, will help you to find your own personal inspiration. Be conscious of what makes you feel excited and ready to work with your dog. If you find an article in a magazine or a passage in a book, keep it and occasionally refer back to it. If you feel inspired by the words someone said, write them down. If you see something inspiring on television, record it on video or write down a description. You'll have a better understanding of where your motivation and inspiration come from and something inspiring to reflect on when your enthusiasm wanes.

Sometimes when I am running, I find my feet getting heavy and my legs dragging. When this happens, I think about an article I read several years ago. In it, a runner described her feelings about running in the most inspirational manner I have ever heard or read. By recalling her description, I, too, feel the beauty and grace as well as the power and pride of running.

The runner described how she holds her head up with pride as she runs. How she absorbs the environment through all her senses. How her arms and legs flow freely from her body in effortless swinging. How her feet gobble up the path below her with long, powerful strides.

When I call her description to mind, my body reacts on a physiological level. My head is held high, my body is more erect, my breathing is easier and deeper, and my legs move more smoothly and are more relaxed. I have shared the runner's inspiration and my mind is more peaceful.

And my dog? The change is amazing. I know he reads my shift in attitude. He perks up, and when he looks up at me, I can almost hear him saying, *It's about time! I wondered when you would get involved in what we are doing here.*

This kind of inspiration need not be reserved for important competitions, although its value during these times cannot be underestimated. It can also enhance training and exercise sessions. Mundane, must-do activities can become something you look forward to—an ordinary walk with your dog can transform into a magical experience—when you take a few moments to find your inspiration.

VISUALIZATION

Wouldn't it be wonderful to improve your chances with the judges or improve your dog's scores while sitting on your couch in your living room? It is possible. The technique is called visualization and it is used by elite athletes all over the world. Nothing takes the place of hard work, but this tool can improve your confidence, skill, and technique.

METHODS OF FINDING YOUR INSPIRATION

1. Prayer
2. Meditation
3. Visualization
4. Reflection
5. Reading of encouraging written material

In visualization, you imagine you and your dog flawlessly performing your selected activity. The key to successfully using this tool is to take your time and accurately and vividly picture your team's performance. Use all of your senses to accurately "see" the perfect training session, event, or performance. Picture the correct body posture, voice, and timing. See it in your mind, feel each movement of your body. Feel the grass under your feet, and smell the air.

To begin visualizing, sit somewhere you can be comfortable and relaxed. You may want to dim the lights. Choose a place away from distractions, where you won't be bothered. After you are comfortable and relaxed, close your eyes and start picturing you and your dog's performance or training session. Start at the beginning and follow through to the end. Imagine every detail. Use only positive images. You may want to use your best performance or a combination of best past performances. Performances of others can also be used, but imagine them as being performed by you and your dog. If you have had the opportunity to videotape your favorite successful dog and handler team at its best, you can watch the tape, and then close your eyes and use the same images to visualize you and your dog giving the same performance.

Visualization will benefit you and your dog if you take the time and put in the energy. If your dog is injured, or if you must take time off for any other reason, visualizing your performances again and again will make great use of your time off. When you go back to the actual physical event, you may find you've improved.

Performance-Enhancing Techniques

Sports psychology has gained acceptance as a performance-enhancing method. While it may have been a fringe movement years ago, it is now a respectable and important part of all elite athletes' training. But the techniques used by sports psychologists shouldn't be available exclusively to Olympians and professional athletes. They can, and should, be a part of your training for canine sporting events.

Especially when sharing the performance ring with your dog, you should remain as calm and confident as possible. This attitude will keep your animal partner focused and relaxed so that she can perform her job. Even people who have been involved with canine events for years will have periods of uncertainty, nervousness, and shyness. Knowing methods you can use to take control of your anxiousness is valuable in achieving your best performance and helping your dog do the same.

"I'M SO NERVOUS!"

It's almost your turn. You and your dog are "on deck" and ready to show the judge what you can do. You have prepared solidly for this opportunity. After hours of practice, you know your dog can do it. She is happy and positive and excited. You, on the other hand, feel like you might vomit. Butterflies? You feel sure that your stomach is full of something more substantial, like sparrows. Your hands are shaking so terribly the leash is vibrating. You're sure that if you take a step, your wobbly legs will collapse, leaving you in a pile for the other teams to walk over on the way to the arena.

The closer your turn is, the more nervous you become. Your dog begins to feel it. She looks up at you, searching for reassurance, wondering what is causing your fear. You have distracted and worried your dog. That makes you even more anxious. She'll surely not be able to do her best if she is nervous. A vicious cycle has started. Where does it end?

A case of the jitters is a normal reaction to the stress of competition. The crowd, the dogs, the judges, and the change of environment are all disconcerting.

You fear you'll fail or embarrass yourself. Although these thoughts may be normal, they will affect your performance and your dog's performance. You will lose focus and not be able to concentrate. Here's one trick: Dogs can smell your nervousness on your breath. If you suck on mints, this may help camouflage your tension and give your dog less to worry about. But to get to the root of the problem, try the following suggestions.

BREATHING

Breathe deeply. Shallow breathing or holding your breath are common manifestations of stress and nervousness. They will hinder your performance and concentration and your dog's ability to relax and perform well. You also won't get enough oxygen. Take long, deep breaths through your nose and exhale through your mouth. Expand your abdominal muscles as you inhale and contract them naturally as you exhale.

Breathing seems so natural that most people don't give it a moment's thought. Practice deep breathing at home, especially during training sessions, and use it at your next event. You'll see the magic that deep breathing can bring to your state of mind.

Just three breaths will help. Breathe in for the count of eight. Hold your breath for the count of eight. Release the breath for the count of eight. If you do this three times, you will feel more relaxed.

REALITY VERSUS FICTION

Constant dialogues with ourselves go on in our heads, but we often take little notice. If you have a case of the jitters, however, you are probably making negative statements about what *might* go wrong. Under stress, your mind may not know the difference between reality and fiction. You can fool your brain by convincing it of a better, more positive, reality.

Never say anything negative out loud. Doing so leads your brain to confirm the statement as truth. Alter the script by changing all negatives into positives and filling your mind with encouraging thoughts.

Instead of worrying about the number of people in the audience, say to yourself, I love big crowds. Do this with any negative statement that enters your brain. This technique won't work alone though. You must follow these positive statements with positive body language. Stand up straight and breath deeply. Put on a calm, confident exterior. Watch others who are calm and confident, and copy their body language. Remember a situation where you felt calm and confident. Mimic yourself in that situation and feel those same feelings again.

BE PREPARED

It is difficult to feel confident and ready if you haven't done your homework. If your dog is well trained, well conditioned, and well groomed, you will feel more sure of yourself and your dog's ability. Know the judge (look him or her up in the booklet you receive listing the particulars of the show, called a premium). Know what this particular judge likes and dislikes and recall any previous experience you have had with him or her. If your memories are negative, put them out of your mind. If you have no experience with the judge, assume he or she will like your dog best.

Understand what's expected. Know the course or the particulars of the individual event. Have you done something similar in the past? How did you respond? Remember the positive aspects clearly. Know how you are going to improve this time and visualize this improved performance.

Being prepared also requires investing time in practice, training, and conditioning. After you've worked hard at home, you can relax at shows, knowing you only have to show the judges what your dog already knows so well.

Come to the show prepared with all the necessary accouterments. Forgetting to bring drinks will distract you when you are nervous, thirsty, and ready to go into the ring or onto the field. Forgetting equipment is even worse. Missing important pieces of equipment could potentially ruin your entire competition. Make a list of everything you will need at the show and cross off the items as you pack them. Then check everything again before you leave home.

ACCEPTING ERRORS

As will inevitably happen at some point, when your dog makes a mistake during an event or performance, forget it—immediately. The difference between a great performance and a bad performance can be your dwelling on a mistake. You can't take it back, so accept it and move on. In your mind, pretend that no one saw it. Chances are very few people saw it anyway. Don't blame your dog, it was most likely your mistake. But then again, don't dwell on your own shortcomings. Look at each performance, good or bad, as an opportunity to learn something that will improve your following performances.

I'm not sure why, but I always get very nervous before I compete in a horse show. What I have done to alleviate some of this fear is to say before each show that I am participating only to learn. "This show is a learning experience. I am going to try my best. Everything that happens, good or bad, will be stored in my memory bank to use to improve my performance, and one day I will be able to *really* show." I always do better with this attitude. I am more relaxed and I try my best. It may work for you too.

THE REWARDS

The feeling of winning is a personal experience to be shared by you and your devoted canine partner. But the ribbons and awards are only the frosting on the cake. The real reward is in improving your relationship with your dog. Your dog will have fun in any competition as long as you allow it. Foremost in what you bring to the team should be the belief

A SUCCESSFUL TEAM: THE 10 ESSENTIAL ELEMENTS

1. Keep a Positive Attitude—Keep your attitude positive even in the face of an important loss. Your dog does not understand that she hasn't won. She may sense that you are upset over something to do with her, but she does not know it is because she has failed to place first. A positive attitude in training and in competition will make a world of difference in her enthusiasm, ability to learn, and cooperation.

2. Set Goals—Setting goals has been discussed (so you know how to create them to benefit you and your dog). This is a reminder of how important they are for you and your dog's success as a team. The keys are to be flexible, reevaluate, be realistic but challenge yourself, and make long- and short-term goals. Enjoy the process, not just the results.

3. Adjust Your Training As Necessary—Have in your training repertoire a bag full of techniques and tricks. Adjust the training style if the one you are using doesn't appear to be working. Try different ways of communicating with your dog if she is having difficulty understanding what you are asking from her. Find out what motivates your dog and apply that knowledge.

4. Commit to Physical Conditioning—Your dog will not be successful in your chosen adventure, no matter how well she knows the skills, if you don't help her achieve the physical conditioning necessary to stay healthy and strong. Keep the F.I.T.T. principles in mind when creating a training program.

5. Allow for Mistakes and Bad Days—When you are or your dog is making consistent mistakes, it is time to reevaluate your program. Something is amiss and it is probably not your dog. Your communication, technique, or plan may need to be adjusted. Were your expectations too high to begin with? What can you change to make the situation better? When you do

that you are there for the love of your dog and for the excitement of the adventure.

Elite Canine Athletes

The elite canine athlete is a special animal. As with an elite human athlete, it takes a unique individual to be extremely successful in a sport.

have a bad day, stop working with your dog and just enjoy her company. If the bad day happens to be the day of an event, write it off as experience and learn from it.

6. *Keep It All in Perspective*—Participating in an adventure with your dog is meant to be fun. If either of you is not enjoying of the process, take time off. Work on problem areas and strive to improve, but stay positive. If you win, stay modest. Next time, even with the same performance, you may not win. Congratulate the winners if you lose. Everyone deserves the spotlight once in a while.

7. *Take Your Time*—Don't rush; there is no hurry to reach your goals. Take training one step at a time. Adjust your expectations if you need to. Take a step backward if necessary. Skip training on bad days, and end training early if it gets difficult. Shortcuts will not benefit you or your dog.

8. *Be Compassionate*—You and your dog are a team—you need each other to accomplish your goals. Your responsibility is to build your dog's abilities, knowledge, and confidence, and you must fulfill this responsibility with compassion. Every action you take should contribute to a mutually respectful relationship. Harsh corrections have no place in building teamwork. Again, don't blame your dog for mistakes. Keep in mind who taught whom.

9. *Keep Records*—A record of your training and conditioning sessions, as well as the shows and events you have participated in, is a valuable tool you can use to improve your interactions with your dog.

10. *Keep Learning*—Learning is a lifelong process. Challenge yourself and your athletic canine friend. Continue your education, keeping an open mind, by attending seminars, reading books, and taking training courses. Some advice you'll find during your quest may be harmful, old-fashioned, or just plain nonsense, so you should know how to weed out what is not relevant to you and your dog.

The physical demands of the activity must be met with a good dose of natural ability, dedication, and conditioning. (For an example of athletic elitism, read the quick peek on dog sledding in part II of this book.) To excel, a dog must be willing, intelligent, confident, and energetic. These characteristics make an extraordinary athlete but can also create unique demands on the dog's caretaker.

Many canine athletes combine high intelligence with assertiveness. If your dog possesses both these personality traits, your firm leadership is crucial. Dogs need leaders and are more comfortable if their humans are the leaders. If you act like the owner in charge and expect proper social behavior from your dog, she will not become too pushy. Keep an eye on your dog's attitude and accept that you may have to remind her who's in charge once in a while. Training your dog and working with her will help you maintain control.

Athletic dogs are likely to be in great physical health. They are able to exert high levels of energy for extended amounts of time, and they are strong and feisty. These qualities are great for participating in events, but during off-seasons and slow periods, you may have your hands full. Consistent exercise will help take the edge off your dog's energy. Bicycling or cart pulling may work well for you because you won't have to exert nearly as much energy as she will. Check with your veterinarian about changing her diet during these down times. A good, balanced diet, one different from her high-energy training diet, may lessen her excess energy and still keep her healthy.

After all the time your elite canine has spent by your side—training and competing and relying on you as her sole companion during times of excitement and stress in strange environments—your bond with her is closer than ever. In fact, at home she may rely on you more than you would prefer. She may want to be by your side every second. Placing your dog in a down-stay on a rug or bed for a periodic break or in a crate for a short time (30 minutes at the longest) may give you those few minutes needed to keep your sanity.

This is not punishment—make sure your dog understands that—so don't feel bad about doing it. I have a dog who lies on my feet whenever I sit down. Often after tripping over him a dozen times because he thinks he must be underfoot just in case I need him for anything, I have to send him away. I use the command "out" and point in the direction I want him to go. He will sulk away in that direction, lie down with his ears back, and look at me as if I have broken his heart, even though I am extremely careful to never use an angry tone with him. In a few minutes, all is forgotten, and he is back as happy as always.

To compensate for the stress of training and competing (even if it is good stress), spend time daily in some sort of relaxed activity with your dog to keep her mentally healthy. Gentle grooming is something some dogs adore and others despise. If your dog enjoys it, she may find it very relaxing. Another rewarding way to give your dog the relaxation she needs, and which I find therapeutic in the giving, is TTouch or massage (described in chapter 4) for your deserving pooch.

If you share your home with more than one dog, it is important to give each of your dogs some one-on-one time with you. It doesn't have to be longer than a few minutes of reassurance and a demonstration of your love. After working hard, you all could use a minute to remind yourselves that your relationships with each other are important.

CHAPTER FOUR

Keep the Engine Running Smoothly: Physical Care of the Canine Athelete

Your dog cannot be an athlete if his body is not in good condition—on the inside and the outside. You will have to decide when to increase or decrease his work, perform precautionary health measures, feed your dog a more nutritious diet, and spot any signs of health problems early and then take care of them as necessary. This is not a responsibility to be taken lightly. It is vital that you have a general understanding of your dog's body and what it takes to keep him healthy.

The Canine Body

The canine body is a wondrous, efficient creation. Domestication allowed people to selectively breed and thus manipulate the canine body. Different structural traits were chosen for specialized tasks. Although many of these tasks are no longer required of dogs, a breed's present structure reflects its past responsibilities. It is amazing to me how seemingly minute differences effectively allow a particular breed of dog to perform its duty.

Although we now call a specific classification of a dog a "breed," that was not always the case. Before the creation of registry organizations such as the American Kennel Club (AKC), dogs were lumped together by type. For example, the turnspit dogs (dogs used to turn a wheel on a roasting spit) were usually shortlegged and longbacked. They all had a similar body structure and appearance, but there could be many differences between dogs in the group.

Currently, the conformations of the different breeds are becoming so strict that a breed's "look" can be extremely limited. Since their acceptance into the AKC registry, breeds that have always demonstrated a range of structural differences are slowly becoming more uniform in appearance. Traditionally, breeding has concentrated on working ability, but many breeders are shifting their emphasis toward looks. Although the longtime breeders of Border collies are breeding solely for herding instincts, the dog is a good example of how fast a breed can be physically manipulated by newer breeders to create a specialized appearance.

What does this mean to you if you're searching for a dog to match your activity? You should loosely divide dogs by types instead of breeds in an effort to organize them by function and ability. From there, you can discern the assets of each individual dog for your chosen activity. A general description of the canine body follows and is meant to give you the basic knowledge you'll need when searching for a new dog or evaluating your own dog.

The breeds' predominant differences are in size—small, medium, and large dogs. Small dogs can be of two different types. An achondroplastic dog has a normal-sized head and body, but his legs are smaller than normal. These dogs do not do well at jumping because their small legs don't provide good leverage. A small dog can also be of miniature *size* with normal body *proportions*.

Large dogs were used for guarding and warfare and were usually fearless and confident. Long, sleek dogs captured and killed predators and game. Medium dogs have been used to find game for hunters to kill. When shotguns came into use for hunting, these dogs fetched the game after it had been shot by the hunters. Dogs resembling wild predators such as wolves were used for herding because they frightened the sheep, while dogs used as the herds' guardians resembled the sheep.

Dogs' coats have always varied greatly among the different breeds and even within a breed. Smooth-coated dogs required less upkeep than some of the more elaborately coated breeds. For instance, small lap dogs often had silky, long hair that was soft and comfortable for the people whose laps were warmed by them. Because the dogs were not outside working hard, their beloved owners could spend more time combing and caring for their coats, and the dogs' luxurious lifestyle kept them from becoming too dishevelled. Dogs who had to work in brush and burs had a feathering of hair to catch the burs away from their bodies. The coat of single-coated dogs is made up of hair that is consistent in thickness and texture and may be of any length. Double-coated dogs have one guard hair for every 10 undercoat hairs. This system traps air in the dense coat, creating insulation. Dogs expected to tolerate cold water have oil in their hair that provides water resistance and maintains their body temperature. There are even breeds that are hairless.

The structure of a dog's legs are critical to his performance. Their movement is complex and they bear the dog's weight. A discussion on optimum leg structure is included in the next section. A dog's spine must be strong enough to support his midsection and yet be flexible. Physically fit dogs have well-developed muscles on their necks, shoulders, loins, and hindquarters. Although dogs use their tails to help them balance during jumping and quick turns, bobbed-tail individuals and breeds don't seemed to be bothered by the lack of a "rudder."

CANINE ANATOMY

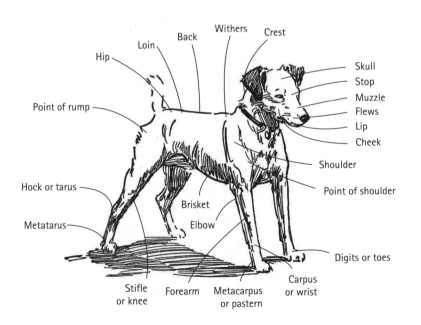

The size and shape of a dog's chest can have on impact on his ability to perform. A large chest permits maximal expansion of his lungs. Fast-running dogs have deep, narrow chests to provide plenty of room for their lungs without increasing wind resistance. Dogs who need stability for their work, such as bulldogs once needed for fighting, have wider rib cages.

Body Structure

The structure of your canine athlete is vital to his ability to perform well in the adventure you have chosen. His structure, and all of its advantages and shortcomings, becomes increasingly important as you strive toward a higher standard of performance. If you are participating just for fun, you may be able to work around some structural defects, depending on their seriousness. But I still suggest that you analyze your dog's structure and understand his faults. Slight structural imperfections may create an imbalance that can result in serious problems. However, if you are aware of any problems your dog has, you can pay particular attention to developing strength in the appropiate muscle groups and can more knowledgeably detect when you have pushed your dog too far or too hard.

HOW STRUCTURE RELATES TO PERFORMANCE

Your dog's movement is supported by his muscloskeletal framework. If this framework has defects and is not strong and balanced, movement will be compromised. After constant stressed movement, the muscloskeletal areas that have been working to compensate for a weaker section can become damaged. Some structural faults are serious enough to make some activities impossible. Remember that no dog has perfect structure and that structure is related to a breed's anticipated function. Different breeds will have different "correct" structures depending on the job they were bred to perform. For instance, shoulder angulation is important in complex movements such as jumping. Since different breeds have different standards of angulation, some breeds are naturally better built for jumping.

Structure is determined mostly by heredity and partly by training. Your dog's natural structure should guide you in choosing an adventure. Your dog will have an advantage if you pursue an activity to which he is naturally inclined. Training, however, can help your dog overcome structural difficulties by strengthening his entire system and reinforcing specific muscle groups.

SOME THINGS TO LOOK FOR

Angulation is one of the most important structural aspects to look for in a performance dog. Angulation refers to the degree of angle created where the bones meet each other at the joints. Too little angulation means your dog will not have much power or leverage for jumping, running, and other dynamic movements. With little angulation, your dog will also experience less flexibility and more concussion with movement. Excessive angulation can also be a problem. It is difficult to develop enough muscles to support bones with excessive angulation, thus stability is reduced and the risk of injury is increased.

The dog's topline is also important. The term "topline" refers to a dog's profile from his shoulders to the base of his tail. The topline can be arched, level, or sloped. An arched topline is great for running long distances. The increased flexiblity of this topline allows a dog to reach with longer strides while running in order to have more power and speed. A level topline aids in galloping short distances or in trotting. A sloping topline is optimum for trotting for long periods and over long distances.

When you are evaluating your dog's structure, look for a wagging tail; an effortless, flowing gait; and a content facial expression. If you don't see these characteristics, look deeper for imperfection in his structure. He may be experiencing pain, or he may have to exert extra effort to perform even simple activities.

Movement

Some activities, such as conformation and walking, require simple movement. Other adventures such as agility and obedience require challenging, complex movement. No matter what the required movement in your chosen activity, it is important to evaluate your dog's motion and be aware of any problems that may arise.

Movement patterns are established in puppyhood and, once ingrained, are difficult to change. For example, if a puppy is raised on a linoleum floor, he may always walk as if he is navigating on ice. Exposing your young dog to a myriad of surfaces, obstacles, and games will counteract many undesired patterns.

THE GAITS

The various means of canine locomotion—the ways a dog places his feet on the ground as he moves forward—are called gaits. The specific manner in which your dog moves at each gait tells you something about his structure (how his joints and muscles are assembled) and physical health at the joints, as well as his overall mental and physical health.

Locomotion is more than just getting from here to there, and many people spend years examining and learning about how their dogs move. As your dog progresses into the status of elite athlete, his health will depend, in part, on how well you understand his gaits and your ability to tell the difference between normal and abnormal movement. A general overview of the five gaits is provided below.

Walk

When your dog walks, three of his limbs bear his weight during each stride. First one front foot, then the diagonal rear foot, then the other front foot, and then the other rear foot hit the ground.

Trot

The trot is the best movement to watch to analyze your dog's structure. This gait is a good gauge of how straight and balanced he is, as well as if his angulation supports increased physical activity and participation in canine sports.

During the trot, one set of diagonal limbs moves forward, followed by the other set of diagonal limbs. Weight bearing happens during two alternating moments. A distinct pattern of one, two, one, two occurs. During the trot, energy is focused on forward motion, and there is little vertical or lateral motion.

A trotting dog should single-track; that is, the dog's feet should fall in midline (the imaginary line drawn down the dog's body from head to tail). The movement should produce footprints that form an almost straight line.

When analyzing your dog's movement, you may find it easier to use an assistant or to videotape the session for later review. Videotaping will give you the extra advantage of being able to stop or slow down the movement to help you gain a clearer understanding of the action.

Have your helper trot your dog toward you, or trot your dog toward the camera. Your dog's front legs should form a straight line from his shoulder to his foot. His elbows should not be bent inward or outward. His feet should not flip out before landing and create a "paddling" effect. Next, have your dog trot away from you or your camera. His rear legs, when you're looking at him from the back, should be straight from hip to foot, not bending at his stifle or hock.

When watching your dog from the side during the trot, you should see his front feet extending to or past his muzzle. This is called the dog's "reach." A dog with a short reach may have a short upper arm or poor angulation in the front. Your dog's rear legs should stretch out behind him. This is called "drive." A strong, powerful drive with the legs extending far back is advantageous. If a dog has good reach and drive, he expends less energy while covering ground and can work longer at a higher intensity.

Pace

During the pace, your dog's front and rear left legs work together and his front and rear right legs work together. Dogs use this gait to conserve energy when they are tired. Dogs will also use it if their feet interfere with each other during a trot. Short-backed dogs and dogs with long or overangulated legs will also use the pace. The pace can be taught by walking faster and faster with your dog. This gait isn't used much because trotting is easier and faster.

Canter

The canter is a three-count gait, with the weight of your dog in contact with the ground during three moments. He can lead with either front leg. If he is on a left lead, his right rear leg hits first, then his right front leg, then his left rear leg, and finally his left front leg. This last weight-bearing moment is the longest and has the most extended reach. Your dog can change his lead as necessary during movement to make sharp turns and to adjust takeoff spots during jumping. Because of his ability to change leads so quickly and smoothly, he can easily adjust his speed, his stride, and the flow of his performance. He can also change leads when tired, thereby working a different set of muscles and giving the others a rest.

Gallop

During the gallop, there are four moments of weight bearing. This is the fastest stride. The motion is left rear, right rear, right front, and left front. Your dog's head and neck thrust forward and down when his rear legs are under his body and up and back when his front legs reach under his body. Dogs require strong heads and necks, flexible spines, and free-moving shoulders for increased speed.

Exercise-Related Problems

The problems discussed below are those that specifically affect canine athletes. They either are induced by particular types of exercise or are a product of too much exercise. By understanding potential problems before they arise, you will be able to notice when they are beginning and prevent any further related problems.

BEHAVIORAL CHANGES

In order to be a competent coach, an effective personal trainer, and a caring friend, you must be an attentive observer, aware of your dog's physical and mental well-being at all times.

A behavioral change in your dog, no matter how slight, can be a warning sign that something is wrong. He may be stressed, overworked, fatigued, or bored, or he may have a physical problem. To be safe, assume a change in behavior has a physical cause. If you don't immediately know what the problem is, then a trip to your veterinarian is in order. Rule out physical problems first, and then you can delve deeper to find what might be bothering your dog. Sometimes the source of an emotional problem can be very difficult to trace. It may help to keep an accurate record of your dog's state of mind for a few days to clue you in to any pattern that has developed. Talking to a trusted trainer or behaviorist may also help.

LAMENESS

Lameness is a decrease in the ability to move. Sometimes lameness is slight and almost imperceptible. Other times it is the result of intense, sharp pain that is immediately apparent. Temporary lameness can be caused by sores, stones, and thorns. Lameness can also be caused by pain in your dog's bones, muscles, tendons, or ligaments. These problems are generally more serious and take longer to heal. Some injuries can cause permanent damage or can develop into more chronic problems such as arthritis.

Lame dogs should not compete or engage in training. Lameness is the manifestation of pain. If your dog is in pain, he should rest and you should search for the source of pain and cure it with your veterinarian's help.

Checking for Lameness

Practice the following check for lameness before you ever suspect that your dog is lame. This way, you will know what your dog's normal body feels and looks like and what to do before an emergency situation occurs and you are worried and anxious.

While your dog is at rest, check to see if he is evenly balanced, bearing his weight equally on all four legs. Run your hands down each leg and check for any areas of swelling or increased heat (especially at the joints). Rub one hand down each front leg at the same time. Compare the legs to each other. Do the same to the rear legs. Is your dog leaning to one side or to the front or back? Subtle lameness can be checked by walking your dog, trotting him in small circles in each direction, or having him go up stairs. View your pooch's movement from the front, back, and each side. With these tests, you should be able to assess how serious the lameness seems to be and which section of his body the pain is in.

A lame dog tries to avoid placing too much weight on the leg experiencing pain. As he walks, he will lift the painful leg as soon as it touches the ground and often wince in pain. He'll raise his head sharply as the painful leg begins to bear his weight. His good legs will be held lower to counteract the withdrawing motion and for added support. He'll compensate with a shortened stride on the painful leg and possibly drag his toenails. He may stumble or cross his legs as he moves about, depending on the severity of the pain.

When you have located the lameness, palpate the area, feeling for any abnormality. Flex and extend your dog's joints to check his range of motion. Compare one leg to another, taking note of the differences. Look for heat, swelling, cuts, and foreign matter. If you still cannot find anything, have your dog lie down and check him again. Taking the weight off of the area can result in different information.

Trust your instincts and watch for even the subtlest of indications from your dog. Unless you are able to fix the problem right away, by removing a foreign object from his paw, for example, stop training or performing. Your dog may need time to heal, or he may need veterinary attention.

Retta's Story

Retta is my Bouvier des Flandres, with whom I at one time did agility. She loved it. In fact, it was the only activity that she really seemed to enjoy, and it brought out the puppy in her.

Retta is not an agility dog though. She is chronically overweight (an inherited condition that five miles of daily running and a strict diet didn't cure), large, extremely bow-legged, and black and shaggy. I just accepted that she had to take it easy and we were doing it just to have a good time.

At home one day, I noticed she didn't seem quite right. She appeared to be favoring a back leg, although the change was hardly noticeable. I thoroughly checked her back legs by running my hands down them and massaging gently to find a possible sore spot. Nothing I did seemed to bother her. She didn't wince, wiggle, yelp, or try to get away. I did notice that one of her legs was a bit smaller than the other—a sign of muscle atrophy.

I took her to my veterinarian. His observations of Retta's condition were similar to mine. He took x-rays and did some tests. He could find nothing. It wasn't until a number of months later that an x-ray of her back showed that she had developed arthritis in her spine. It had affected her ability to use one of her back legs. Of course, she doesn't do agility anymore, and she is on pain medication.

The most troubling part of the experience was that Retta had not been her usual peppy self at agility. I attributed it to the heat—it was summer and she is intolerant of warm temperatures. Although it's true she doesn't work hard in the heat, it was the pain in her spine that was causing her lack of energy. Because of the amount of muscle atrophy, I know she had been experiencing the pain for a while. I felt terrible for not investigating more carefully earlier.

This experience taught me the importance of acute observation, trusting my instincts, and taking my dog's physical condition seriously. It was only a small, subtle difference in carriage that alerted me to a serious condition.

INJURIES

Muscle and Tendon Injuries

The most common muscle and tendon injuries are strains. A strain is an overstretched muscle or tendon and can produce intermittent lameness. Soreness during or immediately after exercise or delayed soreness in two to three days are signs of a strain. The standard treatment for strains is a day or so of complete rest and then a lowering of the training level. Strains generally take four to six weeks of rest to heal and often require anti-inflammatory drugs. To lower the risk of your dog getting a strain, make sure to give him a complete warmup and increase his activity gradually. Stretching after activity will greatly lower the risk of strains.

Another common tendon injury occurs in the digital flexor tendons, which flex the toes. The injury is usually accompanied by a laceration, which must be repaired by being sewn back together.

Your dog may experience an Achilles tendon injury. The symptoms of such an injury are hind-leg lameness and a dropped hock appearance. Your dog may be unable to extend the affected joint, and there will be swelling of the injured tendon. One, two, or all three tendons in the hind leg may be affected. Surgical repair is necessary, and your dog might never be able to return to the same level of performance, depending on the severity of the injury and how soon treatment begins.

Whenever your dog experiences trauma or injury to a muscle or tendon, there is the secondary risk of atrophy. Atrophy, like that which alerted me to Retta's condition, happens in muscles that are not used or when there is nerve damage. The atrophied muscle becomes small and weak. Physical therapy and a progressive conditioning program can reverse the process and help the muscle regain its previous functioning level.

Ligament Injuries

The most common injury to a ligament is a rupture of the anterior cruciate ligament (ACL) in the knee joint. The ACL is often injured during a twisting motion when the knee is weight bearing or hyperextended. The ACL can also be slowly injured over time because of a structural deficiency. If you can't attribute a suspected ACL injury to a traumatic event, you should watch for chronic lameness that worsens after exercise and see your veterinarian.

When your dog receives such an injury, you should immediately apply ice packs. Later you can use heat. For a mild injury, the treatment consists of a few weeks' rest. A more serious injury may have to be splinted for a number of months. Intermittent lameness may require surgery, and if the injury is severe, surgery is the only solution. Future arthritis is a strong possibility due to this sort of injury.

Wrist Injuries

Traumatic injuries to the carpus (wrist joint) are common. Wrist injuries are usually caused by falls or jumps from an excessive height. Traversing uneven, rough ground can also cause injuries to the carpus. Fractures and dislocations of the wrist are less common but possible.

Carpal hyperextension syndrome occurs when the back side of the wrist is injured. Sometimes small chip fractures can occur. A great deal of pain and swelling accompany this injury. Your dog will not be able to bear the weight of his body. The treatment for carpal hyperextension is surgery to fuse the joints, which provides stability and eliminates pain. Your dog's gait will be altered, and high levels of performance won't be possible.

Digit Injuries

Active dogs who do a lot of running and jumping can experience toe fractures and dislocations. Dogs who exercise on uneven, rough terrain are particularly vulnerable. If your dog experiences sudden lameness, suspect a toe fracture or dislocation. The pain and lameness are usually most obvious after activity. Treatment includes splints or surgery. Your dog will be able to return to activity in a month or two.

Chronic and repetitive stress on your dog's feet can lead to arthritis in the digits. Arthritis in his digits requires the same treatment as arthritis anywhere else—rest, moderate exercise, and anti-inflammatory medication. An affected digit can even be amputated. With an amputated toe, your dog can return to high levels of competition without pain.

NERVOUS SYSTEM DISORDERS

Nervous system disorders are fortunately not common, but they can be quite frightening. Falling or bumping into something can cause damage to your dog's spinal cord. He may lose part or all of his ability to function (physically or mentally). If the injury is not too severe, it will repair itself in several weeks or a few months. Your dog may bite at himself if he has nerve damage because he has no feeling in this area. You may have to protect the area by wrapping it. If you do not actually witness the injury and see the immediate results, muscle atrophy will be your first clue that nerve damage may have occurred in an area.

DISEASES AND OTHER CONDITIONS THAT CAN AFFECT ATHLETIC DOGS

The following is an overview of conditions that may affect your dog's ability to perform at his optimum level and diseases and other conditions that can put his life in danger. These are the most common problems for hard-working canine athletes. As your dog's coach, you should be aware of these problems and have the basic knowledge to deal with them if necessary.

Joint Disease

Degenerative joint disease, or osteoarthritis, is common, notably in athletic and active dogs. Arthritis is the wearing of joints as they constantly rub together. Areas where your dog's structure forces two joints to fit together in a less than perfect manner will be worn down sooner than other areas. Excess weight, trauma to a joint, and heredity can also raise the probability of your dog acquiring joint disease earlier in life.

The signs of joint disease include performance changes and an unwillingness to work. Your doggie athlete may appear stiff or lame all the time but more noticeably after prolonged exercise. He can also appear stiff when first moving and mildly lame after rest but not sore at all when he is warmed up. Dogs with arthritis will be especially stiff or lame during cold or damp weather. Your dog will also experience a reduced or altered range of motion. Areas to watch for arthritis are the hips, shoulders, elbows, spine, and patella (knee). Pay particular attention to joints that have experienced past trauma.

The treatment for arthritis will depend on the location and severity of the affected area. Taking periods of rest, avoiding overexertion, and maintaining normal weight will help ease the pain. Sometimes pain medications are necessary. Arthritis has no cure, but heat and massage can help to ease the discomfort. Moderate exercise is possible and often advisable (ask your veterinarian). Activities such as swimming and walking are often helpful.

Heatstroke or Hyperthermia

If your dog's body temperature rises to 105 degrees Fahrenheit or more, he is suffering from hyperthermia. Dogs are not as efficient in dissipating heat as humans. That is why you will see warnings again and again about protecting your dog from hot weather. Dogs cool themselves by panting, and they perspire through the pads of their feet. This is just not an effective way to cool a body with such a large relative size. High humidity makes it even harder for your dog to stay cool. Dogs with short noses, very large dogs, and dogs with dark, thick coats are especially prone to heatstroke. But before shaving off your dog's coat, check with your veterinarian or breeder. Some thick coats actually provide enough insulation to protect a dog from the heat. Individual dogs handle heat differently. My dog Retta cannot cope with the heat. Her half-sister, on the other hand, is also black and shaggy but doesn't seem to be bothered by the heat unless it is extreme (and we get extremes of 105 to 110 degrees Fahrenheit at times).

Avoid overworking your dog on hot days. Proceed with light work on warm days, but watch your dog carefully and offer plenty of water. If your dog appears to be too hot, stop your session and let him rest in the shade. If you are hot, your dog is too hot. At home, you can give him a children's pool with cold water to play in, especially after a workout. Add ice to the water if necessary to cool him. Puppies are particularly prone to overheating. Even a moderate temperature with high humidity is dangerous. Know your dog well enough to recognize when he is getting too warm. Remember that he may do as you ask even if it is too much for him, especially at a show or event. Watch him closely.

If after resting in the shade your dog doesn't want to get back up and resume your session, take a longer break and offer him water. Even if you are in the middle of a run and aren't near home, if your dog needs to cool off, stop and let him rest under a neighbor's tree. Check for signs of overheating that could lead to hyperthermia (heatstroke).

Does your dog have rapid, noisy breathing? Is his tongue red and enlarged and is his saliva thick? Does your dog exhibit staggering and weakness? Are his eyes glassy? Is he dehydrated (see page 132)? Does he have diarrhea or is he vomiting? And lastly, is his temperature over 105 degrees Fahrenheit? These are signs of heatstroke, which is a serious emergency situation. You must immediately cool your dog's body. Wrap him in a wet towel, shirt, or blanket and gently massage his skin. If he is experiencing serious heatstroke and you place him in cold water, you may shock his system. You can, in an emergency, apply ice or ice packs to his head and between his thighs to lower his temperature more rapidly.

No matter how quickly your dog recovers from a case of hyperthermia, take your dog to a veterinarian. Even a seemingly mild bout with heatstroke can cause permanent damage. It is best to let your veterinarian decide if your dog has been unharmed.

Never leave your dog in a car if it is 65 degrees Fahrenheit or warmer. The car quickly heats up and your dog can succumb to heatstroke in a few moments.

Dehydration

The best defense against dehydration is to offer your dog plenty of water, especially when it is warm, humid, or extremely cold or when he is working hard. Check his gums to monitor his state of hydration. Except for naturally dark pigment, his gums should be moist and pink. Tacky, dry, and dark gums are a bad sign. Offer your dog lots to drink. If he begins vomiting, wait two hours and then offer a small drink. If he quits vomiting, increase his water intake. You can use Pedialyte (an electrolyte-replenishment drink) for rehydration. If your dog becomes dehydrated, call your veterinarian for advice. He or she may want you to come in to have your dog checked. Dehydration can also occur in the winter when your dog's water needs increase as his body works to keep him warm. Because it is so cold, he may not drink as much as his body needs. Keep an eye on the amount of water he is drinking.

Frostbite

Frostbite can affect dogs who are unaccustomed to cold or winter sports and exposed to subzero temperatures for several hours. The affected skin will be very pale and cold to the touch. After the area thaws, your dog's skin will be red and dark, and it will begin to peel and scar. If the frostbite is severe, the skin will die. Affected skin should be handled gently and thawed with warm, not hot, water (105 degrees Fahrenheit) for 15 minutes. Do not rub the skin. Gently apply an antibiotic ointment to the affected areas. Your dog's appendages, especially his feet, ears, tail, and scrotum, are all at risk. Dry your dog if he is wet; wrap the injured area lightly with a dry, non-adhering bandage; and see your veterinarian. Frostbite and hypothermia (see below) may or may not occur at the same time, but check for symptoms of both.

Hypothermia

Hypothermia is a condition in which a dog's body temperature falls below 99 degrees Fahrenheit. Like frostbite, it often affects dogs who are unaccustomed to the cold. Hypothermia victims are usually short-haired dogs, small dogs, or puppies. Also affected are dogs who participate in winter sports in subzero temperatures for extended periods or those who participate in sustained swimming in cold water. Dogs can withstand cold better if they are not also wet.

The first sign that a problem may be brewing is uncontrollable shivering. If your dog is wet, dry him as soon as possible. Other signs of hypothermia are shallow breathing and an anxious expression. If your dog becomes depressed, confused, or lethargic, he is headed for serious trouble. He could slip into a coma and die if he's not helped right away. Get him warm as soon as possible with blankets (electric ones get too hot too fast), towels (you can place them in a dryer for a couple of minutes to warm them if you are home), rubbing (avoid areas that have frostbite), a plastic bottle filled with warm water placed against his body, or a blow-dryer. Take him to your veterinarian quickly.

If it is so cold that you can stay outside only for a short period, your dog is going to need extra consideration. Small, old, sick, or thin-coated dogs have a difficult time handling cold weather. Provide a dog sweater or coat for such a dog when engaging in outdoor activity in the cold. (A sick dog should stay where he is comfortable and rest until he is well.) Even larger or double-coated dogs may need a sweater if there is a risk of getting wet. You can hold your dog close to you to warm him *and* yourself. If you are camping in the wilderness and it gets cold, share your sleeping bag with your four-footed friend. This is the best way to keep warm in the wild.

Bloat

Gastric dilation and torsion, commonly referred to as bloat, is a serious condition that acts quickly and jeopardizes your companion's life. Bloat is the distention of your dog's stomach caused by gas or frothy material in the stomach. The stomach then rotates, closing itself off in both directions. It then compresses one of the major veins carrying blood to the heart, which slows circulation and can lead to shock or death. This is an emergency situation with no time to spare.

The main symptom of bloat in your dog is discomfort: your dog may get up and down, attempt to vomit, whine, or pace; he may have a painful stomach and distended abdomen. If you see any of these signs, get help *immediately*. If your dog does not see a veterinarian within a few hours, he will probably die. Once your dog has had bloat, he will be more susceptible to it in the future.

Large breeds, breeds with deep chests, and those with steep angulation between the stomach and esophagus, seem to be at most risk. Dogs who gulp their food and older dogs are also susceptible. Avoiding excessive water intake can help prevent bloat. Before and during exercise, offer your dog small amounts of water at a time. After exercise, offer moderate amounts of water, allowing your dog to drink at will after he is quiet and rested. How soon before exercising a dog eats also seems to affect whether he becomes a victim of bloat. Feed your dog his meal four hours before vigorous exercise. After exercise, wait one hour to feed him. Small snacks during sustained, endurance exercise are acceptable, but control his eating by offering him small bites every few moments.

The best ways to prevent bloat are to keep a consistent feeding schedule, never feed your dog and then leave him (because you can't keep an eye on him), avoid rapid changes in diet, and avoid encouraging food gulping (as sometimes occurs among several dogs eating at the same time).

Sunburn

Sunburn is a concern for dogs who have light skin. A light-colored dog's nose is markedly vulnerable to the sun. When your dog will be outside for an extended amount of time, apply sunscreen to save him from the sun's potential damage. Use a children's sunscreen with a sun protection factor (SPF) of 15 or higher on his sensitive areas.

You should apply the sunscreen to your dog in the same manner you would apply it on yourself. Thirty minutes before you go outside, rub a generous amount of sunscreen on you and your dog. Reapply every two hours or if your pet gets wet.

Some companies are producing sunscreen for pets in spray bottles. This is convenient for large areas, but do not spray his face. Apply the product to your hands and rub it on your dog's face.

Some dogs do not mind sunscreen at all; others will mind terribly. Find the sunscreen with the least scent and gradually accustom your dog to wearing it on his skin. Use small amounts at first until he can tolerate a greater amount. Use treats and praise to encourage him and distract him if necessary.

Care of the Canine Body

As you have already discovered by reading this chapter, the canine body is an intricate and finely tuned machine. When you ask your dog to work hard and perform, support his efforts by taking good care of his body to help him acheive and sustain optimum health. This section explains how you, as caretaker and friend, can perform this important duty.

TOUCH THERAPIES

When your dog's activity results in an injury, you will most likely use some sort of physical or touch therapy in his rehabilitation. You and your vet may decide to use any combination of the therapies discussed below.

Your immediate goal will be to restore full function to the injured body part(s), and your ultimate goal will be to restore your dog's elite physical condition.

Because you cannot simply give your dog a list of therapy exercises for him to perform on his own, you will be an intergral part of his therapy. You will be dealing with a creature who does not understand that you are doing these things for his own benefit, so you must develop an effective program with your vet that your dog will tolerate. As the one in charge of your dog's therapy, you must be sensitive to his pain threshold and know when he is experiencing discomfort.

Extremely aggressive or fearful dogs should not be forced into touch therapy.

Physical Therapy

Physical therapy is a widely accepted method of touch therapy used on dogs. Since you cannot explain to your dog what you would like him to do, physical therapy is beneficial because you use passive movement, producing movement for your dog by manipulating his body. You are responsible for flexing and extending the various parts of his body that have been injured to bring back the full range of motion and flexibility to the area.

Physical therapy improves your dog's circulation and promotes healing. It helps reduce the development of stiffness in the joints and muscles and halts decreasing flexibility associated with injuries. By preventing a muscle from shortening and keeping a joint's range of motion from decreasing, physical therapy is invaluable in the recovery of many injuries.

Physical therapy includes heat and cold therapy. Cold therapy reduces swelling and numbs the area. Ice packs, cold wraps, or cooling blankets are most effective if used in the first three days after an injury. Heat therapy reduces pain and muscle spasms. Gentle heat such as hot towels, heating pads, hot water blankets, and warm baths can be used.

When using heat, be cautious because your dog may not feel the heat and could be burned.

High-tech methods of physical therapy are being increasingly used on canine patients. Ultrasound therapy is a form of massage that uses high-energy sound waves that are converted to heat by tissue. It is often used for the treatment of tendon and ligament injuries, as well as muscle spasms. The equipment is expensive, so the treatment may not be available from your veterinarian or the cost may be prohibitive.

Atrophied muscles can be stimulated electrically by neuromuscular stimulation. This therapy uses a pulse generator and electrodes on the affected area. This form of therapy is especially useful on spinal injuries.

Massage

Massage is also highly effective for certain injuries. Massage should be performed two or three times daily. Massage and whirlpool baths are a great combination for treatment.

You don't have to be a licensed, trained massage therapist to make your dog feel better with your hands. Through a little trial and error, you will find the method that your dog enjoys and that makes him feel better. After you have discovered the magical benefits of massage, you may want to increase your knowledge. Find a book on canine massage, or use a book or video on massage for humans and adapt the techniques for use on your dog. You may want to attend a class on massage for people. If you can find a massage therapist who treats animals in your area, you may be able to learn some of the techniques from him or her.

To start getting your dog accustomed to massage, approach him when he is in a calm, relaxed mood. Don't force him. Take your time. Make the atmosphere relaxing with soft classical music and dim lighting. Your dog should be comfortable and you should be prepared with any equipment you may need. Experiment with your touch. Learn to read your dog's preferences—where he likes to be massaged, what method seems to work best, and how much pressure he prefers. The more relaxed and calm you remain, the more your dog will do the same.

The results of starting a touch therapy program may be dramatic, but chances are the results will be subtle and gradual. Keep up with the program, and eventually you will notice a difference in the way your dog feels.

But how can you tell if he likes massage? If your dog likes it, he will become more and more relaxed. He may roll over and let you rub his belly. If he doesn't like the touch, he may flinch or his skin may ripple—you may have found a sensitive spot. If he paws, mouths you, or walks away, he really doesn't like it. Keep alert for tenderness, lumps, or changes in the skin so you can report them to your vet.

Be careful around your dog's hips as he may be sensitive here. If you dog has a disc problem, avoid massage unless you have discussed it with your veterinarian. After surgery you should be particularly careful, and again, talk with your veterinarian before beginning massage therapy. Leave surgically repaired limbs and incisions alone.

Even if your dog does not need massage for a particular injury, you may still want to learn the techniques. Massage may change behavior by calming a fearful or excitable dog. Weekly massage will build trust and increase your bond with each other. Your dog works hard for you, and the more competitive you are, the more stress (both physically and mentally) he will experience. A massage or a whirlpool bath every now and again is a caring way to say thank you and help your dog relax.

TTouch

Linda Tellington-Jones first developed this method of touch for horses and has discovered its benefit for all animals from dogs to monkeys to dolphins. This is not a form of massage intended to affect the muscular system; it is a method of touching that activates the nervous system.

TTouch is a series of specific touches given gently to an animal at varying pressures. Learning this method is easy, and if you read Tellington-Jones's book, you will find some interesting information. For example, you will learn the various areas on your dog's body that connect with certain emotions and pain centers.

You can also purchase a video on giving dogs TTouch that shows you the touches and how to apply them to your dog. TTouch proponents claim that it will help many conditions, both physical and behavioral, and although the claims may appear inflated, I have seen this method work miracles. If nothing else, it will build a trusting bond between you and your dog.

Acupuncture

Acupunture was developed in China and has been used for over 3,000 years. It is commonly used for pain management, but it is also used as a form of holistic therapy for other problems. Acupuncture involves the insertion of small needles into specific points on the skin. In canine therapy, these points are carefully and skillfully chosen by veterinarians.

Although it is gaining in popularity, acupuncture is still considered by some to be quackery or at least something to be suspicious of. Naysayers attribute success stories of this therapy to coincidence or the caretaker's trust in the procedure and excitement over the possibilities of success. More and more veterinarians, animal caretakers, and researchers are finding that, in truth, acupuncture can make a difference in the lives of animals who suffer from pain.

Even normally conservative veterinarians are being trained in acupuncture and finding it not only helps ease the pain of dogs (and other animals) who suffer from chronic pain such as arthritis, but it helps ease pain after surgery and can even be used as an anesthetic in weak or older dogs.

Only veterinarians specially trained in acupuncture should perform this therapy. Make sure the veterinarian you choose has the knowledge and the experience to perform acupuncture correctly.

Acupressure

Acupressure is an ancient art from the Chinese that uses hand and finger pressure in specified body areas to affect disease and to relieve pain. The addition of a few acupressure techniques can enhance a massage program. Acupressure strengthens the circulation and flow of energy. A veterinarian that practices acupuncture can teach you acupressure.

Chiropractic Therapy

Veterinary chiropractic therapy adjusts your dog's spine and other bones, placing them into proper alignment. Misalignment can cause much pain and affects the dog's movement, muscles, and internal organs.

Veterinary chiropractic therapy requires extensive knowledge and should only be performed by a certified veterinary chiropractor.

VACCINATIONS AND PARASITES

Vaccinations are particularly important for athletic dogs because they are exposed to other dogs and unfamiliar locations. Dogs who spend time in the untamed outdoors need vaccinations because of their contact with wild creatures.

DISEASES PREVENTED BY VACCINATIONS

These diseases can be fatal:

➤ Distemper

➤ Parvovirus

➤ Rabies

These diseases can cause severe permanent damage:

➤ Parainfluenza

➤ Leptospirosis

➤ Adenovirus

➤ Coronavirus

➤ Bordetella (kennel cough)

➤ Lyme disease

Adult dogs need almost all their booster vaccinations yearly; their rabies vaccinations may be good for two to three years. They should also have an annual stool specimen tested for the existence of parasites.

In general, puppies require their first vaccination at the age of 6 weeks for distemper, adenovirus, parainfluenza, leptospirosis, parvovirus, and coronavirus. The vaccinations should be repeated at 9, 12, and 15 weeks of age. Additionally, a booster parvovirus vaccination should be administered at 5 to 6 months of age. Your dog's first rabies shot should be given at 14 to 16 weeks of age and is good for one year. Bordetella vaccinations are given at 6 weeks with the first booster shot at 9 weeks and the second at 12 weeks. Lyme disease requires two vaccinations 3 weeks apart beginning when the puppy is 12 weeks old. Your puppy should also have a stool sample examined for parasites. Discuss this vaccination schedule with your veterinarian and your dog's breeder. These are only general recommendations and may not be appropriate for your dog.

Heartworms are parasites transmitted by mosquito bites. If you live in an area that has mosquitoes, your dog should be taking a heartworm preventative. If mosquitoes leave larvae when they bite your dog, these larvae will migrate to his heart, where they will grow into long, spaghetti-like worms that damage the heart and cause lung problems. Heartworms are very difficult to treat once they have taken refuge in your dog. Prevention is the best way to protect your dog. Your adult dog will probably undergo a test to rule out the existence of these parasites and will be put on a heartworm preventative program with a once-a-month pill. Young puppies are routinely placed on the preventative program without being tested first.

FEEDING YOUR DOG

The health of your dog's digestive system is critical to his performance. He must get the maximum benefit of the nutrients he takes in. Canine nutrition is, unfortunately, complex and controversial. Almost any opinion about it can be supported by research and success stories. The confusion becomes greater when you consider the nutritional needs of different breeds.

Many good books exist that attempt to explain canine nutrition, and because your breeder and veterinarian are also good sources of information, this book will not discuss the specific nutrient needs of individual dogs. I know from my education as a personal trainer that each person seems to operate best on a diet that is specifically geared to his or her needs and that allows optimum performance. I am sure that the same is true of dogs. If your dog is experiencing a lack of energy, frequent sickness, breeding difficulties, skin and coat problems, or personality problems, a change in diet may help solve the problem. You may have to research and experiment to find a better diet to feed your dog.

What follows are some general guidelines on feeding your athletic dog.

Calorie Counting

An athletic dog will require more calories than an average dog to have enough energy to perform optimally. If you need to increase your dog's amount of food, do so gradually until you have increased it to the most beneficial amount. You will know you have done so when you observe your dog consistently performing at a high level. If you are not presently feeding your dog a high-quality, nutrient-dense food, you may need to change to a better quality food first before you increase the amount.

When winter sets in and your dog is active outdoors, you may need to increase his calories by 10 to 20 percent. These extra calories are needed for coat thickening and muscle maintenance, as well as energy to generate body heat.

Don't go by the package instructions to find out how much to feed your dog. Use trial and error to establish the optimum amount to feed him—an amount that gives him enough energy and nutrients to stay healthy and at his ideal weight but doesn't add extra fat to him. The amount your dog needs will depend on his metabolism, his energy output, and the quality of the food you feed him. Talk to your veterinarian if you are unsure how much to feed your dog. Make certain that you explain your training regimen so that your vet can adjust the suggested amounts accordingly.

If your dog is going to be exerting himself steadily for more than one hour, you may want to provide him with an energy snack during the activity. A light snack such as Milk-Bones dog biscuits, granola bars, or energy bars without chocolate are handy and will give him the boost he needs. The company Dog Power also produces a sports bar called Power Bone made especially for your four-footed friend.

Quality Is What Really Counts

How do you know which foods are of better quality? You shouldn't rely on advertising or cost; you should read the packages for yourself. This can be an overwhelming task. However, reading the books listed in the appendix will help you understand the nutrition panels on packages of dog food and teach you how to tell a bad food from a good food. To begin with, find a food that does not list by-products in the ingredient list. Dog food is allowed to include ingredients that are not approved for human consumption such as the hair, eyes, bone, and other undesired body parts of animals used as food by humans. These by-products do not supply healthy, adequate, usable protein.

Too much protein, on the other hand, may damage kidneys and cause cancer. You may need to increase protein and carbohydrates to compensate for higher energy needs, but you don't want to overcompensate. In the same vein, avoid oversupplemenation (giving your dog overly high amounts of vitamins and minerals). Dogs need calcium and phosphorus for healthy bones and joints, but oversupplemenation causes rapid bone growth in large breeds and can cause harm in any dog. For this reason, some dog breeders do not recommend puppy food for large breeds. Talk to breeders, other participants in your sport, and your veterinarian to get information on the percentages of the various nutrients that will be best for your dog.

The Chunky Pooch

Obesity is a condition that causes real problems for canine athletes. The increased physical exertions required to perform the same maneuvers as a lighter dog will put your dog at a disadvantage. An overweight dog will become tired more quickly and won't have the same physical prowess. He'll be less agile, his performance will have less vitality, and his body will suffer (either immediately or over time) from the added concussion due to his weight.

Keep your dog's weight in check by visual and tactile observations. You should be able to feel his ribs and pelvic bones with no more than a quarter- to a half-inch of tissue between his bones and skin. You should be able to see an indention between his flank and ribs. A dog at his ideal weight may appear to be too skinny to those who base their impressions of the "perfect" dog on what they see at dog shows, where dogs tend to be a bit heavier than they should be.

Be assured that once your overweight dog begins his exercise program, he will begin to lose weight. (If not, check with your veterinarian; there may be a medical reason he is holding on to his extra weight). But you can help hasten the process by decreasing the amount of food that you feed him. Start by eliminating a quarter of his current amount. Stop feeding him those high-fat snacks and instead offer him carrots, apples, and other healthy, low-fat fare. You can add rice, potatoes, canned pumpkin, green veggies, and bananas to his food to fill him up more without adding empty calories and fat.

How to Feed Your Dog

Dog caretakers feed their dogs by using one of two methods: free feeding (having food always available for your dog) or schedule feeding. How should you feed your nutrient-needy canine athlete? It depends on what is convenient for you and your dog and what you and your veterinarian and breeder decide is best. The "best" way to feed a dog is a topic that generates plenty of controversy in the dog world. You will hear persuasive arguments for both feeding methods. Only through experimentation will you find the way that makes your dog flourish and fits your lifestyle best.

I feed my dogs twice a day on a set schedule. I am a routine-loving person. I'm lucky in that my lifestyle also affords me the opportunity to stick to that schedule, which is an important consideration if you are going to feed your dog at a particular time. Dogs tend to do best—physically and psychologically—with a routine, especially when it comes to their tummies. So if you choose to feed your dog at a certain time of day, stay as close as possible to the same time each day.

What are some of the arguments for the different methods? Feeding your dog on a schedule is a good way to know exactly what your performance pooch is eating. You can more easily control the amount of food your dog is getting. If your dog is a bit pudgy, then you may need to closely regulate the amount of food that he is consuming. (Although, if like me you have children offering your dog crumbs and spills, you can never know *everything* your dog eats.) If you are feeding your dog on a schedule, then you should feed him twice a day. This will assure that he has more energy stores to make it through his day, and it will help prevent him from gulping his food in a famished frenzy that could lead to bloat.

Athletes, whether on two legs or four, have higher energy requirements than sedentary individuals. The harder your dog works, the more food energy his body requires. If your dog is engaged in vigorous activity throughout the day, he may need a more steady stream of energy-providing foodstuff. A hard-working canine may require two to four times the amount of food energy a less-active pet needs. One way for you to ensure that such an active dog meets his constant energy requirements is to allow free feeding throughout the day. Another way is to offer snacks to your dog as needed, following the advice to keep bloat at bay by not feeding large amounts of food too soon before vigorous activity.

WATER AND HYDRATION

The importance of keeping your dog hydrated is mentioned in several places throughout this book, but I will recap the basics for you here.

Offer your dog a little bit of water before and during strenuous exercise. After he is finished exercising and has cooled off, you can offer him a more moderate amount of water. To prevent dehydration, make sure that you offer him more water when it is hot, very cold, or humid.

If you are going to be exercising your dog for longer than 30 minutes and you will be away from home, bring water with you in a squirt bottle or sport bottle.

Dogs generally don't like ice-cold water to drink (although many love ice). If your dog is outside often in the winter, you may need to buy a water heater to keep his water at a temperature he will drink. Remember that dogs can get dehydrated in the winter as well as the summer.

PAW CARE

Just as with active people, active dogs must protect their feet. A dog's feet absorb the impact as he runs, and his paws take a beating. You can protect his feet by performing routine maintenance, and with a bit of extra effort you can keep his paws in tough, healthy condition.

The paw pads are the thickest skin on your dog. The pads offer protection, shock absorption, and traction (with claws). The carpal pads, at the back of his front legs, serve as bumpers or cushions and as brakes during running and turning.

When you begin a conditioning program, your dog's paws may be sore at first. He will gradually develop calluses to protect them. If you build up slowly and don't push too hard too fast, your dog's feet will be fine. You shouldn't apply any type of oil or lotion to his feet—his pads need to harden.

If your dog has long hair, trim the hair from between his toes regularly for the best traction. Hairy paws are magnets for stickers, burs, and those nasty foxtails that can cause so much damage if left undetected. In cold weather, fur between the toes can become an ice pack.

Once a week, check your dog's nails for growth and his feet for dirt, foreign matter, and cuts. Keeping his nails trimmed will allow his foot to fall in a natural position when it strikes the ground. Long nails are a danger because if they get caught in something, they can be torn, ripped, or otherwise damaged. Well-trimmed nails also give your dog better traction.

Trimming Your Dog's Nails

When you trim your dog's nails, you must be careful not to cut the "quick," the vein of blood and nerves that feeds the nail for growth. If you cut the quick it will bleed and hurt. Accidents can happen even to the best of us, but you should be as careful as possible, especially with a puppy. A bad experience when he is young will ruin all future attempts to trim his nails without trauma.

When a dog has light-colored nails, you should easily see the quick through the nail as a dark vein extending down the nail. Trim away the excess nail beyond the quick. If your dog's nails have been allowed to grow, the quick will be close to the tip. Cut off this small section of nail. The quick will then recede, and you can cut the nail a bit shorter during your next weekly exam. The quick will recede further until you are able to cut the nail to an optimum length.

If your dog's nails are dark, finding the quick will be more difficult. You may be able to see it if you shine a flashlight from the nail's under-side. I cannot see the quick in my Bouvier's nails at all. I simply keep them regularly trimmed and cut off only the very tip of the nail. I once heard a dog "expert" recommend that you simply cut a dog's long toe-nails down as short as you want and let them bleed. The resulting blood loss from this practice could be considerable. But more importantly, the pain is unfair to your dog. I can't imagine a dog ever cooperating with nail clipping again after an unnecessary and cruel procedure like this.

Paw Injuries

If your dog damages a nail or nail bed during his adventures, clean the injury with Betadine antiseptic and apply a systemic antibiotic. If you can, have your dog avoid rough surfaces for a while, and if necessary, have him wear a bootie on the injured foot to protect his healing paw.

Winter brings special challenges to keeping your dog's paws and pads healthy. When your dog goes from water to snow or ice, or from one frozen condition to another, his feet are vulnerable. As he runs, his feet spread out and snow can cut into the wedges between his toes. Ice balls can form between his toes. To prevent ice balls from forming, apply petroleum jelly between your dog's toes before going out or have him wear booties.

Booties

Booties may seem like the ultimate canine luxury, but active dogs should probably have a pair or two. If your dog is recovering from a nail or pad injury, he can wear a bootie on the affected foot and still participate in his exercise routine. Booties allow the injury to heal faster. You can also use them to protect overworked feet or during your beginner's acclimation period to minimize wear and tear until your pooch's paws are ready for a full-time beating.

A bootie should fit just right. If it's too loose, it will move around and offer little stability. A loose opening at the top will allow debris to fall into the bootie, and the traction won't be as good when the bootie slips around on the foot. If it's too tight, the bootie will cut off the circulation in your dog's foot.

Where winters are fierce, booties protect your dog's feet from salt and de-icing chemicals (which when ingested can irritate the dog's gastrointestinal system). Sometimes dogs have a difficult time adapting to icy, snowy conditions. Until your dog gets used to being active on icy surfaces, you may want to provide him with booties that have a rubber tread. Winter booties should not have ventilation holes.

If you spend time in rough, rocky terrain, you may want to have a pair of booties with rubber treads. In warm climates, you will want the booties to have ventilation holes.

EARS

Dogs who participate in water sports or activities and have long, dangling ears are prone to ear infections and other problems with their ears. So are dogs who have allergies, small ear canals, or hair in their ears. Cut away the hair on your dog's ear flap, around the canal, and in the canal for better air circulation.

During your weekly exam (described on page 150), check for foul odor and for red or painful ears. You can clean dirty ears with cotton balls. A dog's ears are L-shaped, so you won't puncture his ear drums. Talk to your veterinarian if your dog experiences chronic problems with his ears. Your vet may be able to provide you with a special wash that you can use to keep your dog's ears clean and healthy.

TEETH

The importance of caring for your dog's teeth has just begun to get the attention that it deserves. Although tooth care sounds intimidating, it is very easy. You can purchase several different types of equipment to help you with this chore. Brushes, soft tips that fit on the end of your finger, or gauze pads can be used to wipe and brush your dog's teeth. You can even purchase doggie toothpaste in canine-pleasing flavors such as chicken and beef. Don't use toothpaste made for humans; it will give your dog an upset stomach.

Cleaning your dog's teeth once a week is often enough. Accustom your dog to the process in stages, doing the work only as he allows it. If you let him slowly adapt to this cleaning, he will not resent it and the chore will be easy for him and for you.

While cleaning, check for broken, loose, or discolored teeth. (Your dog's teeth should be white.) If your dog appears to be in pain, he may have an infected tooth. If his gums are red or swollen, you should take him to your vet. In older dogs, you may see the growth of benign bumps. These should be removed only if they interfere with your dog's eating.

HEAT CYCLES

Taking a bitch in heat outdoors for exercise presents difficulties. You will attract many males, and fights could easily be instigated. Dog fights are a nasty business whether your dog is the instigator or the victim. Keep your bitch at home when she is in heat, or better yet, get her spayed if she isn't an integral part of a breeding program. Many competitions will not allow a bitch in heat to compete, so make sure you understand the rules for your chosen activity.

AIR POLLUTION

Because we don't feel the effects of pollutants and environmental hazards immediately, we often ignore them. However, these same pollutants affect your dog more quickly than they affect you because of his smaller respiratory system.

The most common pollutant is carbon monoxide from vehicles. This compound is especially dangerous for dogs who spend time exercising on roads. During exercise, your dog's respiratory system (like yours) works harder and takes in more air to get the oxygen needed for energy, and he absorbs a larger concentration of air pollutants in the process.

If you must expose your dog to areas traveled by vehicles, choose a time of day with less traffic, and if possible, stay on roads that have the least amount of traffic.

WEEKLY EXAM

Weekly examinations of your dog will help you catch problems before they become serious, check on old injuries or problems, groom your dog well at least once a week, and keep your dog accustomed to being examined. This last benefit will make your veterinarian happy.

Make a list of the items you will need when examining your dog (see the next page for suggestions). Check off each item as you progress through the examination, and add any condition or special circumstance that you need to. Take notes so you can refresh your memory during the next exam.

Find a quiet place that is well lit but not too bright. Soft classical music can make most animals feel more relaxed. Have your tools ready and laid out within your reach. Take your time; this should be a relaxing, positive encounter. Make it gentle and comforting.

THE WEEKLY EXAM

EQUIPMENT YOU WILL NEED

➤ Nail clippers and nail file—for trimming nails and filing rough edges

➤ Brushes and combs—for grooming

➤ Mat breaker—the gentlest way to remove mats

➤ Flea comb—in case you find the nasty little pests

➤ Scissors—to trim hair from inside the ears or around paw pads or to cut out foreign matter in fur

➤ Small flashlight—to shine behind toenails to avoid cutting the quick and to look in ears

➤ Cotton swabs—for cleaning, for applying necessary ointments, and for applying styptic powder

➤ Cotton balls—for cleaning or for applying necessary ointments

➤ Toothbrush—to brush your dog's teeth

➤ Dog toothpaste—this item is optional, but your dog may tolerate brushing better if you use it

➤ Towel—for a myriad of uses

➤ Vitamin E oil or capsules—to help clean your dog's ears

➤ Styptic powder—to stop bleeding; apply to the nail tip with a cotton swab if you accidentally cut into the quick

➤ Treats—for reward and distraction

THE EXAM

Check each of the listed items and take notes on what you find. Take care of any developing problems right away.

➤ *Skin and coat*—Feel for bumps, lumps, abscesses, sores, mats, and hot spots. Check coat condition. Look for hair loss, scratches, other sores, and pests.

➤ *Feet*—Look for splits in skin between toes (webbing), hair growth between toes, and damage to nails or nail beds. Trim long nails.

➤ *Ears*—Check for discharge, foul odor, redness, and soreness.

➤ *Eyes*—The eyes should be clear. Check to see if they are watery or red or have any discharge.

➤ *Teeth*—The teeth should be white. Check for cracks or breaks, changed gum condition, and soreness. Clean the teeth.

➤ *Anal area*—Be sure the area is clear of feces. Check a male's anal glands for swelling.

➤ *Weight*—Record your dog's weight.

What to Do in an Emergency

Knowing what to do in an emergency before it happens is comforting. Throughout this book I include measures to take in an emergency. Heatstroke, hypothermia, lameness, snake bites, and wild animal bites are discussed in their appropriate sections. The following are other kinds of emergencies that you may have to deal with.

WHAT YOU SHOULD KNOW

No matter how loving your dog may be, when he is in intense pain, he may not act like himself and he could bite you. Therefore, muzzle any injured dog, including your own.

The rule of thumb for quick action in an injury emergency involving a sprain, strain, or break is easily remembered with the acronym RICE—rest, ice, compression, elevation. Rest your dog, even if you need to carry him to keep him from moving around too much. Apply ice to his injuries until you can get him home or to your veterinarian. Keep a moderate amount of pressure on the affected area, and keep it elevated to reduce bleeding and swelling.

Check your dog's pulse by gently pressing your thumb near his elbow or on his inner thigh. A normal pulse rate is 80 to 120 bpm. If his pulse is low, he may be going into shock. This must be dealt with right away (see below). You will need to calm down a dog with a high pulse rate.

Know your dog's normal body temperature. You should also know how to take his temperature rectally (your veterinarian can show you how) so that if you need to, you can monitor his condition.

BROKEN BONES

Fortunately, broken bones don't occur with great frequency, but just in case, you should be prepared to take care of your dog until you reach your veterinarian's office. This is especially important if you will be journeying outdoors and will have to bring the injured animal out of the wilderness before you can seek help.

Before moving your dog, carefully splint his broken limb. Splinting is used only to provide support and to prevent further damage; it should not be used to help your dog walk farther. You will need a flat stick, board, cardboard (if you have nothing else), or other flat, strong object. For your dog's comfort, wrap the splint in a towel or clothing to pad it. Tape your dog's limb to the splint; the tape should be placed above and below the injury. If you can, transport your dog on a flat surface.

A break can be complete or incomplete. You will know a complete break has occurred if you see the bone protruding from the injured area. If there is a complete break, place the bones as close as possible to their original anatomical location before you splint the limb.

Your veterinarian will apply an external splint or brace and may need to surgically apply wires, screws, or plates to repair the damaged area. Check the injury at least twice daily. Call your veterinarian if you observe swelling, heat, or odor at the injured area; if your dog experiences fever, depression, or a change in appetite; or if your dog is chewing the site.

CUTS AND ABRASIONS

The first thing to do for a cut or abrasion is to apply pressure and elevate it. Clean out the wound with water. A jet-like stream from a water bottle or syringe works great. Follow this up with Betadine antiseptic. Wrap the area in gauze, Ace elastic bandage, or vet wrap. It is easy to apply vet wrap too tightly, so be careful. Remain calm and get your dog to your vet.

SHOCK

Shock is a serious condition that can lead to coma and death. It is important for you to be able to recognize the symptoms of shock.

Any time your dog suffers an injury, you should check his pulse. A low pulse can signal the onset of shock. Other symptoms include white gums and mucous membranes, hypothermia, reduced urine output, slow capillary refill, fixed and dilated pupils, and loss of consciousness. To test capillary refill, press on your dog's gums for a moment. Release the pressure and see how quickly the gums refill with blood and return to their normal color. (You will have to know what is normal for your dog, so practice this under nonemergency circumstances.) They should refill very quickly.

WHAT TO INCLUDE IN A CANINE FIRST-AID KIT

emergency phone numbers written on a card
Betadine antiseptic
antiseptic soap
blunt-end tweezers
blunt-end scissors
rectal thermometer
gauze roll
1-inch bandage tape
3-inch x 3-inch gauze pads
elastic bandage (vet wrap)
triangle bandage
safety pins
cotton swabs
wooden tongue depressors
plastic eyedropper
measuring spoon
activated-charcoal tablets
baking soda
antibacterial ointment
3% solution of hydrogen peroxide
lubricating gel (such as K-Y jelly)
Kaopectate antidiarrheal medicine
Pepto Bismol upset stomach remedy
milk of magnesia
cold pack (chemical type, activated by manipulation)

If your dog is in shock, he needs to see a veterinarian immediately, as there is little you can do to help him. While transporting him to your vet, keep him warm with blankets or towels. Many people believe that by gently rubbing a dog's ears, one can help him relax and possibly protect him from the complications of shock. Start at the base of his ears and use long, firm strokes along the ear to the tip of his ears.

CPR

If your dog experiences a lack of heartbeat or breathing, you will have to perform CPR (cardiopulmonary resuscitation) immediately. If your dog is not breathing, check his mouth for any obstruction. If after you remove the obstruction your dog's chest begins to rise and fall, you do not need to apply rescue breaths. If he is still not breathing, apply rescue breaths. Place your mouth over your dog's nose, and exhale into his nose. Apply one breath every two seconds. You should be able to make his chest rise and fall with your breaths.

Deliver five rescue breaths to your dog. If he does not start breathing on his own and there is no heartbeat, begin chest compressions. With your dog lying on his side, place your hand just behind his shoulder blades and administer gentle but firm compressions. For large dogs, press two inches down with both hands. For toy dogs, press half an inch down with two fingers.

If you are working with a partner, apply one rescue breath every five compressions. If you are alone, apply two breaths every 15 compressions. Every two minutes, stop and check to see if your dog is breathing on his own or has a pulse. If not, continue CPR, but after 10 minutes you should give up. If you check his pulse and he has one, no matter how slight, do not perform compressions. Take him to your veterinarian as soon as possible.

Care of the Canine Mind

The canine mind is complex and mysterious. People can only make assumptions about what dogs are thinking. Some thoughts, emotions, and feelings are obviously expressed through behavior. And others are "known" because of the close bond that people share with their dogs. Although science has yet to prove it, those of us who share our lives closely with our dogs know that canines have elaborate emotional lives.

WHAT STRESS CAN DO TO A DOG

Dog owners know that dogs feel stress. Not all stress is avoidable, but continued extreme stress can cause many problems. Stress produces the fight-or-flight adrenal hormones. When there is no outlet for these hormones (the dog can't fight or flee), the overworked defense response mechanisms damage your dog's physical and emotional health.

Your dog's immune, cardiovascular, respiratory, circulatory, and gastrointestinal systems are all affected by stress. Prolonged stress also affects the release of neurotransmitters in the brain. These substances regulate emotions such as happiness, fear, and apprehension. Long-term, extreme stress seems to affect these neurotransmitters in negative ways, making your dog unable to cope with many of his emotions.

Stress can increase the likelihood of heatstroke and the frequency or severity of conditions such as epilepsy. Behavioral problems are frequently the manifestations of stress.

Some dogs handle stress more easily than other dogs. The same dog may react to the same stressor differently at different times. Older dogs are usually more susceptible to stress.

The Immune System and Stress

The strength of your dog's immune system is vital to his health and longevity. Stress can be very detrimental to an immune system.

It is your responsibility to keep the anxiety your dog experiences within acceptable limits. Remember, a dog with a strong immune system may withstand an environment that is laden with germs and still retain his health. An animal with a weakened immune system may succumb to minute amounts of germs in the cleanest of environments.

The Source of Stress

You may be able to tell *when* your dog is stressed, but it is harder to diagnose the *source*. He cannot verbally tell you what is bothering him, but he can help you understand by giving you clues. Always check with your veterinarian first because the problem could be physical. Otherwise, use your sharp intuition and acute observation to find out what is bothering your dog.

Many different sources of stress can cause your dog problems. Dogs can become stressed because of lifestyle changes—a change in routine or environment, a new addition to the family (animal or human), or a loss in the family. Your dog may be stressed because you are stressed. He may be succumbing to the pressure to perform. He could be suffering from a mild or chronic illness or experiencing nutritional stress. The heat or the cold could be playing havoc with his ability to cope well. A performance dog must deal with many expectations. Performance dogs also travel frequently, which can be stressful. Usually with experience, dogs can learn to adapt to the above situations more quickly and with less trauma, although some poor dogs never adapt to the pressures of performance. Training and performing are stressful, but your dog should be happy, willing, excited, and healthy. Unless you are placing too much pressure on him, the amount of stress a canine athlete experiences is necessary for learning and performing.

The Signs of Too Much Stress

What are the signs that your dog is suffering from too much stress? How will you know when you need to help your dog? The following is a list of signs that he may be suffering a high level of stress:

PHYSICAL SIGNS OF STRESS

- gastrointestinal trouble
- diarrhea
- inflammation of the large intestine
- vomiting
- excessive gas
- elevated blood pressure
- skin problems
- eczema (hot spots)
- lick granulomas (bunk sores)

BEHAVIORAL SIGNS OF STRESS

- change in eating habits (eating less or more)
- overexcitement outside the ring or field and sluggishness during a performance
- housebreaking accidents and marking
- excessive sleeping or insomnia
- continual whining or barking
- sudden aggression
- self-mutilating behaviors (including sucking his flanks, constantly chewing or licking, biting his own legs, chomping his jaws)
- hyperactivity
- out-of-control behavior (not listening to your directions)
- roaming
- destructiveness
- tail chasing

WHAT YOU CAN DO

What can you do to help your pooch maintain his emotional health? Prevention is the best medicine. Choose a confident, secure dog with a solid but flexible temperament and socialize him well (see chapter 2). Emotional stamina to handle the stress of competing is vital, but early socialization is the crucial component in having a confident, outgoing dog.

You can use a number of techniques to help your dog stay relaxed. First, know what stresses your dog and learn ways to avoid or counteract that stress. Moderate exercise can be relaxing, but if you have been working your dog hard, lower your expectations awhile and let your dog rest his mind and body. Reduce or vary your training and show schedule if the pace gets too hectic. Massage and TTouch can calm your dog, as can gentle brushing and grooming. Give your dog quiet, quality time daily. Soft music can often help, especially when accompanied by low lighting and a relaxing environment. Good health care is a must—overlooking a slight physical problem can produce a stressed dog. Keep your dog at a steady, lean weight and give him consistent exercise. If your dog is stressed, maintain a routine, feeding and training at the same time every day until your dog feels better and acts like his old self again. No matter how busy you are, show your dog the attention he is used to. If you live with more than one dog, don't forget to show each of them plenty of attention.

Your dog should be allowed time to be a dog. The greatest competitor or performance dog still needs time off to engage in doggie behaviors just for fun, to play with other dogs, or simply to "hang out" with his favorite person—you.

When competing or venturing from your home, bring things with you that comfort your dog. His regular food and water from home, along with his favorite toys and blankets, will help him relax. Developing a pattern or routine for competition days will also help your dog feel more comfortable. Controlling your own excitement will make it easier for him to cope. In fact, if your dog is experiencing heightened anxiety at shows and events, look first at yourself. Are you sending negative emotions to your dog? If you are nervous, anxious, and uncertain, your dog will be too.

Talk to a canine sports veterinarian regarding changes you can make in your dog's diet. Incorrect amounts of particular vitamins and minerals as well as food allergies may be affecting your dog's state of mind. Offer your dog steady, confident leadership so that he can be released of the responsibility of making his own rules. Of course, lots of love and attention are great stress relievers. Take a few minutes to tell your dog how wonderful he is. Appreciate every minute of your adventure together and your dog will also.

CHAPTER FIVE

Rules of the Road

You wave to your neighbor and her cute, fluffy pooch as you jog down the tree-lined street, your dog proudly trotting beside you. As you turn the corner past the park, you watch as a dog and her owner happily play a game of Frisbee. Completely engrossed in the action and excitement, the dog slides to a stop, spins around, and catches the Frisbee in her smiling mouth, then returns it to her proud friend to throw again. Farther in the distance you see a beautifully muscled sighthound running beside her caretaker's bicycle, covering ground quickly as they head in your direction. They pass you with a swish and a nod. As you travel the last couple of blocks before you reach your home, a pair of dog-human teams pass on your left—one dog pulling her handler on a skateboard and the other pulling her caretaker on skates. To top off a great run, you get to see the final touches on Mr. Johnson's new garden, the blooming rose bushes at your son's teacher's home, and the new neighbors moving in down the street.

Participating in an activity that leads you out into your neighborhood is enjoyable and rewarding. Once you have dedicated yourself to an adventure on the street, you will become a familiar sight to many people along the way. As you and your dog venture out during your regimen, your presence will become an expected part of someone else's day.

On my run, I see the same people again and again. When I had to leave my Bouvier home while she recovered from an injury, I was frequently asked where she was and how she was doing.

Dogs are also a catalyst in forming friendships with your neighbors. Many people are friendlier when you have a dog with you. It gives them something to comment on or ask questions about. This kind of communication and friendliness instills a true sense of community.

As your human-dog team hits the pavement with all six feet, it is important to remember that you are heading into public domain. You are sharing the same trails and roadways with many people and animals. Give-and-take, as well as respect, are demanded if you want to retain your neighbors' friendliness.

Because of insensitive, unknowledgable, and uncaring dog owners, many streets and other public places are banning dogs. A town not far from me in northern California does not permit dogs on the street at all. Dogs must remain in their yards at all times. They can't even be taken for walks! Why are so many municipalities forced to impose such restrictions on dog caretakers? Why do some ban various dog breeds?

These restrictions are a direct result of irresponsible dog owners. Even if most dog owners take their obligation to ensure the comfort of their neighbors seriously, it takes only a few bad experiences with reckless owners to raise the hackles of the general population and lawmakers.

Some of your responsibilities as a dog owner are obvious, and most are simply common courtesy. Caretakers and their dogs should work to create a reputation for being kind and considerate of the sensitivities of their dogless neighbors. In this chapter, I will expound upon these virtues.

I will also discuss the concerns that confront those people who explore the roads and streets with their canine athletes. Many situations are unique to city street surfaces and populations. You should also know how to stay safe when venturing near automobiles.

Getting out and about may be a necessity for you. If you live in a large metropolitan area, an apartment, or a house without a yard, hitting the streets with your canine is unavoidable. You may use the streets and trails to be with your dog outside or to ensure your dog's and quite possibly your own fitness. Whatever the reason you put your feet to the street, this chapter will assist you in your adventure.

Shared Space—Why We Should Think about Others

If you live in a densely populated area, you must share the road with pedestrians, automobiles, bikes, and skaters, as well as other dogs. The need for cooperation among road users is obvious. Following the rules of the road helps dogs remain a welcome sight on the streets. The areas that have made it illegal to walk dogs in public have done so for two reasons: lack of cleanliness and fear of physical threat.

STRAIGHT TALK ON CLEANUP

I believe one of the main reasons that dogs become unwelcome on the road and in neighborhoods is because of the messy deposits they leave behind. It is the caretaker's responsibility to pick up after his or her dog. Although I live in a dog-friendly neighborhood, I too have been the target of negative thinking.

Once while running with my dog, I was stopped by a walker who took it upon herself to personally remind me to pick up after my dog. I kindly told her I always picked up after my dog and continued on my run. I have to say that the confrontation left me a bit rattled. I showed the woman my pooper-scooper bag and I think I was able to convince her of my good intentions, but the fact that someone would think I would leave behind such an obvious sign of my dog's presence bothered me greatly.

Jumping over a pile of poop while picking up a good pace in my run is one of the most annoying experiences I can think of. I hate it! Because I am so bothered by dog waste on the street, sidewalks, and paths, I will always pick up after my dog. Besides, it is the law and the ethical thing to do. Don't you feel the same way?

Picking up after your dog is a simple, painless task. No matter where you go with your dog, you must bring a pooper scooper of some sort. A dog-supply catalog or a well-stocked pet-supply store will have some fancy versions. My personal favorite, and the one I now use exclusively, comes in a small plastic container (the kind that you get cheap prizes in from vending machines). A blue plastic bag is stored inside; you just scoop up the feces and tie the end of the bag. I like these bags because they easily fit into my pockets or even the neoprene belt that holds my tape player.

So the last thing you want to spend money on is pooper scoopers? Well, I understand. Although the commercial versions are not that expensive, you can use an even cheaper method. Plastic sandwich bags are small, lightweight, relatively inexpensive, and always on hand. If your dog decides to stop and have a bowel movement while you are out and about, take out your plastic bag and turn it inside-out over your hand. Pick up the poop, turn the bag right side out again, and seal it shut. Because sandwich bags are clear, and for added protection for your hands, you can put the sandwich bag in a small paper bag. You can then dump it in the next available trash receptacle, or you can carry it back home with you.

Make sure the bag is well sealed and you'll be fine. I can tell you from experience that it is not great fun to jog with a bag full of dog poop. But I'd much rather carry it a mile or so than go out alone without my faithful canine companion!

The best solution is to train your dog that your daily excursion is not the time to relieve herself. Give your pooch time to do her duty before you leave home. If you have taught your dog to go on command, this is a useful time to use that option. After your activity, your dog will need another opportunity to defecate. Oftentimes the physical exercise will wake up bowel activity. Excitement and nervousness can also speed up your dog's digestive system. If your dog knows that she will have an opportunity to empty her bowels as soon as you return home, then you can stop her in midaction during your exercise. I have taught my dogs not to relieve themselves when we are running. They have plenty of opportunity before and after (and we are only gone an hour). I am especially adamant about my male dog marking territory along our route. Even so, I always have a pooper scooper ready. I never leave home without one, and neither should you.

FEAR OF PERSONAL ATTACK

The fear of being attacked by a dog is a serious problem to many people. I have met people in my neighborhood who will cross the street when they see me and my friendly dog coming toward them.

Constant media tales of aggressive dogs have heightened society's concern and paranoia. If your dog is a member of a perceived "vicious" breed (there are no actual vicious breeds, only vicious individual dogs who have inadequate guidance or other problems), or even resembles one, you can be the victim of discrimination. In many cases, all dogs are simply lumped together as uncontrollable, savage killers.

You can take measures to counteract this societal bias. A cute bandanna or bow around your dog's neck makes her appear more approachable. Your dog should be trained and under your control at all times. One important reason to have a leashed dog is that a loose dog always makes people more nervous. Of course, a friendly smile and warm greeting from you will help relax people who may be fearful around your pooch.

It appears that particular types of dogs scare people more. Obviously, larger dogs frighten more people. Other characteristics are black fur, black fur trimmed in brown, and pointed, upright ears. If you are concerned about your personal safety, having a dog who has one or more of these characteristics may keep the "bad guys" at bay, but be aware that your dog may frighten the nice people also. Sometimes you have to work harder to socialize these types of dogs because people don't naturally gravitate toward them.

If you do have a dog who has an aggressive tendency, avoid potential problems. For instance, a dog that detests children should not be walked past an elementary school playground at recess time. If your dog is truly aggressive, you have a serious problem, the complexity of which cannot be addressed in this book. Seek professional help from a trainer or behaviorist. Your veterinarian or Humane Society should be able to make a referral for you. Check the bibliography for other sources.

If we, as a society, do not begin to understand aggression in dogs and take actions to control the rise of problems associated with this aggression, dog ownership may become uncomfortably restricted.

COURTESIES

Good Manners

Your dog must be well mannered to be out in a public place. If your dog frantically circles you, pulls on you, tangles you up in the leash, and trips you or pulls you down, you won't enjoy yourself and your dog will frighten other people and be a danger to them. Your dog could just as easily trip an innocent passerby as he could you. As a courtesy to your community, keep your dog under control.

Loose Leash

I am a firm believer in allowing my canine buddies to have a sense of freedom while out and about. I do not make them adhere to a strict heel while walking or running. A loose leash has many benefits. Your dog will be able to enjoy the hundreds of interesting smells and the ever-changing scenery. On a loose leash she will be calm and relaxed. Dogs at the end of a tight leash feel threatened because they cannot control their distance from objects that frighten them. This leaves them no choice but to fight if they are truly fearful. If your dog is on a tight leash, she may also feel the need to protect you from passersby and other animals.

My dogs are allowed to go to the leash end (no tugging allowed) or stay close to me. They are not allowed to walk in front of me or to change sides in front of me. Safety always comes first. I do use the heel command and believe all dogs should know this important position. You can use this command if you encounter a situation where you want complete control of your pet, such as when others pass you on the road. This gives the passersby confidence in your ability to handle your dog and keeps your dog out of the way and in control. If you are coming to a busy intersection, use this command to get your dog in check and remind her to pay attention to your direction. Be attentive to what is going on around you. If you see a loose dog or other powerful distraction in the distance, you can get control over your dog before coming upon the problem, or take an alternate route to get away from potential danger.

I have taught my dogs the classic heel position—the dog's right shoulder in alignment with my left leg. I have also taught my dogs the opposite position—the dog's left side in alignment with my right leg. I call this position "side." Originally taught during agility training, it is extremely useful to me while participating in activities in my neighborhood. I can choose the side that is farthest from a passerby or distraction and therefore place myself between it and my dog. I truly believe this gives people added comfort when they must pass close to me.

A dog out of control on a leash is no fun. Constant pulling and tripping will become a massive battle of wills, with you as the discouraged loser. This kind of arm-lengthening exercise is frustrating, and you may simply decide to forgo taking your overly excited pooch out. I can't tell you how many times I've heard, "I can't take my dog for a walk because she pulls on the leash." But it doesn't have to be this way. Try using a head collar described on the next page. If your canine terrorist is truly out of control, get help from a trainer.

Some little techniques can help you take control of your leash-pulling canine right away. At the beginning of your workout, when your dog has high energy and excitement, you must have a tighter hold on the leash. Toward the end of your workout, you will be able to loosen your grip as she relaxes into a comfortable pace. Consider starting out when the traffic is lighter, avoiding high traffic or highly populated areas until your dog puts less strain on the leash.

Leashless—The Unpredictable Dog

View the leash as a life preserver. You are protecting your dog and keeping her safe when you place a leash on her. The world is a scary, dangerous place. Cars and other people pose the worst threats.

A dog is an animal, and animals tend to take the most rewarding course of action without considering the consequences. If you are walking, with even the most reliable, obedient dog, and a cat runs across your path, what do you think your dog will do? You may, with all cockiness, answer that she would stay right with you. But chances are there will be one time,

THE HEAD COLLAR

The head collar is a handy tool that can be used to control your dog's behavior. Although there are several different brands that fit slightly differently, all head collars affect the dog and her behavior using the same concept.

The head collar does not fit around the dog's throat like traditional dog collars. Putting excessive pressure on a dog's throat can actually promote aggression because dogs will instinctually pull against pressure. Pressure on the neck can upset a more sensitive dog, possibly frightening her, so that she cannot concentrate.

The head collar fits around the back of the neck, behind your dog's ears, and around the muzzle of your dog below her eyes. Looking at the dog from the side, the head collar appears to make a Y shape. The leash then connects to the ring on the section under her chin.

The head collar looks like a muzzle, but it's not. Your dog can eat, drink, bark, play, and defend herself if necessary. If you choose to have a head collar on your dog while you are walking her, some people may think she is muzzled. They may be frightened of your dog or tell you they think a muzzle is cruel. These problems will eventually fade as head collars become more common.

The idea of the head collar is the same as that used in the horse world for centuries—where the head goes, the body follows. Redirecting your dog's head will redirect her focus. This is handy when a confrontation is impending. Only a little force is necessary. In fact, the leashes that are made specifically for the collar are thin and lightweight. The head collar influences the behavior of overly excitable and physically active dogs. It can really help you while walking your dog or when you need to control her in the house, such as when visitors arrive.

If you are going to use a head collar on your dog, give her time to get used to it. In the beginning, most dogs will try to get the collar off by pawing at it or rubbing it against things. After a couple of sessions, they will relax.

Give the head collar a try. Most people are amazed at the difference in their dogs.

maybe in the distant future, when your dog will choose to go the cat's way. Wouldn't it be nice to have a leash on her at that moment? You can protect your dog from running in front of a passing car, from being shot by a farmer or hunter as she runs through forbidden territory, from confronting a rabid wild animal, and from getting lost. She is worth it, isn't she?

Unleashed dogs, as I have already mentioned, also stress other people. Even I cringe when I see a loose dog while I am on the road, and I am a true dog lover. Imagine what goes through the mind of someone who is terrified of dogs. Not having your dog on a leash while you are out, no matter how well she is behaving, will alienate your neighbors, risk the safety of your dog, scare people, and get you in trouble if your community has leash laws. Keep your dog on a leash.

The Ultimate Safety Device—A Reliable Recall

Imagine peacefully walking your dog down a country road. The sweet air, the blooming trees, the gentle breeze, and a well-behaved canine friend lull you into a state of serenity. Then—zoom!—a rabbit dashes in front of you. As quick as lightning your dog is off. You lose your gentle grasp on your dog's leash and your dog is running full force through an orchard. Do you have a reliable recall to get her back?

Coming to you when called is probably the most important skill a dog can have. It could quite possibly save her life, especially in crowded areas. Put yourself in the above scenario and add a passing vehicle and you will see the importance of having a solid recall. A dog running loose will win you no points with your neighbors and can even injure people.

People are often confident that their dogs know how to "come." Your sweet little puppy happily runs to your arms as you squat down and enthusiastically beckon her with your outspread arms. This is how puppies act. They want to be with you above all else and will gladly come to a happy, inviting caretaker. It is as they grow up that the problems start. Your puppy, believe it or not, is not trained to come to you. She does it because it is the most rewarding action to take. When she is older and more confident, there are more rewarding things stealing her attention. For example, it is more fun to run to play with a group of children in a park than it is to come to you. And inadvertantly, you may be reinforcing this belief by calling her to you to cut her nails, give her a bath, or put her leash on and end her romp, or worse, by reprimanding her for not coming the first time you called. Call your dog to you only for favorable things. Call her during her playtime and then release her after a moment of petting to fortify the idea that coming to you doesn't always mean "the end." Don't call your dog unless you can reinforce the command if she doesn't comply right away. Enroll in a class, get the help of a trainer, read training books or magazines, and get your dog trained to come to you, no matter what!

Your Safety on the Street

Many people avoid "taking it to the streets" because of fear for their personal safety, but you can arm yourself with knowledge and lessen your risk of attack considerably. Attacks include verbal or physical harm and may take the following forms: inconsiderate drivers, whose lack of responsibility puts you at danger; hostile or sexual verbal comments; gestures or verbal comments instigated in an effort to start a fight; or a direct physical assault. These attacks are major concerns for women, but men can also be victims. Having your canine friend with you is a great deterrent to would-be assailants, but knowing how to avoid becoming a victim is important for everyone who spends time on the streets and trails.

Here are some tips to stay safe:

- Use attitude to your advantage. A confident attitude projected with strength and awareness will deflect most attacks. Would-be attackers would rather find an easier target.

- Stay alert to your surroundings at all times. If you are like me, you use your exercise time for escape. For me, it is a form of meditation. I have my most creative insights while I am running or bicycling. But being in a state of mental separation from your surroundings makes you vulnerable. I have learned to be completely aware of what is going around me while letting the creative side of my mind be free to wander.

🐾 Be smart about where you are going and at what time. Dusk, darkness, and quiet areas may be unsafe.

🐾 Let someone know where you are going and how long you plan to be gone. Leave a note if no one is home. Let those who are close to you know which routes you frequently use so they will have an idea of where you will be.

🐾 Consider taking along a self-defense spray such as Mace tear gas or pepper spray so you can protect yourself and your dog from attacks. Learn how to use the spray most effectively. You may also want to learn self-defense techniques, which are offered in many communities.

🐾 Invest in a rearview mirror so you can safely and easily see what is happening behind you. CycleAware makes the ViewPoint, a mini rearview mirror that attaches to the inside edge of your sunglasses. It is adjustable, comes off easily, and isn't distracting.

🐾 If ever you feel uncomfortable, trust your intuition and avoid the situation. Don't worry about insulting someone. Stay calm and act confident. It's better to be safe than sorry.

🐾 Travel in the same direction as vehicle traffic. Much safety advice recommends that you face traffic so that you can watch approaching vehicles. However, I have found that drivers are more cautious when they are coming from behind you rather than toward you. When you face traffic, the driver may not see you as quickly because he approaches you quicker. Your dog may also have a preference. She may become nervous with vehicles coming at her from one direction or another.

🐾 Be alert to which direction the sun is shining. Drivers facing the sun may not be able to see you. Take extra precautions when crossing the street.

🐾 Be aware of drivers making a right-hand turn in your direction. I have found those making a right-hand turn will look left and then start to roll forward before looking right. If you aren't paying attention, you will be right in their path. Never assume that a driver has seen you unless you have made eye contact with him or her.

Dog Meets Dog on the Road

While venturing on the road, chances are you will come across other dogs. Most of the time, you and the other human-dog team will simply pass each other. Once in a while, you may want to introduce your dog to another. Meeting other dogs can promote friendliness in your dog; constantly passing dogs and never getting to meet them is frustrating for her.

There is another reason you should take time to introduce your buddy to other dogs during your outings and conditioning sessions. Your canine athlete will be around many strange dogs when competing, and she should be used to meeting new dogs beforehand.

It is difficult, without a lot of experience, to judge the friendliness of strange dogs. The barking, lunging, muscle-bound, spike-collared dog may be an obvious one to avoid, but sometimes even passive-looking dogs can create problems. Dogs who have been properly introduced to others in the past, who have good doggie manners, and who are not shy or fearful are your best choices for introductions. If your dog is all these things, then even if something goes wrong during the introductions, she will be fine. You can make sure everything goes well if you follow some specific suggestions.

Wait to make contact with a dog and her caretaker until you have seen them a couple of times and can tell how the dog acts when you and your dog pass by them. Make friendly contact first through smiles, waves, and small talk. When you are ready to introduce your dog, ask the owner if it is okay and if his or her dog is friendly and accepting of strange dogs (although many people will not admit their dogs have a problem).

WHAT TO DO DURING A DOG FIGHT

If a dog fight breaks out, the first thing you should do is the hardest—stay calm. Yelling and frantically trying to separate the dogs will only encourage their excitement and could get you seriously injured. Prevention is the best way to avoid injury to a person or dog. Attentiveness will help you sense when a fight might happen, and you and the other owner can distract the two dogs and break their concentration on each other.

If a fight does occur, you won't have much time to think about what to do. Your rational mind will give way to your emotions, but you must consider the danger of stopping a dog fight. It is a difficult task when two dogs are full of fighting energy. No amount of yelling, calling, or physical abuse will get them to willingly stop. If you decide to get involved, you must understand that you could be injured. No matter how much your dog loves you, during a fight she is not in a rational state of mind.

If you decide to stop a fight, or one has just begun and you think you can nip it in the bud, some techniques may work. Separate the dogs by grabbing a back leg or the base of a tail and pull them apart. This way you will be less likely to be bitten. If you have a hose or water, spray or splash the dogs to break them apart. Give both dogs time to calm down, and never give the instigator of the fight any attention, even negative attention. Don't reprimand, sweet talk, or in any other way interact with your pet until she is completely calm and relaxed. She will be too excited and may not be reliable in her actions.

Of course, you may be asked first to let your dog meet someone else's dog. Use your judgment and make a polite excuse to avoid pushing your pooch into a meeting you would rather avoid.

Pay close attention to the dogs' body language. If your conversation with the other person is too distracting, you may miss the subtle signs of incompatibility in the dogs.

Start with a loose leash. Remember, tight leashes cause more problems than they cure. Many owners who claim their dogs don't like other dogs are amazed by the results when they loosen up on the leash. The dogs get along fine.

Be an acute but relaxed observer. Being tense, worried, or distrustful produces a dog who will act the same way. You want your dog to be confident, comfortable, and curious, so act that way yourself.

Does the dogs' initial interest appear friendly? Mutual? Are they greeting each other with their noses? What is their body language saying? Look for signs of stress in either dog.

Getting along with strange dogs is so important to a well-rounded canine athlete that you should go out of your way to meet other dogs (especially while your dog is still young). But you should be aware that some dogs have never been allowed to be around other dogs because of their caretakers' unfounded fears. These dogs are not socially knowledgeable. They can become fearful and try to drive your dog away. Your dog could get hurt in the process. Remember when you are introducing dogs to each other that they will work to find a balance in the relationship that suits them, so there may be some posturing between the two. Stop the introductions and continue on your way if the situation begins to look risky.

Road Conditions

Spending time with your dog exercising and training on roads presents special circumstances such as the types of paths you travel on as well as different weather conditions. This section assists you in dealing with these variables so that you can stay motivated to continue toward your goal of peak canine physical fitness.

THE PATH YOU TREAD

Beyond the confines of your living room, paths of many compositions await you. Grass, concrete, asphalt, dirt, sand, and snow are some of the many surfaces you may discover in your neighborhood. If you have access to a variety of paths and trails, your training life will be more interesting.

If you are like me, the path you choose may become a habit. While getting dressed to run, I tell myself to take a different route and plan it in my head. Then out the door I go, and within five minutes I realize I am on the same path I always run. When I do remember to change my trail, I feel somewhat out of sorts.

I created this habit when I first started running. I set a route, measured it, and knew exactly how fast I had to go at any particular point in the run to make the time I was attempting. My emphasis has changed, and now I just enjoy my run and go at the pace I feel like at the time. I use my run as a way to spend time with my dog and to relax. But I still find myself heading off in the same direction on the same measured route.

My experience taught me a lesson—start with several different routes. If you need to measure and pace the distance for conditioning purposes, have several options to choose from. Alternate these routes regularly.

This alternating of routes has many benefits. The psychological one is especially important, I believe, to your dog. If I happen to take a different turn in our route, my dog Cody perks up and accepts his self-imposed mission of taking notice of each new sight, sound, and smell. He loves to explore new venues. A change in path also balances out your physical conditioning. Different surfaces, slopes in the road, and hills give both your bodies new challenges and work different muscles, helping you and your canine to keep physically balanced.

To keep you and your dog interested and enthusiastic, jump in your car and explore a different area once in a while. You will both appreciate the change.

Concrete

Concrete, the material sidewalks are made of, is the most readily available path. Unfortunately, it is also the most wearing on your and your dog's bodies.

The advantage of concrete trails is that you will find them quite easily in most neighborhoods. Sidewalks are smooth for skating and other such activities, but sidewalks are intended for pedestrians. Be considerate and give them the right-of-way.

Sidewalks are also generally flat, which allows you and your dog to remain balanced and lowers injury risk. Then again, cracks and unevenness in sidewalks can present challenges.

Concrete absorbs heat well; it will be hot when it is warm, scorching when it is hot, and cold when it is cool. If you use only concrete for your path, protect your pup's feet from extreme temperature conditions.

The most significant disadvantage of concrete is the shock to your and your canine athlete's bodies. Concrete is the worst material to travel on if you are engaging in high-impact activities such as running.

If you have no other choice but to walk or run on concrete, take the necessary precautions. Find a shoe store that specializes in athletics. The professionals in such a shop should be able to analyze your feet, your movement, and the level and intensity of your activity to help find you the best shoe available. You will, of course, need to replace these shoes often. If you find the soles of your shoes wearing out, you are in need of new shoes. There is a difference of opinion on how long good running shoes are usable, but generally assume you will have to replace them every 300 to 400 miles.

You may also want to have your gait and running style evaluated. Make an appointment with a running coach or a personal trainer who can help you analyze your strengths and weaknesses. The correct movement while running will definitely make a difference in the wear and tear on your precious body. The coach or trainer should be able to show you specific techniques and exercises to increase your effectiveness and decrease the chances of damage to your body.

As for your dog, you will have to take the same precautions as you would with any activity. Watch for lameness and unbalanced movement. These signs of stress on the body should be attended to immediately.

Time off from this running, some stretching, cross-training, and a check with your veterinarian if a problem persists or appears serious are good damage control measures. See chapter 4 for more information regarding lameness and structure evaluation. The structure and movement of your dog can influence her ability to handle the constant concussion of running. If you can find a trainer or veterinarian who specializes in canine athletes, you may get assistance in planning specific exercises to help your dog weather the streets' impact.

The more impact involved in an activity, the more damage that can be done. Try to contain your dog's excitement and keep her from jumping, especially up and down curbs. Do your best to keep the movements fluid and graceful by regulating your pace and choosing paths with as few curbs to jump as possible.

Running shoes for your dog aren't available yet. At present, you can only purchase booties for your dog that protect against abrasions and hot or cold surfaces, but a shock-absorbing shoe for dogs cannot be far behind.

Asphalt

Like concrete, asphalt is a widely available surface. Asphalt, the material used to pave streets, has more shock-absorbing properties than concrete. Concrete can be as much as 10 times harder than asphalt.

Still, paved roads are harder on you and your canine athlete than grass or dirt. You also risk potholes, and in some areas the streets seem to be made entirely of interlocking potholes. Because some of the "repaired" potholes are overfilled with asphalt, the bumps make the road more treacherous than the dirt shoulder beside it. Also, after running on newly paved streets, dogs will track black footprints. This problem decreases as the roads are used more.

Most streets have decidedly sloped shoulders, which can cause both dog and human to move their legs in less-than-perfect alignment (with the foot or feet near the gutter always in a lower position), increasing the risk of injury. You may be able to compensate for this imbalance on the trail by alternating directions from time to time. If it is safe, switch sides of the road several times during your outdoor activity. If you are riding a bike or carting, the impact and sloping won't be factors in *your* physical condition, but they can cause problems for your dog.

The advantages of asphalt usually outweigh the disadvantages. The biggest advantage is that asphalt is usually a more predictable surface than natural trails. Streets are also easy to measure for distance, so you can keep a more accurate record of your progress.

Traffic is the most significant problem. You must share the streets with vehicles, some with less-than-considerate drivers. Beware of someone opening the door of a parked car just as you careen by on your bike with your dog in tow. You may have to stop to let someone turn into a driveway just when you and Fido have finally picked up a nice pace on your skates. An insensitive driver who prefers to speed by you, missing you by a foot, rather than cautiously going around you, is always a risk.

Gravel

Gravel is difficult to evaluate because there are so many different kinds of gravel that produce a variety of surfaces.

Small pieces of gravel, called pea gravel, covering a dirt surface may have considerable shock-absorbing properties and be quite comfortable underfoot. On the other hand, large, irregularly shaped gravel rocks placed over an asphalt or hard-packed surface may be uncomfortable and put you and your dog at risk for injuries caused by twisting and slipping. The rough surface can also be hard on the pads of your dog's feet.

Dirt

You will find numerous advantages to using dirt paths. The biggest payoff is often the scenery. Perhaps you can find a trail near you that wanders through parks, past tree-filled groves, and along soothing streams. Maybe your dirt trail will be the shoulder of a country road. All-natural terrain will enhance your spirit of adventure.

Taking advantage of a dirt path near you will give your and your dog's bodies a break from the pounding they take when you travel on concrete or asphalt. This respite from impact will lessen the risk of injury and general wear and tear. Both your bodies will appreciate it.

Dirt trails include ruts, rocks, holes, and other obstacles for your added "excitement." This decrease in predictable surface conditions can add to the impact of your trek, especially if your avoidance techniques involve hopping and jumping. Even so, traveling on dirt trails results in less impact than on harder surfaces.

By adding rougher terrain to your dog's program, you may increase her risk of digit and carpal injuries. Pay particular attention to her feet and always stop to examine your dog at any sign of lameness. Booties may be in order if the path is especially treacherous or your dog is particularly susceptible to foot injuries. Unanticipated obstacles may also cause you to fall and sustain an injury. If the path is wet, slipping can be a concern. Gradual acclimation to uneven terrain is your best defense against problems for you and your dog.

An advantage to this uncertain footing is the recruitment of numerous muscle groups to support your body and maintain balance. For example, your ankles will adjust to the subtle twisting and turning by becoming stronger. This increase in muscle strength and recruitment of other muscle groups applies to your dog as well. Be prepared to slow your pace at first until your body, and that of Fido, has adapted. If you and your dog become regular trail runners, you may want to look into special trail-running shoes for yourself (they have a tougher, waffled outsole and offer more stability). For extreme cold or areas with abrasive rocks, you may want to get your dog some protective booties as well.

A trail may contain steep areas, which are great for training and strengthening. Running up and down a hillside works muscles in an efficient and concentrated manner. Hill work will also increase the strength of your and your dog's respiratory and cardiovascular systems.

If you have access to a true wilderness trail, the pathway may be narrow and winding. These conditions present extra challenges and the possibility of running into another dog or other outdoor explorers as you round a blind curve. Your dog's good manners and your courtesy are valuable in these situations.

You may be surprised to learn that natural trails are available in your area. Even big cities such as New York City and Chicago offer trails. Start your search by contacting the local agency that maintains the parks. You can also contact a local running group or mountain biking group. A sporting goods store that is actively involved in these activities should be able to direct you to a nearby trail.

Unless you are fortunate enough to live close to a natural trail, you will have to drive to enjoy one. Do it at least once in a while. Your dog will greatly appreciate it. The fresh sights, sounds, and smells will make you both feel rejuvenated. Any means to keep boredom at bay and excitement in your quest for fitness should be used to its full advantage.

If the trail you traverse leads you into a section of wilderness, read chapter 6, which discusses the special considerations that confront those who venture into the home of wild creatures and plants.

Grass

Golf courses, fields, and parks offer some of the best surfaces for running and walking. After you've run on concrete or asphalt, you'll think sprinting across grass is like trekking on clouds.

The slight undulations of a grass surface will strengthen the muscles in both you and your dog. Until you have adjusted to grass underfoot, you may get tired more quickly. Decrease the intensity or the duration of your activity until you both have adapted.

Watch for holes and other obstacles. Wet grass is slippery, so be extra careful after watering or rain. You or your dog may also suffer from an allergic reaction if you are prone to hay fever. Your dog may be delighted to run on such comfy terrain—be prepared for an increase in her excitement level. Parks and fields may also contain other dogs playing with their owners, so be watchful around these interesting distractions.

NIGHTTIME

Being on the road after the sun goes down requires increased safety precautions. Darkness makes it difficult for others who are using the road to see you. You should also take more seriously the general safety measures discussed at the beginning of this chapter. Streets at nighttime can be more risky than during the day.

The most important issue facing nighttime-adventuring dog-human teams is being seen in the dark. If you are the caretaker of a white dog, you have a natural reflector. Otherwise, you will need to take measures to make your dog more noticeable. A reflective collar is definitely worth getting for your dog. Make sure that it can be seen through her fur if she is fluffy. If you train predominantly during dusk and dark, buy or make a reflective vest of some sort for your dog. You can simply attach a white towel around your dog if you wish. Consider adding reflective trim available from fabric or sporting goods stores for extra visibility.

Also take precautions to make yourself more visible. Wear light-colored clothing, possibly with reflective strips added. When my husband goes out at night, he wears a small flashing light that clips onto his clothing. One of these lights can also be attached to your dog or her vest. Even if your dog is decked out appropriately and you are wearing a light, it is still important to dress in light-colored clothes. The increased visibility will greatly improve your safety. Also remember that traffic will be coming from both in front of you and behind you, so you must be visible from either direction.

THE WEATHER IS NO EXCUSE

If you avoid going out and conditioning your dog when the weather isn't perfect, you will hardly have time to exercise at all (unless you are fortunate enough to live in a dream climate). Participating in your favorite adventure is possible in most weather conditions as long as you take steps to assure your comfort, as described in the following sections.

If you are going to compete, your adventure may take place on the scheduled date no matter what the weather. If an important trial or show falls on a cold, wet, or windy day, you won't have to give it a moment's extra thought if you and your dog have already trained on similar days. When you are accustomed to various weather possibilities, you will be less distracted by the sudden occurrence of a snow flurry, as will your dog.

Keep your commitment to your dog and her conditioning and training, whatever the weather. As you and your dog become acclimated to changing conditions, you will hardly notice the difference between fair weather and foul.

Refer to the section on motivation in chapter 3 for some ideas to use on those days when you feel you need an extra shove to go out and face the weather.

Rain

The worst part about rain, I think, is coming home with a muddy dog. Most dogs are like children when it comes to puddles and mudholes. Each puddle brings indescribable joy, beckoning critters to stomp and splash. I always have a towel ready by the back door to wipe off those sopping wet paws before letting my dogs back in the house.

Even a dog who can normally tolerate low temperatures can be intolerably cold when wet. You may find your dog shivering. Dry her with a towel as soon as possible after you finish your exercise session and get her into the house so she can warm up.

You could outfit your dog with a raincoat, available from pet supply stores and catalogs. Like any kind of garment for your dog, a raincoat has to give her room to move, stay secure, and be out of her way.

Roads and trails are slippery when they are wet. Some doggie booties have rubber soles for traction. You should also be equipped with shoes that have good traction. Avoid obviously slippery surfaces, such as steep driveways, and be extra careful wherever you go. Do your best to avoid puddles because you don't know how deep they may be.

Staying comfortable when it's raining is vital to your continued commitment. Invest in good rainproof clothing for yourself. Your head and your upper body are the most important areas to cover to prevent excessive heat loss.

Don't let the rain decide when you are going to exercise your dog. Get out and get used to it.

Heat

Heat is probably the most dangerous weather condition to work your dog in. Overheating is definitely a risk if you are not careful, don't take extra precautions, and don't carefully observe your dog. See chapter 4 for more information on working in the heat and what to do in an emergency situation.

If you are too hot, your dog is feeling worse. The canine body is a wondrous, efficient machine, except for its insulation system. Dogs have inefficient heat control mechanisms. They do not dissipate heat through their skin, like we do; they sweat only through their paws and tongue. You must take extra care to protect them from overheating.

Dark-colored dogs are at higher risk. Dark colors absorb the heat from the sun while lighter colors reflect the heat. You can put a white vest on your dark-colored dog to reflect some of the heat. If your dog is a hairy beast, you may think the solution is to shave her. Before taking that drastic measure, discuss this with your veterinarian and breeder. Some breeds have a double coat that provides insulation, and they are actually better off in their natural state. Some types of hair, once shaved, are never the same again. Hair may grow back coarse, shorter, a different color, or thinner.

For long treks into the wilderness or an area away from home in warm weather, bring an ice chest with ice and water. Before you leave home, wet some towels and throw them in another ice chest. You may also want to bring a chemical cold pack to use in emergencies if you venture from your ice chest for longer than an hour.

Engaging in your training or conditioning session in the early morning or at night will keep your dog more comfortable and possibly keep her from getting ill. Before you hit the road in sunny weather, hose off your pooch's paw pads, groin area, and stomach. Avoid spraying her back, especially if she is dark, as the wetness will absorb the heat from the beating rays. By the time you get back home your dog will be dry, but she will have been spared much discomfort.

If you are going to be out for longer than 45 minutes, it is important to bring some water for you and your dog. Read chapter 4 for tips on bringing water along for your dog.

Concrete and asphalt can become extremely hot in the summer. If you can feel the heat radiating off these surfaces, imagine what your dog's paws are going through. While you run on the sidewalk or street, you can let your dog run beside you in the grass of adjacent lawns to give her feet a chance to cool. My dog Retta loves to run in the gutters. In the summer, we jog early in the morning after automatic sprinkler systems have watered the neighborhood lawns and there is still water in the gutters. If we chance upon a sprinkler still spraying, I let her dunk her head in it and get a quick drink. Retta is a black dog and she gets quite warm, so the momentary breaks and the wetness help keep her cool.

Fog

When it is foggy, you must worry about being visible to others. Red or orange clothes will be more visible than clothing of other colors. You should make sure that your dog is visible too. Follow the suggestions given for nighttime workouts, such as using reflective trim and wearing a light. When it is foggy you will want to protect yourself from the wetness also.

Cold

When it's freezing outside, the last thing you may want to do is leave the comfort of a glowing fire and tread outdoors with your reluctant pooch. Here are a couple of suggestions to help you and your dog handle the weather.

Your pooch can maintain her body heat while exercising, but you must protect her from losing body heat while resting or following activity. When you reach the end of your workout, have a blanket or towel waiting to warm her. Wool is the best material for capturing warmth. If it is windy and cold, you can reduce the chilling effects by protecting your dog with a sweater or other garment. As previously mentioned, the combination of cold and wetness is especially troubling. Some breeds are more susceptible to cold than other breeds. The Nordic breeds, such as Samoyeds and huskies, require less extra protection than thin-haired breeds like boxers or Dalmatians. If you must take extreme measures to stay warm yourself, then your dog may be at too great a risk to go outside. Take the day off when it is this frigid.

You know how important drinking water is when the weather is hot, but it is just as important in the cold. Fluid intake is a consideration whenever a body must work hard to maintain a normal temperature.

Wind

I really must force myself to go out and train on windy days. Something about moving the hardest I can and not going very far makes my frustration soar. A nice, gentle breeze is one thing, but a 25-mile-per-hour wind is another.

However, you may one day have to compete in the wind, so you may as well get used to it.

If you are engaging in a long conditioning session, it is best to head out with the wind at your back, pushing you, and give yourself a chance to warm up before you have to fight the wind in your face. I have a special route I run when it is really windy. The route has many turns so I never run directly into the wind for long periods at a time, and I get a break now and again.

My dog doesn't seem to be bothered by running against the wind at all. It doesn't tire him out like it does me. Even so, be aware of how your dog is doing (although you'll probably be ready to head home well before she is).

The main concern with being out in the wind is flying debris. I've had to stop conditioning sessions when there was too much sand in my eyes and I couldn't see well enough. Your dog is closer to the ground and catches the flying dirt and sand more easily than you do. Watch her carefully for signs of irritation, especially in her eyes.

Snow

Training in the snow takes special consideration. Like rain, snow can be quite slippery. Not only do you have the obvious slippery ice, but melting snow, especially when mixed with mud, makes for treacherous footing. If you regularly train in the snow, special dog booties with "knobbies" for traction may be necessary. Even seasoned Iditarod sled dogs wear booties, so you needn't feel embarrassed if your dog wears them.

A common problem in snowy regions is the salt that is placed on the roads to melt the snow. Rinse your dog's feet when you return from your outing. If your dog licks the salt off (which she will do), she can get sick.

Most of the suffering that can occur during the snowy season has to do with your dog's feet. When you are finished with your workout, check your canine's feet to make sure that they are in good condition. Check for ice balls between the toes. Check for signs of frostbite (described in chapter 4), although this condition is uncommon. After you have

OTHER TIPS FOR TRAINING OUTDOORS

➤ If you go anywhere near sticker bushes, check your dog thoroughly when you get home for stickers, especially foxtails.

➤ Watch for glass, nails, shredded metal (such as soda cans), and other debris on the trail.

➤ When a vehicle passes wide around you, giving you plenty of room for safety, wave thank you to the driver. Let him or her know you appreciate the consideration.

checked your dog's paws, wash and dry her feet. Keep the hair between her toes and on her feet trimmed to lessen the chance of developing ice balls. You can also place Vaseline petroleum jelly or Pam cooking spray between her toes. (Avoid getting anything slippery on the pads themselves.) The best solution is to get her a pair of booties and get her used to wearing them before the first snowfall.

Before you go out in the snow and ice to run your dog five miles, you should take some time to prepare her. Practice walking on icy surfaces. If your dog is going to wear booties, have her practice with those on. Walk her around your yard and neighborhood so that she has an opportunity to experience the different feelings under her feet. Take your time with her when the mercury first drops. She needs a while to acclimate, and so do you. Take her for short, slow walks until she has adjusted to the temperatures. Vigorous exercise in subzero temperatures can cause pneumonia and respiratory problems if your dog works too hard too soon. Again, offer her plenty of water.

CHAPTER SIX

Never Take a Short Cut and Other Advice for the Great Outdoors

Throughout both part I and the quick peeks in part II, you will find references to enjoying activities with your canine friend that take you away from civilization and into the wilderness. Whether taking a short hike, dogsledding through new-fallen snow, or camping deep in an untamed forest, you will fare better and stay safer if you have some knowledge about the special circumstances presented in the great outdoors.

When venturing into the wilderness, it is important to remember that each time you travel is unique. Your experience can include different types of weather (extremes of cold or heat), encounters with wildlife (some that are possibly threatening), and unfamiliar terrain. In other words, never take anything for granted and always be prepared for any situation. This chapter will give you some basic information to begin your outdoor adventure with your canine athlete.

The Advantages of Taking Your Pooch Along

The great outdoors offers a change of scenery, a new environment, and interesting sights and sounds. Exposing your dog to all these wonderful stimulations can produce a happy and satisfied dog.

When you take your dog into the wilderness, you will share a unique experience with nature. Your canine's keen senses will alert you to things that you may have missed had he not been with you. He may even alert you to danger. One of the best arguments for taking your dog is the comfort he can bring you. Not only will he keep you company, but he can fulfill practical roles also. On a freezing "three-dog night," at least you will have one dog to keep you warm.

Bringing your dog with you will make your adventure much more rewarding—if your dog is ready for it. He must easily tolerate changes and be enthusiastic about traveling and exploring. Your dog should be friendly toward strangers and accepting of strange animals. A dog who is reserved about using his voice and who listens to your direction will be much appreciated by those you meet along your path.

The Risks

When you take your dog on a wilderness outing, you are taking a certain amount of risk. Snakes, cliffs, predators, and ticks are all reasons to be concerned. Dogs don't always scare away predators and wildlife. Many wild animals are actually attracted to dogs out of curiosity, which can possibly create trouble.

When your adventure takes you into the great outdoors, you may not be able to get veterinary care as soon as you need it. The nearest veterinarian is likely to be quite a distance away and not easily accessible. If you plan to take your dog for an extended hike, consider taking a wilderness first aid course for yourself (which is a wise idea anyway). Most of what you learn can be applied to dogs also. Simply ask your veterinarian for specific recommendations, and most importantly, know how to give your dog CPR (see page 154).

Some places that you may wish to visit simply aren't safe for your canine friend. You will have to weigh the dangers against the potential for enjoyment. The smartest, safest course of action may be to change your plans and go somewhere closer to home and less hazardous.

Before you make plans to bring your dog along, consider where you are going, what the terrain and weather conditions are like, the altitude, the availability of water or your ability to carry the extra water and supplies necessary for your dog, the purpose of the trip, and your dog's fitness level. If you are planning a week's trek into remote mountain areas with high altitudes and extreme weather fluctuations, taking your inexperienced, out-of-shape dog would be cruel. But even an older, sedentary dog can come along if you are planning a weekend of relaxation at an established campground.

Never take your dog trekking in wild areas during hunting season. Hunting accidents are all too common, with hunters sometimes mistaking each other for animals. Your furry, four-legged buddy is in even greater danger of being mistaken for in-season game. Leg-hold traps and poison bait are other perils that may be present.

Is Your Dog Ready for the Great Outdoors?

Venturing into the wilderness requires more forethought than taking a jaunt around the block. Many aspects of preparing for a trek into the woods, or other natural and remote places, take specific consideration. For instance, your dog's breed and his individuality will make a difference in how you prepare.

The first thing to evaluate is how rigorous and treacherous you plan on making your forays. Your dog's physical prowess should match the demands you expect to place on him. If you want to participate in skijoring with your dog, a dog who is a fit, healthy, natural athlete is necessary. This is especially true if you plan on taking skiing trips into deep parts of the wilderness for long stretches of time on more challenging trails. An occasional casual trip to the hills with your dog in the snow doesn't require as much athletic ability.

Winter sports like sled pulling and skijoring, or even high-altitude snow camping, lend themselves naturally to the arctic breeds like Samoyeds, huskies, and malamutes. Of course, many short-haired breeds have successfully particpated in these adventures, so if recreation (rather than competition) is your purpose, then not having an arctic breed shouldn't put an end to your interest.

A thick coat is not an asset in the heat. Black, hairy beasts, like my Bouvier, just don't handle the heat as well as other breeds. A summer hike with my dog Retta can be hell for her, so she stays home if the conditions are extreme, even though leaving her behind is hard for both of us. For tolerating heat, a short-coated, light-colored, thin dog is best.

If you plan on hiking or riding your bike with your dog off leash, you had better know your dog well. He should be obedient and should look to you for guidance. Independent individuals may not be the best dogs to take with you on these types of excursions. Sighthounds, who aren't bred to look to their guardians for direction and have an instinctive need to chase small moving animals, are often unreliable in the wilderness. Dogs who are closer to their wolf ancestry, such as wolf hybrids and some dogs in the arctic breeds, are also less trustworthy off leash in wild environments.

Having an obedient dog can contribute to a relaxing, enjoyable, and safe trip. A reliable recall is essential. If your four-legged friend goes exploring and fails to come back when you call, the trip will become your biggest nightmare. Going home and leaving your dog behind because you could not find him in miles and miles of wild territory would be heartbreaking.

The Park System

The rules of parks today may change tomorrow with nary a public notice posted for you to discover. Checking the current rules before you leave for your adventure will spare you the distress of having your pooch rejected at the park's entrance. Even if you have a special place you go year after year, it is still wise to contact the park during your planning stage to verify your dog will still be accepted.

Each park that allows dogs will also have a series of regulations concerning the conduct of your dog, so make sure that you understand these specifics and are willing to abide by them. Although the rules may seem overly strict, they are established to protect the wildlife, habitat, and other people, as well as you and your dog.

NATIONAL PARKS

National parks have the most strict rules governing doggie visitors. For instance, Yellowstone National Park allows only leashed dogs, and only in areas within 25 feet of the roads. Dogs are not allowed on hiking trails in any national park and they must always be on a maximum six-foot leash.

That is just the beginning of the list of rules and regulations you are obliged to follow when visiting national parks. Your dog must be quiet at all times. You cannot leave him unattended or tied up. No dogs, except service dogs, are allowed in public buildings. He cannot swim at the designated swimming spots.

The National Park Service authorities have the right to impound animals running free and can destroy a dog that hurts wildlife, people, or livestock. The rules are extremely strict. If you don't think you can abide by them, then you should find a different place to go or leave your dog at home.

NATIONAL FORESTS

Generally, national forests allow dogs as long as the owners are able to keep complete control of them. Here, dogs are most often allowed on the hiking trails. To be on the safe side, call the particular park you are planning to visit and find out if dogs are allowed and what the governing rules are.

REGIONAL AND STATE PARKS

The rules governing dogs vary greatly at regional and state parks. Some may be more strict than others. As always, check with the park rangers before you make plans.

BUREAU OF LAND MANAGEMENT

If you want to go where your dog is more generally welcome and the rules and regulations are more relaxed, then find out the locations of Bureau of Land Management (BLM) areas near you. The BLM permits your dog to be off leash in its wilderness areas, although he must be leashed when in public areas. If you are going mountain biking with your dog (where a leash can be troublesome at times), then BLM lands are ideal for you. Rules regarding where you can ride, what speeds you can travel, and other regulations are more lenient here.

GENERAL CAMPGROUND RULES

When you think of camping, do pictures of isolated regions of untamed wilderness enter your mind? Do you imagine you and your dog sitting near a warm, glowing fire, the clear sky lit by a full moon and millions of glowing stars, the sounds of wild animals filling your ears? The reality is that few will be able to experience this kind of scene without going deep into the wilds. Most people are not knowledgeable enough or simply do not have the time for such adventures. When you go camping at an established campground, you may feel you are alone, but someone else will probably be close by. Because of this, it is important to know the campground's rules, as well as general camping-with-your-dog etiquette guidelines.

Many campgrounds will charge an additional fee for your dog. Some also limit the number of dogs per campsite. Check into this when you are making your reservations or doing your precamping research.

Keep your dog inside your tent or camper at night. Even if you don't let your dog in the house with you at home, being out in the wilderness is a very different situation. Strange animals of all sorts can make your dog's night a nerve-wracking experience. The unknown is quite anxiety-provoking, and unless your dog has been in the wilds many times before, he will be nervous. His barking, whining, and agitated movement can all disturb your neighbors.

Inexperienced campers are often unaware of how cold the wilderness can become at night, even during the warm season. It is unfair to leave your dog outside on his own. Your dog can also attract unwanted and curious creatures. If you don't want your dog sleeping with you, purchase a tent with a vestibule. Since you made the effort to bring your dog, why not take advantage of a little shared body heat and let him sleep with you? That way you will both feel warm and cozy all night long. You can protect yourself from shedding hair by using a blanket especially for him.

RULES FOR CAMPERS

Keep in mind the following key rules for responsible campers:

1. Treat your camping neighbors with respect and keep their comfort in mind.

2. Leave the wilderness as you found it, with no traces of you or your dog.

3. Protect your dog from dangers in the wilderness such as wildlife and plants.

4. Protect the wildlife and plants of the wilderness from your dog.

5. Follow all rules and regulations of the area.

Don't leave your dog alone during the day. If you are camping in a trailer, leaving your dog alone in it can be dangerous. Even if you leave an air conditioner on when the weather is hot, something could happen and your air conditioner could stop working. Leaving your dog unattended in a campground, even tied up somewhere outside, is against the rules almost everywhere. Think about the trouble he could get into. Someone could let your dog free, or a wild animal might attack him and he would be virtually helpless. Because camping is a strange situation and your dog may be nervous, he could be overly protective of your camping area and hurt someone who approaches. If you leave the campsite, take your dog with you. If you think you will have to leave him unattended for any length of time, then maybe he should be left at home.

Keep control of your dog at all times. Loose dogs scare children and adults. They may urinate on people's tires (everyone hates that) or on their possessions. They can cause disruption, steal food, defecate in others' campsites, and scare, chase, or kill wildlife.

Discourage your dog from digging. Leaving your camping area with a new landscape of potholes is not acceptable. All wilderness adventurers should strive to leave the area as it was when they arrived.

Keep your dog out of harm's way while cooking. The flying sparks from a campfire could cause problems to a curious dog, and singed hair is not a desired reminder of an otherwise joyful trip.

Remember, when you lock your food away from unwanted visitors (from squirrels to bears), to put away the dog food as well.

Equipment

What follows is a discussion on the equipment you will need for you and your dog as you venture into the wilderness. Even if you are planning only a short hike lasting a few hours, there are basic supplies necessary for your trip. As you gain more experience and more knowledge, you will be able to tailor the list of equipment for your individual adventures.

KEEPING CONTROL—LEASHES AND COLLARS

A halter or quick-release buckle collar is a safer choice for the wilderness than a choke or traditional buckle collar. Dogs instinctively pull away from pressure on their necks, so if your dog gets his collar caught on a tree limb, he will likely pull until he strangles himself. When hiking or biking, your dog will be safest with a halter because it will not choke him or interfere with his movement. Also, the halter collar will help you pull your dog to safety if he falls over a cliff or into water.

A bell on his collar will alert you to his whereabouts if he wanders off and will alert people and wildlife of your dog's presence. Attach some form of identification to his halter. His identification should have the phone number of someone who is home, not necessarily your phone number. That way, a person who finds your lost dog will be able to reach someone, and you will have someone to call to see if your dog has been found.

Bring two leashes and collars in case something happens to one. The traditional 6-foot leash is necessary, but in the wilderness, you may also want to have a tracking lead. These lightweight leads start at lengths of 10 feet. In the outdoors, your lead should probably be no longer than 10 to 15 feet; otherwise, you will have to worry about the lead becoming tangled in the foilage. Using a tracking lead will give your dog more freedom but still allow you some control. An extendable leash is also a good idea if you are not going to be participating in a vigorous activity and will be able to carry it. One brand has a tether that attaches to your wrist with Velcro fasteners.

The leash should be considered extra safety equipment—a backup to use if something goes wrong—and not a control device for your dog. If you treat the collar and leash as a control device, you can inadvertantly cause problems. If the ground is rocky or uncertain, your pulling on the leash could cause your dog to fall. If your dog does not walk or run loosely on the leash, then go back to the basics and teach him his manners.

A PACK FOR YOUR DOG

Imagine if you will a small, agile animal wearing saddle bags, eagerly tromping over even the most harrowing trail conditions, loyally going wherever you ask. A horse? A mule? No, it's your tail-wagging, face-licking canine companion. I've explained how dogs like to be useful, and what better way to assist you on your great outdoor adventure than by carrying part of the load. Before you throw a fully loaded pack on your dog's back, take into consideration the following advice.

Choosing the Best Pack

The dog pack is a handy piece of equipment for the outdoorsy pooch, but only as long as it fits well. The dog carries the pack on his back with the weight of the pack resting directly on his spine. To get an exact fit, it is best to take your dog into the store for a fitting. Try the pack on your dog instead of relying on weight recommendations. You may find dog packs at well-supplied pet stores; you are more likely to find them at sporting goods or outdoor supply stores. (Get your dog fitted for booties while you are there.) You can purchase packs (and booties) through catalogs also.

The dog pack should sit well forward, over your dog's shoulders at the base of the neck. The pack should not interfere with your dog's elbows at the front.

The pack should have at least two wide, soft straps: one around his chest and one or two under his belly. The chest strap should rest directly in front of your dog's chest. These straps can be made more comfortable with covers of lambskin or other soft material. The straps should adjust snugly enough to keep the pack from shifting, causing abrasion and falling off, but it should not be so tight as to cause discomfort. Many packs use Velcro fasteners, but Velcro may become encrusted with mud and not stay securely attatched. Look for D-rings and other fasteners on the outside of the pack so that you can attach objects to the pack.

It's a great advantage to have a pack that comes in two pieces. This allows you to take the panniers (saddle bags) off the harness in a snap during breaks. The pack is more comfortable when the panniers are attached to a solid surface resting across your dog's back rather than straps. Your dog may overheat if the pack lacks ventilation, so look for a saddle area made of an open material such as lattice webbing.

The amount of weight a dog should carry in his pack is still being debated. Suggestions range all the way from 10 percent of your dog's body weight to two times his weight. Consider these questions as you decide how much your dog can carry. Where are you going? How long will your dog carry his load? What is your dog's fitness level? Is he structurally sound? Is he an experienced backpacker? The best advice is to start with a minimal weight. As your dog gains experience, you can have him carry more and see how he does. Also ask your veterinarian for advice. Watch your dog's attitude. He should be energetic, willing, confident,

TIPS FOR USING A PACK ON YOUR DOG

➤ The weight of the pack must be balanced. Whenever you take something out of the pack, rebalance the load.

➤ Place softer items against the dog and harder items toward the outside of the pack.

➤ On warm days, store frozen, refreezable cold packs in the panniers against your dog's sides. Be sure that the area underneath the cold packs is not too chilly for your dog.

➤ Your dog's body is so warm that whatever you put against him in the pack will be affected by his body heat. Perishable food and camera film can be ruined.

➤ When you stop and take a break and remove your pack, also take off your dog's. Allow him a break from the load and time to cool his back.

➤ Inspect your dog at least twice a day for sores under his pack. Gently rub his back as you look for sore spots and tenderness. If you find sores, give him a break from carrying the pack. When you replace the pack, check the fit and readjust it where necessary.

enthusiastic, and curious. He should have a wagging tail and an effortless gait. You know your dog—is he happy? If he seems to be struggling, lighten his load. If you really want a pack animal, get a llama.

Getting Your Dog Accustomed to the Pack

Suddenly throwing a full backpack on your dog may terrify him—he may never accept the pack without a struggle. Spend the extra time to slowly accustom your dog to the pack.

The very first time you lay the pack on your dog's back (which will likely be in the store when you are trying one on), have treats readily available. As you lay the pack across your dog's back in a slow, steady movement, offer him treats as a distraction and to say thank you for being such a good boy. In the beginning, you should avoid moving and adjusting the pack on his back, especially if he is showing signs of anxiousness. Leave it on for the shortest time possible and give him a treat when you take it off. If he was calm and comfortable with the pack, you can leave it on a bit longer next time. If he is concerned and uncomfortable, then use the following advice to slow down the process.

Leave the pack on the floor and scatter treats on it. This will attract your dog and give him positive reinforcement for approaching. Being close to the pack will show him that it is harmless. After you observe your dog readily approaching the pack without concern, then separate the harness from the pack and place just the empty pack on his back. Give him treats and praise him the entire time he is wearing the pack. If he shows any hesitation at all, take the pack off, praise him and give him a treat, and try again the next day. As he accepts the pack, try using the harness and increase the length of time the pack stays on.

After your dog wears the pack with no problem, then you can take him for walks when he is wearing it. While the pack is off, test your dog's tolerance of the noise of the buckles or other fasteners. He will probably have no problem with these sounds. While the pack is on his back, accustom him to your adjusting and reaching into the pack. Slowly add weight, making sure that both sides of the pack are balanced. Gradually build up the weight he carries, the duration of your walks or hikes, and the difficulty of these excursions.

This process may seem tedious and time-consuming, and you may be eager to start on your trek. But it really is better to take the process one step at a time. If your dog is relaxed and accepting, you may be able to go through all the steps in one day.

HIKING GEAR

This book is meant as a general guide regarding your canine friend, not as a comprehensive guide for you. If you are already an avid hiker, camper, and outdoors person, you know what is necessary for your comfort and safety. If you are a beginner in the wonderful world of outdoor adventure, you'll soon learn what is important to keep you comfortable and safe.

WHAT YOU NEED TO BRING

➤ A topographical map that you can read and understand.

➤ A compass in case you get lost or to get your bearings.

➤ Water bottles or canteens with water from home for you and your dog. You can put some of his water in a spray bottle and use it to spray his pads and face to cool him off.

➤ Calorie-dense, nonperishable food and snacks for you and your dog. You will burn many more calories than you realize while trekking. Choosing calorie-dense foods allows you to save on weight and space.

➤ Sunscreen for you and your dog. Use it whenever the sun is shining, whether it is cold or warm outside.

➤ A small flashlight.

➤ Insect repellent.

➤ A jacket that is windproof and waterproof—an absolute must no matter what the weather is like when you begin your adventure.

➤ A sturdy, comfortable backpack. Again, check mail-order catalogs and magazines and guides, or ask a well-educated salesperson at a outdoors store for help in choosing a pack.

➤ A fanny pack for short excursions.

➤ Rain gear, including several waterproof tarps to put under and over your tent and your other possessions.

➤ Comfortable, waterproof shoes. Those with a Gore-Tex fabric outer lining are dependable as well as comfortable. Buy your shoes a half-size bigger than normal to give your toes plenty of room.

Reading backpacking and hiking magazines and books will give you great ideas on necessary equipment for yourself. My favorite information sources are magazine articles comparing equipment. Catalogs are useful for comparing prices and individual products' components. Of course, visiting a well-stocked outdoors store is pure inspiration! The well-trained staff at such stores is a great source of information.

> A hat. For cold weather, bring a hat that is warm and comfortable, preferably one that covers your ears. If it is warm, wear a hat that shades your head from the sun. Choose a light color for reflection.

> Tights or gaiters made of synthetic ripstop material to protect your legs against scratches, ticks, and poison ivy. Gaiters are lightweight, socklike booties that cover your legs from knee to ankle.

> A long-sleeved synthetic tee-shirt to protect your arms from exposure to the sun, scratches, ticks, and poison ivy.

> Lightweight cotton gloves. These can protect your hands if you fall.

> Plastic bags to store supplies, especially anything you place in your dog's pack. Your dog may suddenly decide to take a swim or chase a fish in the crystal clear waters of a stream.

> A well-stocked first-aid kit (see the sidebar on page 154). One first-aid kit that you and your dog can share is fine.

> A quick-reference first-aid book for you and one for your dog.

WHAT YOUR DOG WILL NEED

> Flea and tick repellent.

> Two sets of collars and leashes. The collars should be a quick-release or halter style or a pulling harness. You will need one six-foot leash as well as a tracking line, expandable leash, or another six-foot leash.

> Booties.

> Pooper scoopers or a small shovel for digging a hole to put your dog's excrement in.

> A collapsible bowl for your dog to drink from. If you are camping in very cold weather, don't bring a metal bowl.

The above lists (one for you and one for your dog) include suggested items that you should bring when traveling in the great outdoors. Keep in mind that even a short jaunt on a trail can be ruined by accidents, getting lost, weather changes, or other unforseen problems. Be prepared. Some items may seem unnecessary, but they could save your life.

The Wilderness

A healthy respect for the wilderness is paramount to your enjoyment of it. Understanding that you are in untamed country and that you must abide by the rules of nature will keep you and your dog safe while allowing you both to appreciate the beauty around you.

ALTITUDE

The higher up you go, the less oxygen there is. Whenever you travel to higher elevations, you will both have to adjust to the difference. Altitude sickness can give you headaches and make your dog feel tired and lethargic. If you notice your dog dragging and looking forlorn, he needs some time to adjust.

Your heart rates must increase in an attempt to get adequate oxygen for muscle activity, so begin any activity at a lower intensity to ward off exhaustion. Your respiratory systems will compensate by becoming more efficient and stronger. When you return home, a residual affect of your bodies' adjustments will allow you both to perform at a slightly elevated intensity. Unfortunately, once you have been home for a few weeks (usually three to four) both of you will once again adjust to the more oxygen-rich air, and you will return to your normal performance levels.

At higher altitudes, you will see improvements in your and your dog's performance in four to five days. Complete adjustment will occur in two to four weeks. The exact length of time depends on how high you are and what altitude you are accustomed to at home.

WEATHER

Experienced back-country adventurers know that they are at the mercy of nature when they leave civilization behind. The weather in remote areas is erratic and unpredictable and can be extreme. For this reason, it is important to be prepared for any weather.

Imagine that the day you leave to begin a five-day hike to the mountain top is sunny and warm, but by nightfall on the second night, you're facing 20-degree temperatures and winds of 20 miles per hour. Are you prepared? Did you bring the right clothing to protect yourself from the wind? Did you bring enough of the right kind of bedding to be comfortable as the wind howls at your tent, lifting the edges several inches off the ground? Do you know how to protect your dog in inclement weather?

Always be prepared for an extended stay. You may be temporarily trapped somewhere, disoriented, or slowed down by foul weather. Packing extra clothes, food, and water is the most vital step you can take to make it through difficult weather conditions. Extra tarps will help keep you dry and therefore more comfortable and healthy. They will also help keep your valuable resources dry and usable.

When pitching camp, look for a place that will protect you from high winds and snow or rainfall. Stay out of valleys to avoid water runoff from rain and flash floods, but stay off the highest areas to avoid lightning. Trees will protect you from the onslaught of rain, wind, and snow, but the tallest tree will attract lightning.

Respect the wilderness. Nature is beyond our control. And above all, be prepared.

Cold

Some dogs can handle the cold easily, and others shiver at the slightest coolness in the air. If your dog has trouble with cold temperatures, you will have to take more precautions or else leave him at home if you will be venturing where you expect the weather to turn nippy.

A dog's underbelly is the most vulnerable area. You can bring along a special coat for your dog to wear that protects this area. Don't see this as a frivolous garment for lapdogs. This apparel serves a very useful purpose and can possibly save your dog from undue discomfort. The same is true of booties.

Additional information on how to keep your dog comfortable in cold weather is included in chapter 5.

Heat

If your dog is especially sensitive to the heat, you will have to decide if he can withstand the trip you are planning. A hiking trip in July may be out of the question, but a camping trip in September may be comfortable. Heat is not to be taken lightly. Your dog could suffer greatly from becoming overheated.

Chapters 4 and 5 include more information on exercising in hot weather and what to do if your dog should overheat.

Keep in mind the present physical condition of your dog, the availability of water for him to cool off in, how long you will be gone, and the activities you are planning when considering whether to bring your dog along.

WATER

It is tempting to think that your dog can drink from the water sources provided by nature when you venture into the wilderness, but this is not a safe practice. Your dog could contract anything from a stomach ache to a life-threatening disease. You can't tell by looking at the water if it is safe or not. Even water sources in remote areas may not be safe to drink.

Giardia lamblia, a parasite that causes dangerous gastrointensinal problems, is a very real threat. *Giardia* is encased in a cyst. When the cyst is ingested by your dog (or yourself) by his drinking from a contaminated water source or licking off his wet fur, it is broken by stomach acid and begins its active phases. In two weeks, 10 cysts can become a million active trophozoites in the small intestine. In one to two weeks after exposure, diarrhea (possibly bloody) develops. *Giardia* is highly infectious. It is usually treated with antibiotics and can reoccur in periods of stress.

The rule of thumb is don't drink out of a natural water source unless you did your research before you left home. This means knowing where you are going and questioning a ranger about the results of the latest water testing. Polluted and contaminated water sources should be avoided during your trek. It will be difficult to keep your dog from drinking from these sources unless you stay away from them.

Even if it's safe to drink, unfamiliar water can cause stomach upset. The best way to assure your dog's good health (and ultimately your own) is to carry your own water from home. To keep your dog from drinking from other sources, offer a small amount of water on a regular basis, at least every 90 minutes and more often if the temperatures are high, your dog is working hard, or it is humid.

To offer your dog water, keep some handy in easily accessible containers. While hiking, you can wear a special belt pack that holds sports bottles with squirt tops. Before leaving home, make sure that your dog understands how to use these bottles. If you are bike riding, you can attach more water-bottle holders (called "cages") to your bike frame. You may want to mark the water bottles so that you can keep track of which bottle is yours and which is your dog's.

Keep a watchful eye around waterfalls and rapids so that your dog doesn't fall in and get swept away. If your wilderness adventure takes you near the water—from calm, pristine lakes to roaring rapids—your dog will need a life vest, even if he is a strong swimmer. A life vest is a simple safety precaution that can mean the difference between life and death for your dog.

ILLNESS

Rabies

A curious dog and wildlife can be a dangerous combination. If your dog is bitten by a wild animal, get him to his veterinarian as soon as possible. He will be considered to have been exposed to rabies. If he has been vaccinated, he will need to be revaccinated and confined for 90 days. If his rabies vaccination is not current, he will be euthanized. (The only way to tell for sure if an animal has rabies is to perform a brain autopsy.) Keep your dog current on all his vaccinations, especially when you are exposing him to possible danger in the wilderness.

Other Diseases

The wilderness, although beautiful, contains a certain amount of possible danger. Some potential diseases are listed below.

- Blastomycosis is contracted from inhaling airborne spores of fungus. Symptoms include a raspy bark, audible respiration, fever or lethargy, and no appetite. Your dog may also have oozing sores somewhere on his body.

- Histoplasmosis is common in the Mississippi River basin and the Great Lakes area.

- Aspergillus is usually benign. A dog may develop lesions and have mucous-like discharge from his nose.

- Coccidioidomycosis is most common in the water in Texas, New Mexico, Arizona, California, and Nevada. Older or sick dogs may exhibit a cough or labored breathing.

- Salmonella usually shows up as diarrhea, vomiting, loss of appetite, depression, dehydration, and weakness.

If your dog gets sick even a month after a trip, tell your veterinarian about your excursion. Was your dog exposed to ticks? Did he drink lots of water or swim frequently? Did he have a confrontation with a wild animal?

PLANTS

Plants can cause problems for your dog in two ways: through physical contact and through ingestion. Plants that can cause physical discomfort include cactus, Jumping cholla, thorns on ground, Southwest stinging nettles, and Canadian thistles. To keep your dog from getting ill, don't let him eat any plants in the wilderness. Some poisonous plants, such as poison oak, poison ivy, and poison sumac, don't affect dogs, but dogs can transfer the irritating plant sap from their coats to you.

Creatures of the Great Outdoors

Venturing into the wilderness means sharing your surroundings with a myraid of animals—large and small. You most probably will not come face-to-face with any of the large animals, and the pests may be hardly noticeable, but you should know what dangers the creatures can bring and how to deal with their presence.

WILDLIFE

It is imperative that you do not allow your dog to chase wildlife. Your dog could be injured if the animal decides to fight. Rabies is once again spreading, and your dog is at risk when he travels in the great outdoors. Vaccinations are not always 100 percent effective, and as mentioned previously, if your dog is bitten by a wild animal, he will have to be quarantined (a most unpleasant experience for both of you)—at best.

Most wild creatures will attack only if they feel threatened. Give them plenty of room and you and your dog should be safe. Staying alert is important so that you can notice a wild animal before you have stumbled too close. Pay attention to your dog; he will sense the presence of an animal before you do and give you fair warning.

Bears and cougars are the most dangerous predators you may encounter. If your dog runs after a fleeing predator, he will probably, in the end, lose his life. If your dog runs from the animal to you (his natural reaction) then he will put you at risk also.

A concern for the wild animal is that your dog will have forced a creature to use its valuable energy to escape from him. What if a natural predator now tries to catch the creature? His energy may be spent and he may be unable to defend himself.

If during the night your dog makes a ruckus, don't let him out. Shine a light from inside your tent or trailer to see what is causing the uproar.

If your dog is bit by an animal, thoroughly clean his wound with lots of water and soap or Betadine antiseptic. Wear gloves for added protection against any diseases the wild animal may have been infected with.

Bears

Most bears would rather stay away from you than confront you. Keeping your dog on a leash will keep him from encountering a bear on his own.

If you do meet a bear, don't run. Even your dog would not be able to outrun a bear, and running will only stimulate the bear's instinct to chase you. Making noise will alert a bear of your presence, and he will more than likely keep away from you. However, grizzly bears are highly unpredictable. If you are heading into areas occupied by grizzlies, you should consider leaving your dog at home.

Eagles, Hawks, Vultures, and Owls

Large predatory birds are dangerous because they may see small dogs as prey. Keeping smaller dogs close to you and out of open areas will help protect them.

Alligators

Alligators are found in the southeastern United States in the Carolinas, Florida, and Texas. Stay away from water known to contain alligators. During heavy rains and in flooded areas, these beasts can make their way closer to civilization.

Porcupines

Porcupines will lash out with quill-laden tails if they feel threatened. If your dog is attacked by a porcupine, find a veterinarian. Removing porcupine quills is a tricky business best left to a calm professional. If you know that you will be far from a veterinarian, ask your vet to teach you how to remove porcupine quills, and then take the necessary equipment with you.

Skunks

Not every confrontation with a skunk ends with the dog being sprayed, but it takes only one time for the scene to be etched clearly in your mind forever. A skunk will usually stamp his front feet as a warning before he sprays. Take heed of this warning. If your dog is sprayed in his face, wash his eyes out as best you can. If you don't want to cut your trip short, you'll have to live with the odor. When you get home, you can use a descenting solution such as Odormute, tomato juice, or liquid dish soap to try to get the odor out.

Opossums

Opossums are not aggressive but will fight if cornered. Try to keep your dog from confronting an opossum. The biggest dangers from opossums, other than rabies, are fleas, ticks, and mites.

Raccoons

Raccoons hate dogs. These crafty creatures have been known to lure dogs to water and drown them, fighting aggressively. They are carriers of parvovirus, distemper, leptospirosis, and rabies (especially in the northeast United States). This is reason enough to keep dog and raccoon well clear of each other. A messy campsite will attract raccoons, so keep your provisions locked up at night.

Rats and Mice

Rats and mice transmit rabies, distemper, leptospirosis, anthrax, tularemia, murine typhus, salmonella, rickettsial pox, and rat-bite fever. As if that isn't enough, your dog could also get pests like fleas and ticks from rats and mice. Your dog could contract these diseases if he is bitten by a rat or mouse, if he bites one (even if he chews on a dead one), and sometimes even if he sniffs the rodent's urine. Do your best to keep your dog away from these pests.

Cougars and Bobcats

Cougars and bobcats are shy and will try to avoid you as much as possible. In the last few years in my area, there have been more attacks and deaths due to these cats than ever before recorded. While biologists try to figure out why, it is wise to take extra precautions. Ask the local rangers what precautions they suggest.

These predators are powerful animals capable of amazing feats. A cougar pulled a horseback rider off her horse last summer. Keeping your dog with you and being attentive may save you and your dog from danger. As with bears, don't run away. You'll never outrun one of these cats and you will only stimulate his predatory instinct further. Try to frighten him off with noise.

Deer, Elk, and Moose

Deer, elk, and moose are generally quite shy and will quickly turn tail and run if you encounter them. Deer are the gentlest of these creatures, but during rutting season they can become quite aggressive, and their hooves and antlers can cause damage to your dog if a fight ensues.

Elk and moose can be ornery and have a short fuse. They are larger than deer and can cause more damage. In many parts of the United States, if your dog is caught chasing these animals, the rangers have permission to shoot your dog. If deer, elk, or moose are around, keep your dog on a leash.

Coyotes and Wolves

The wild cousins of your sweet canine athlete are not creatures to be toyed with. Coyotes are common throughout most of the country, but they rarely cause problems. A bitch in heat or food and garbage left out may attract them to your campsite, but they will leave if you demonstrate your presence. Wolves are not as common. They are shy and would rather stay clear of you and your dog. Because they are related to the domestic dog, many common dog diseases can be transmitted from coyotes and wolves to your dog, so avoid contact at all costs.

Badgers

Badgers are mean and tireless fighters. They come equipped with sharp teeth and deadly claws. If your dog corners one of these animals, he is sure to be badly beaten. The badger will likely fight to the death—the death of your dog, that is.

Domestic Animals

A loose dog chasing after domestic lifestock can legally be shot on sight by ranchers. This is a real danger in the wilderness because many areas and parks allow private lifestock owners to graze their herds on public property. If this is the case where you plan to visit, keep your dog on leash.

CREEPY CRAWLERS

The best way to keep your dog safe from the following list of creepy-crawly animals is to keep him from being too nosy. Dogs are curious by nature. They put their noses in places they should stay clear of, and that is how they sometimes get into trouble. Do your best to keep an eye on your dog, and stop him from digging around in shadowy areas and places where these animals might hide.

Snakes

If your dog is bit by a poisonous snake, you must get him to a veterinarian as soon as possible. Time is critical. Antivenin should be given within two hours of a bite. Antivenin is expensive, and because of this, many veterinarians don't keep it in their offices. Your vet will probably provide aggressive fluid treatment and monitoring. Once your dog has gotten through this critical period, subsequent supportive measures will be taken. One serious problem with snake bites is infection at the bite site. All venomous snakebites cause tissue damage at the bite site, so antibiotics are necessary.

If your dog comes back to camp after a romp in the underbrush and is whining, how will you know whether it's due to a snakebite if you didn't witness the bite itself? Extreme swelling within 30 to 60 minutes of the suspected bite is the telltale sign. The swelling is often so severe that a bite to the neck may require a tracheotomy. Swelling starts at the bite and expands in every direction. The skin will seem like it is going to split. Your dog will also be in extreme pain. There may be bleeding—a small, slow seepage—unless the bite came from a coral snake. The two small puncture wounds from the bite will often be on a curious dog's face or front legs. If you aren't sure what kind of snake bit your dog, don't worry, just get him to the vet. If you witness the bite and are able to kill the snake, take the snake with you to the vet. But don't take the time to hunt the snake down.

What can you do 20 miles from civilization if your dog is bitten by a snake? Although there are steps you can take to heighten his chance of survival, your role is to rush him to the closest veterinarian.

If your dog goes into cardic arrest, perform CPR. (See chapter 4.) If your dog has received massive amounts of venom, he probably won't survive more than a few hours. But you can't be sure, so get him to the vet's as soon as you can.

Carry your dog if you are able to because his walking will only spread the venom more quickly throughout his body. For the same reason, do your best to keep your dog calm and unagitated. Gently rub his ears with long strokes from the base to the tip whenever you can. This action calms dogs. Also keep your dog warm to ward off shock. If the bite is on a limb, use a makeshift splint to immobilize the area.

Although it seems like the natural thing to do, don't use ice or tourniquets. Snake venom constricts the blood vessels; ice further constricts them and the whole area will slowly die. Tourniquets stop the flow of blood. The body's natural immune system will help fight the venom's effects, but if you cut off the flow of blood, you cut off the immune system's ability to do the job it's supposed to. Using a tourniquet can also cause complications more difficult to treat than the snake bite itself. Don't clean the wound or administer any medications.

The danger of a snake bite is determined by the size of your dog, the kind of snake, the location of the bite, and how soon you can reach a veterinarian. A few of the more common snakes you may encounter are listed below.

- Coral snake—The coral snake is found only in the extreme southeast. There is not always swelling at the bite of a coral snake, so look for other signs that your dog may have been bitten such as vomiting, dizziness, nosebleeds, convulsions, and coma.

- Cottonmouth, or water moccasin—This snake lives in swamps, ditches, and rice fields and near lakes and ponds. Cottonmouths are fearless, excellent swimmers.

- Copperhead—Copperheads live in fields. They are slow to move and are easily stepped on.

- Rattlesnake—Rattlesnakes are found everywhere in the western United States from deserts to mountains. They don't always rattle before striking, but if you hear that infamous sound, stop! Don't run. Back up slowly and try not to initiate a defensive reflex in the snake. Rattlesnakes can bite without poisoning their victims.

Bufo Toads

These toads are found mainly in southern Texas and southern Florida. They are fat, lethargic creatures with thick, milky poison on their backs. If your dog licks or bites a Bufo toad, he will die within 15 minutes.

Scorpions

Poisonous scorpions live in Arizona, New Mexico, and California and along the Colorado River. Symptoms of scorpion stings include immediate pain, restlessness, agitation, and jerky head or eye movements. Take your dog to your veterinarian if he is bitten by a scorpion.

Brown Recluse Spiders

Following the bite of the brown recluse spider, the skin in the bite area swells, turns black, fills with blood, and ruptures, leaving an ulcer. The area will need a skin graft. The bite will take months to heal.

Black Widow Spider

If your dog is bitten by a black widow spider, he will be overly excited, shiver intensely, have seizures, experience breathing trouble, and salivate uncontrollably. Apply a cold compress to reduce swelling. Take your dog to your veterinarian as soon as possible, where he will be treated with antivenin.

THOSE PESKY PESTS

Fleas, ticks, and other pests are always a problem with dogs. When you take your dog to the great outdoors, you will have to be more diligent than ever. Many of these pests are carriers of a variety of diseases. Just one tiny bite can lead to all sorts of problems. The bites and stings can also cause discomfort, itching, and slight allergic reactions. Severe allergic reactions are rare, but if your dog has a reaction, the swelling can restrict the passage of air and he may not be able to breathe. If he is allergic, his head and legs will swell and feel hot to the touch.

Fleas

Although fleas carry many diseases, the most serious is bubonic plague. The signs of bubonic plague are fever, swollen glands, and pneumonia-like symptoms. If your dog contracts bubonic plague, he can die in as few as five days. The Sierra Nevada in the western United States and other areas that have rodent fleas are the prime areas for this disease risk.

Before you leave on your trip, wash your dog with a flea and tick shampoo that has some residual affect. Take a repellent with you to apply to your dog regularly. Using a fly repellent made for horses will repel as well as kill fleas. Repellents containing pyrethrins as an active ingredient are relatively safe. When you return home, bathe your dog once again with flea and tick shampoo before letting him in the house.

Ticks

Ticks love heat and humidity. In many areas, ticks are a problem mainly from early April to late October. But in mild climates, they are a worry all year round.

Ticks must feast awhile before spreading most diseases, so check your dog daily for these bugs. While in the back country, you should check for them twice a day, especially in the ears and eyes. If you feel even the tiniest of bumps on your dog, take a closer look. Many ticks are extremely small.

When you find a tick, it should be removed. If you are home and feel squeamish about removing the tick, take your dog to the veterinarian to have the tick extracted. If you are far from home, use tweezers and avoid contact with the fluids at the bite site. If you have tick repellent, use it to kill the tick first. Grasp the spot where the tick attaches to your dog's skin. Pull straight out using a steady, gentle pull. Wash your hands thoroughly and disinfect the tweezers and bite area.

The following is a list of possible diseases your dog could get from ticks:

- Lyme disease—Lyme disease is predominantly spread by deer ticks, but it is not limited to them. Symptoms include fever, sudden and severe lameness, swelling in the joints, and lethargy. Lyme disease can lead to arthritis, heart and or kidney disorders, and damage to the nervous system. It can also be chronic and come back to victimize your dog again and again. Your veterinarian will treat your dog with antibiotics.

- Rocky Mountain Spotted Fever—Symptoms include a 104-degree temperature, loss of appetite, listlessness, coughing, labored breathing, abdominal pain, swelling of the face or extremities, and a rigid neck.

- Tularemia—Tularemia is a bacterial infection of the blood. Symptoms include fever, swollen lymph nodes, and bleeding from the nose.

- Ehrlichiosis—This is a disease that is difficult to diagnosis because each dog seems to show different symptoms. Some possible symptoms include loss of appetite, weight loss, lethargy, swollen lymph nodes along the back or legs, occasional stumbling or limping, and nosebleeds. If your dog experiences serious nosebleeds, they will often be fatal. Ehrlichiosis can spontaneously reoccur, and sometimes an organ can be chronically affected.

- ❂ Tick paralysis—This disease is also seen in people. A neurotoxin from the tick's saliva creates the problems. One week to 10 days after the tick begins feeding, your dog may become lame and listless and may not be able to bend down to eat or drink. He may also have a high temperature.

Mosquitoes

Mosquitoes can inflict painful bites. Depending on the level of allergic reaction in your dog, he may have to deal with itchy, irritating welts and hives. Mosquitoes also carry heartworms. Your dog should be tested for heartworms and then begin a heartworm preventative program before going into the wilderness.

Bees, Yellow Jackets, and Wasps

Many dogs will try to catch these flying playthings with their mouths and can get swollen and sore mouths if they get stung. If your dog experiences a sting, he may still have the stinger in his skin. Squeezing the upper portion of the stinger spreads the venom, so scrape or grab the stinger close to the dog's skin. You can apply a cold compress to ease the pain and swelling. If your dog begins showing signs of allergic shock, take him home and to your veterinarian as soon as possible.

Generally, your dog's allergic reaction will get worse the more times he is stung throughout his life. If you know your dog is allergic, talk to your veterinarian about taking and administering an antivenin kit or immunizing your dog. For some dogs, even their first reaction can be severe or life threatening. Unfortunately, allergic reaction shock can set in within half an hour, and if you are far from home, you may not have time to get your dog to a veterinarian.

Yellow jackets are more of a risk than bees and wasps because they will sting again and again, causing even more problems and pain.

Killer Bees

Africanized bees, commonly known as killer bees, attack in swarms and can kill your dog. Killer bees are slowly working their way northward from Mexico and have established colonies in Texas and other areas. A single sting to your dog's head, nose, or throat can cause swelling and make breathing difficult. Apply cold compresses, even cold mud, to control the swelling and pain.

Fire Ants

Treat fire ant stings like bee stings.

Cleanup on the Trail

I once heard a fellow dog person say that he didn't really like to spend time with dog people because all they talked about was excrement. That's an exaggeration, but it is a topic that we must discuss at times.

You cannot let your dog relieve himself where he wants in the wilderness and leave the result there. In highly traveled areas, this is just as rude as leaving feces on a city sidewalk. If you are going to be in one location just for the day, then you should bring plastic pooper-scooper bags and pick up the waste to pack it out with you along with your garbage.

If you are farther into the wilderness, you may not want to pack all that poop out, and you can leave it behind if you follow these rules. Dig a narrow hole 6 to 10 inches deep and a minimum of 100 feet, but preferably 200 feet, from any water sources. Of course, if you don't know where your dog is at all times, you won't know if he has left a piece of himself somewhere—another good reason to keep track of your dog.

When It's Time to Go Home

It's your last evening in camp and it's been a wonderful time for both you and your dog. The weather has been as perfect as you could have imagined, with gentle breezes encircling you with pure air and the sweet smell of pine. You planned well so you had everything you needed to enjoy the great outdoors. Eating yummy food at the end of a challenging physical day has brought contentment, and now you sit by the fire that illuminates your dog's face. He looks at you gratefully for allowing him to come with you. You give him nibbles of graham crackers and marsh-mallows (no chocolate) while you're making s'mores. Then someone suggests singing campfire songs. Through the vast expanse of the night air your voices carry across the grassy meadow, "Michael, Row the Boat Ashore."

Now that you're ready to head home, remember the wilderness rules mentioned earlier in this chapter. Clean up your campsite, and pack out everything you brought in.

When you get home, it is vital to brush your dog to remove any weed seeds stuck to his fur. Give him a bath with a flea and tick shampoo. Check him thoroughly for ticks and other pests, and then allow him into your home to relax and daydream about his grand adventure—all of this before you even get a shower. It is worth it though, isn't it?

CHAPTER SEVEN

People and Events
in the Dog World

Participating in canine sports and activities is a learning experience—for both you and your dog. It teaches the value of facing a challenge head on and learning from it. It also increases the physical and mental abilities of your dog.

Now that you have come this far, you probably understand the skills needed of the activity you wish to pursue. What level of education should you acquire? It depends. If you plan to add walking through your neighborhood to the time you and your dog spend together, your education may consist of taking a basic obedience class so that your dog is under control and well behaved, talking with a knowledgeable salesperson about an appropriate walking shoe for you, and learning some of the basic precautions and special considerations for walking on the street. If you decide to make week-long excursions into the remote wilderness, your education will have to be more intense. Wilderness safety classes and first-aid classes could prove invaluable. Your education might also include books on wilderness hiking, canine first-aid, backpacking, remote camping, conditioning your canine athlete, and other relevant subjects.

The Quest for the Perfect Instructor

If you have decided to try an organized dog sport, you will almost certainly need an instructor, especially in the beginning. You could pick up the phone and call one listed in the phone book. But will you know what kind of instructor you are talking to? Not if you don't ask the right questions and know what a "good" instructor is.

Don't wait until you have spent much time and money and your dog has learned bad habits to find out that your instructor was not the right one for you. Put a little effort into finding an instructor who will treat you and your dog with respect, keep you both motivated, and teach you what you need to know to be successful.

FINDING A TRAINER

Anyone can become a dog trainer. One does not have to be licensed, and most states have no requirements. Any person who can run an ad in a newspaper or have flyers printed up can claim to be a dog trainer. But you need a trainer who has more to offer than sales savvy.

Find an individual who has had extensive experience handling dogs. This experience can come from training guide dogs, therapy dogs, dogs for the military, or police dogs. The trainer should also have extensive experience in your chosen adventure.

Get references from the trainer and make some phone calls. It is useless to get references if you are not going to call and see how the former clients felt about the training. A competent trainer will be glad to offer you references, so don't be afraid to ask.

WHAT TO LOOK FOR

Attend one of the trainer's classes. What is the overall feeling you get from the instructor, the handlers, and the dogs in the class? Is the class taught in an upbeat, encouraging way? The dogs should look interested, not bored; they should be enthusiastic, not frightened. Trainers usually bring their own dogs to use for demonstrating the lessons. Is the trainer's dog well behaved and obedient?

Does the instructor guide the people with respect and kindness? The instructor should be encouraging, not insulting or patronizing, to the people in the class. In group instruction, the distractions are many and dogs may learn little in the class itself. The purpose of a group class is to train the people to train their dogs in the quiet, controlled environment of their own homes. Does the instructor give the people the confidence necessary to follow his or her advice and train their pets when they leave?

The cost of the training course is not a measure of quality. Many good trainers who have been training dogs successfully for many years teach classes just for the fun of it because they love it so much. Their fees may be small compared to those of a trainer who is teaching only for the money and who has little regard for the dogs or their handlers. Some communities may offer dog training classes at no charge as a service to their dog-owning citizens.

TRAINING METHODS

Different breeds of dogs have different learning styles and rates. Each dog is an individual with a different set of life circumstances and personal characteristics. Does the instructor take these differences into consideration? If the instructor offers only one method to teach a command and attempts to make each dog adhere to this method, find someone who is more flexible and better educated.

Attending an obedience class where punishment is the training method of choice can do more damage than good. If you see any loss of temper from the instructor or any physical roughness, leave. These training methods have no place in a respectable obedience class. They only cause harm and mask problems. You want your dog to work with you as a team member. Trained with respect, your dog will learn more and be more obedient at all times, rather than just when a choke collar is around her neck.

If you sign up for an obedience class and have a bad experience, don't give up. There are many caring instructors whose main goal is to provide you with the tools to shape your dog into a wonderful companion. Search out these instructors; they are worth the effort.

Guarantees and Quick Fixes

How reliable is the training advice you receive? If the trainer offers you a guarantee of success, be suspicious. No one can guarantee anything when it comes to a team of living beings. Be cautious of quick fixes to any problems you are having. Quick fixes don't exist; if they work at all, it is only temporarily. Quick fixes tend to use coercion or punishment, both of which can damage your animal's psyche in the long run. You need to treat the underlying cause of a problem. A quick fix treats only the symptoms.

Communication

When the trainer gives you advice on training, make sure that you fully comprehend the techniques and suggested actions. Do you feel comfortable asking questions? Does the trainer respect even the most simple questions and answer them without being derogatory?

Evaluate the trainer to see if his or her animal ethics mesh with yours. Finding someone who believes with you that animals should be treated with respect and concern is paramount. Listen for expressions of affection and respect for your pet.

The Trainer's Philosophy

Does the training and advice better your relationship with your dog? Any punishment or treatments that seem harsh or unnecessary should alert you to a possible conflict with the trainer. You don't just want control—you want mutual respect and a bonded relationship.

Any actions or advice that threaten your dog's sense of security should be avoided. Choose your actions wisely—your dog depends on you.

Is the advice based on generalizations and misconceptions? Does it seem outdated and in conflict with what your intuition tells you? You should search for a trainer who takes your individual animal and your life situation into account and gives you advice relevant to your situation.

The Role of Clubs in Canine Activities

Throughout history, clubs and organizations have played many roles in dog sports and activities. Even in medieval times, haphazard, politically motivated groups would get together for what were often completely rigged and violent events to demonstrate the prowess of an individual line of dogs.

With the formation of kennel clubs in the 1800s, a more structured network of organizations was established. Early kennel clubs throughout Europe and North America kept records of lineage and held shows to evaluate the structure and appearance of their breeds as well as the expertise of the dogs in the work they were developed for.

At present, clubs exist for just about every sport or event that pertains to dogs. Some of these are small groups of like-minded individuals; others are complex organizations that set rules for membership, govern titles, organize events, and publish information.

National clubs often oversee smaller, local clubs. Depending upon which activity you are pursuing, you may be required to join the governing club, but it is in the local clubs—where your participation is necessary to their survival—where you will receive unlimited benefits.

Clubs combine learning with social interaction, continued education, and input from others, among many other things. What are some of the benefits you can gain from joining your local affiliated club?

- Rules—Local clubs can help you comprehend the governing club's sometimes jumbled, confusing rules. Instead of a rules pamphlet to decipher on your own, you will have experienced people to talk to.

- Code of ethics—Many clubs have a code of ethics that has been established to govern the conduct of its members. Reading a club's code of ethics will help you choose an organization that matches your and your dog's personalities and your personal beliefs.

- Events—Local clubs organize many events. During these events, you will come to understand the sport in a new, more enlightened way. Many local clubs hold "matches"—practice shows that don't award points but give you and your dog a chance to prepare for the real thing.

- Training—Many clubs are set up as training clubs. The members benefit from training their dogs at the club with the club's equipment and assistance from experienced trainers. The clubs may offer classes to the public.

- Moral support—When your training or competition is not going well, you can talk to someone with experience who shares your enthusiasm for a particular activity.

🐾 Friendships—When people share the same commitment and excitement for an activity, it is natural that they become friends. Whether the friendships are casual or become deeper, they are rewarding and worth pursuing. At the very least, you will meet others who share and understand your passion for your dog.

🐾 Enthusiasm—Spending time with someone who is devoted to and excited about your adventure will build your enthusiasm. Enthusiasm is contagious, and it takes just a little to create an aura of excitement. A club can often offer this help to keep you committed.

🐾 Networking—You can learn about veterinarians and other professionals in your area. Many times these important people are members of the club. Networking can be especially important if you are new to the area, to the activity, or to dogs or if you need a change in your support team. Word of mouth from your fellow members is the best reference.

🐾 Emergency care—In times of trouble such as a natural disaster, your club can communicate with other area clubs to arrange temporary foster care for your pet. Clubs also develop assistance programs for fellow members and dog lovers. You'll meet people who can help you when you need a sitter for your dog. You can even work out a co-op or trading system for dog sitting.

🐾 Event information—This is an especially valuable asset of belonging to a club. Once you start your quest for events in your chosen activity, you will quickly discover how secretive the dog world can seem. It is sometimes difficult to find out where and when events are taking place. I often learn about local dog events after the fact in the local paper. Your local club will have better access to a list of events and will keep its members up to date on these shows. Also, once you are a member of a group, you are often placed on mailing lists for other local organizations and will get their flyers on upcoming events.

 Education—If people from your club want to attend continuing education seminars and workshops, you can share the monetary load and have more fun if you team up and go together.

 Parties—You also get the benefit of attending great parties. Remember, you share a common bond with these people.

HOW DO I FIND A CLUB TO JOIN?

Finding a club to join may be a challenge, depending on where you live and what activity you are interested in. For the more popular activities and in the more populated areas, you will probably have a number of clubs to choose from. But even if you have little choice, you can still get support and information from a small, practically inactive, not-so-local club, especially if you are new to your activity.

Begin your search for a club by attending local events. Ask what club is putting on the event and request its membership information. Of course, word of mouth is the best recommendation; if you have a friend, or a friend of a friend, who enjoys your chosen activity, ask him or her. Keep your eye out for information about dog training classes. These are often held by training clubs as another way to bring in income and share knowledge.

If you are having no luck finding a local club this way, contact the national club, if there is one. Finding the name and address of a national club is usually quite simple at the library or on the Internet. The quick peeks in part II include a list of the organizations that govern each sport or activity. By writing to these clubs, you can find out if there is a local club in your area.

Books on your chosen activity are very helpful for finding information not only on organizations but also on the activity itself. However, many of the addresses and contacts, especially of the smaller organizations, change so frequently that if a book is not exceptionally current, you may come to a dead end. Again, try the Internet.

When you find an organization, you'll want to check it out to make sure you would be comfortable as a member. Attend a meeting, training session, or event put on by the club. What is the atmosphere? Are the people friendly and do they welcome you? Are they cliquey and unfriendly? You will want to feel accepted so you can easily take advantage of the benefits of belonging to a club and willingly reciprocate by helping out. Most clubs will gladly welcome you. They are usually thrilled to have new members because they love their activity and want to share it.

You don't have to stop with one club. Active dog lovers often belong to many clubs. If you participate in different adventures, you can belong to a club for each activity, a breed club, and the national club. Don't overdo it though. If a club doesn't prove helpful or you don't participate very often, then feel free to drop your membership. Spend your money, time, and energy wisely.

HOW DO I JOIN?

How do you go about joining a club? Often it is as simple as mailing in your membership fee. Other times there are more extensive requirements. The following is a general outline of how to join a club:

1. Write the national club for membership guidelines and an application for membership.

2. Locate a local club and find out how to join.

3. Decide whether you meet the criteria for membership.

4. Send in your application, fee, and any necessary paperwork.

5. Find a sponsor if the local club requires one. If you don't know anyone in the club, attend a meeting and talk to some members. Because clubs usually appreciate new members, you shouldn't have trouble finding someone to sponsor you.

6. If required, attend the designated number of meetings or training sessions or participate for the stipulated number of hours before becoming a full-fledged member.

YOUR CONTRIBUTION

Participating in a club is a give-and-take situation. You will get many benefits from belonging to a group or organization, but you will also have to do your share to support it. Clubs would not exist if it weren't for the dedication of key members. In most clubs, a few extradedicated individuals always seem to perform most of the work to keep the club alive and functioning.

As a club member, you will have to choose carefully your level of participation. You don't want to become so heavily involved that you have no time for training and participating in your adventure, but you do want to add your support and help the club function smoothly.

At the very minimum, you should attend as many meetings as you can. This way you will know what is happening within the organization. You can just listen or you can become an influential participant.

If your club holds events, it is especially important that you help out at them. It takes many people to put on a successful event, and a club relies heavily on membership participation to do so. Even if you are completely new at the activity, you can still help. In fact, helping out at an event is a wonderful way to gain firsthand knowledge. Beginners can get used to being at an event in a nonthreatening manner. You won't have your dog with you. You will be calm and observant and will get a front-seat view of how the event is run and what is expected of you as a competitor.

Offering your professional expertise is another way to help your club. If you are a writer, you can help out with articles, publicity flyers or brochures, or a newsletter. If you are a carpenter, you can be assured that sometime the club will need something built. A lawyer can offer his or her services by reviewing contracts. Whatever you do may be needed at some time or another. Offer your personal expertise to your club or organization.

Show Etiquette

Attending a dog event can feel like entering a foreign world with its own rules of behavior. As with any specialized activity, there is some truth to this statement, but you don't have to be an "insider" to start participating. The following section will give you a general idea of what to expect so that when you attend your first couple of dog events you will feel more comfortable and have a more enjoyable time. Nothing is more educational than experience, so just jump right in and have fun.

HOW TO FIND A DOG SHOW OR EVENT

Finding a dog show or event can be a challenge. The larger shows will be listed in national magazines (see the appendix), and if you find a sport-specific magazine, you will find more local or smaller shows listed. Again, the Internet is a great place to search. For example, if you are searching for an event sponsored by AKC, you can check out its web site. When you attend a show you can usually pick up flyers for other shows in the area. Once you are on a mailing list, you will receive premiums (the pamphlets or brochures that tell of upcoming shows and give a description of the planned events) through the mail. Calling a specialty dog store (or sometimes other smaller pet stores) may provide you with information on events. If you are looking for a more specialized event such as a dog-sledding trial, contact the local club for information.

HOW TO ASK FOR INFORMATION

Perhaps you found an event but still aren't sure what to expect—the whole place seems overwhelming. Everyone else seems to belong to some special secret group. They are running around with purpose, their dogs in tow. Everything seems to have a rhyme and reason that you don't understand at all. You are there to find out specific information and get a feel for the event, yet you feel like such an outsider, and everyone looks so busy.

They *are* busy. Experienced competitors each have a routine and a schedule, and they know what they have to do and when. Time for dawdling is usually scant. Even the people who have only one dog will be busy. Practicing, warming up, grooming, and mental preparation all take time and effort.

Will competitors have time to talk to you? Will they want to? How can you possibly ask for a few minutes of their time when you are obviously a beginner? You must plan your questions so you waste as little time as possible. Some of the competitors may have the time and inclination to chat away, generously sharing their experience and knowledge. Others may offer only a couple of quick answers and want to be bothered no more. Others still may be willing to answer your questions but at a later time. Knowing that you may get a variety of responses and having a plan will ease your anxiety.

Arrive at the show or event early. Many competitors will leave as soon as their turn is over. You may not know ahead of time when a particular person and dog will be competing. A list of times may be printed in the newspaper, or you may be able to get this list ahead of time from the show organization, but it is only an approximation.

If you can, buy a show catalog that lists the dogs and breeders or handlers that are competing. This will give you a way to identify the many people who are competing.

Choose a team that consists of an owner-handler and dog to interview. This means that the person handling the dog also owns the dog and is not hired to handle the dog. This team lives together, trains together, and performs together. An owner-handler is the richest source of information for your own team. If the show catalog lists the competitors' addresses, choose a team that lives close to you and start with them.

Find out where they are on the grounds, asking other people if necessary. Once you find them, see if they are about to compete or not. It would be extremely rude to bother them just before their turn. They need to focus and be ready to enter the ring or field when necessary.

If the owner appears to have a minute, walk up to the team, introduce yourself, and ask if this is a good time to talk. If the person does not have time to talk at that moment, ask if you can call at a later time. Don't forget to ask what would be the best time to call. While talking to the owner, avoid touching the dog until you have asked permission. The dog may be ready to go into the ring, and nothing will turn off a potential information source faster than if you ruin the dog's hair or concentration.

It can be difficult to talk to other dog owners at first. Some people can be snooty or they may be too focused, busy, or distracted. In order not to waste their time, do your research first. Then you will know what questions you really need answered. Write down your questions and take notes when you get answers. Ask for a business card from the person or write down his or her name and phone number. You may want to call and ask a follow-up question at a later time. Ask your most important or difficult questions first, and then ask others if you have more time.

When asking for information, you are asking for a favor. Be courteous and thankful. People will be more willing to help you if you take their feelings into consideration.

In the dog world, as in many segments of society, if you ask 20 people one question you will get 20 different answers. If you probe the minds of too many trainers and handlers—say more than 10—you will only confuse yourself, especially in the beginning.

Some people will keep asking the same question until they find someone who agrees with them, then they stop listening and questioning. This won't help you at all. Stay open minded.

In the same vein, it is no use to argue with someone you are talking to. Since you were the one who asked him or her for an opinion, respectfully listen. You won't make any converts anyway. You can mention that you have heard advice to the contrary, but don't press the issue. Dog people can be bullheaded. If you think you are dealing with a less-than-enlightened dog person, ask your question, get your answer, thank the person, and leave.

WHAT TO BRING

Going to a dog show or event is a special treat. For some events, you can make an entire day of it, bringing the whole family to watch marvelous dog-and-handler teams performing their magic. Other events seem to happen too quickly. Some are held in such uncomfortable surroundings—a conformation show in a large parking lot or a dog-sledding race in below-freezing temperatures—you will want to spend as little time as possible there.

If you are going to spend the day, or even a few hours, with your dog at a show or event, you will want to be prepared. The following list will also assist you when you and your dog are ready to compete or participate. By then the activity itself will dictate much of what you bring, especially in the way of dog equipment.

Attend the first couple of events without your dog. When you are just exploring potential adventures and getting a feel for the way the events are run, bringing your dog is too distracting. Later you may want to bring your dog to see how she reacts, but first make sure that dogs who aren't competing are allowed. If they are, yours must be well mannered and well behaved. When you begin to participate, you should attend a few small events or matches first to get your dog accustomed to the ruckus and commotion.

TIPS FOR COMPETITIONS

The hallmark of a seasoned competitor is being prepared. Of course, no matter how long you may have competed or how experienced you are, there will be times of chaos, but being organized will prevent you from wasting energy that should be spent on bringing out the best in yourself and your dog.

WHAT TO BRING TO A DOG SHOW

➤ Leash

➤ Pooper scooper

➤ Extra clothes. It may be cold in the early morning hours and warm in the afternoon.

➤ Sunscreen, even if it is cold outside. You will probably be out in the sun all day, and you should protect your skin and your dog's if she is light colored.

➤ Water from home for your dog.

➤ A hair clip or rubber band. Wear your hair up if it is long to keep it out of your way and neat in appearance.

➤ Extra shoes and socks if it is wet or dewy.

➤ A crate or exercise pen to hold your dog while you are signing in and taking care of other duties. Make sure your dog is trained to stay in a crate or pen.

➤ Waterproof and comfortable flooring for the crate or exercise pen.

➤ Treats and toys for your dog.

➤ A large shade tent or sheets to provide shade. Large clamps work well to attach the sheets to your dog's crate or pen.

➤ Snacks and drinks in an ice chest for you and your dog.

➤ Folding chairs. It is amazing how few places there are to sit at dog-related activities.

➤ Towels for cleaning up, drying off, or wetting and cooling your dog.

➤ Brushes and other grooming equipment.

➤ Any equipment you need for you and your dog specific to your activity.

➤ First-aid kit for you and your dog. You can share one as long as it has everything that is listed on page 154.

Review your premium at home the night before the event. Check your name and address and verify that it is correct. While looking through the event premium or catalog, see if you are eligible for any special prizes that require you to sign up ahead of time. Know the times, rules, locations, and classes that you will be participating in. You will have enough to worry about without feeling lost and confused.

Have all your paraphernalia organized and know where everything is. Arrive an hour earlier than you think you need to. Find the area where you will be competing and where you should set up your temporary camp.

The extra hour will give you plenty of time to register and take care of any preshow business, settle in, get ready without being hurried, and maybe even have time for a snack. Just before your turn in the ring or on the field, give your dog a brief warmup.

Be a respectful competitor. Be courteous while awaiting your turn or while in the ring or field. Don't get in the way of dogs exiting the ring before you. It is important to walk your dog before entering the ring so she has a chance to eliminate any bodily wastes. Of course, don't chew gum. Respect the judges' decisions. After your dog's class has finished participating, you may approach the judge to ask about your scores. The judge is not required to discuss your scores, but if he or she is willing, you can learn much from this debriefing. If you and your dog earn a title, a photographer will be on hand to take your photo, so stay around and get your picture—you deserve it.

Be gentle and kind to your dog (as you always are). Be a good sport and accept a less-than-perfect performance as a lesson to learn from. Always clean up after your dog and yourself. And most of all, be friendly!

Remember that there is no reason for what you are doing if you and your dog are not having fun. Enjoy the shared experience with your most beloved canine athlete and appreciate her for all that she gives you. You know you are lucky to live with such a wonderfully dedicated and brilliant pooch, and you should make sure she knows it.

Good luck!

Part II

Quick Peeks

God made the earth and sun and moon. He made man
and bird and beast. But He didn't make the dog.
He already had one.

NATIVE AMERICAN FOLKTALE

Introduction

Welcome to part II of *Canine Adventures* where we offer you a teasing taste of various dog activities and sports that you can investigate further. These quick peeks were designed to give you just that—a quick peek. If one or two or three or four activities sound interesting to you, turn to the sources of information listed following each entry.

These sources were verified prior to printing, but some of the groups and organizations frequently change officers, and addresses and phone numbers change also. Fortunately, the organizations are usually extremely helpful, so it's worthwhile to track them down.

I was not able to actually participate in or observe each activity listed in part II, although I did try to talk to or correspond with as many people involved in the activity as possible. I was able to get much first-hand experience in many activities. I hope to have personally seen each activity by the next edition of this book. I sincerely and enthusiastically welcome all input. If you have an activity or sport that you think should be mentioned or would like to add more information about those already included, please contact me.

Cynthia D. Miller
c/o Animalia Publishing Co.
P.O. Box 1390
Yuba City, CA 95992
530/755-1318
530/755-2695 fax
888/755-1318 toll free
animalia@jps.net

I've included in the appendix a list of books and resources that you should seriously consider adding to your library. These are the ones that I consider the most valuable and necessary to understanding your dog. I have also included a list of sources for a wide range of supplies and accessories for you and your dog.

Each quick peek begins with a rating system fully explained below. Please don't reject an activity on the basis of its rating alone. Many highly intense activities can also be participated in casually if you want to cross-train your dog or just to try something new. Read the quick peek though, because some activities are complex and difficult for a beginner.

Here is an explanation of the rating system. The ratings are based on the best information I could garner from a variety of sources.

Level of Commitment

🐾	This activity is just for fun.
🐾🐾	This activity is mainly for fun, but you will have to make some commitment (which usually involves teaching your dog some simple commands).
🐾🐾🐾	Although this activity requires more serious commitment on your part, you will still have time for other doggie-related activities.
🐾🐾🐾🐾	You must be dedicated to fully participate in this adventure. It requires more training, more time, more travel, and/or more money.
🐾🐾🐾🐾🐾	Your entire life will revolve around this adventure. It is intense and highly involved.

Training Level

🐾	Little or no training is involved except basic obedience. (If your dog does not have basic obedience, he will not be fun to do anything with.)
🐾🐾	You will have to engage in formal training for this adventure.
🐾🐾🐾	Your dog will need to earn his "college degree" if you engage in this activity.

Level of Physical Fitness

🐾	To participate in this activity, your dog does not require any special level of fitness. This is a good activity to use to begin conditioning an out-of-shape canine or rehabilitate an injured one.
🐾🐾	Your dog must be physically fit enough to handle some low-key exercise.
🐾🐾🐾	Your dog has to be in good, healthy, strong condition and ready to engage in intense exercise.
🐾🐾🐾🐾	Your dog must be energetic, healthy, agile, strong, and flexible and in great cardiovascular condition. This adventure is going to require a lot from your canine athlete. Is he ready?

Time Investment

🐾	You can engage in this activity less than three times a week or for less than 30 minutes a session. It involves little or no travel.
🐾🐾	This adventure requires a daily commitment or at least one hour per session. Travel may be involved.
🐾🐾🐾	This activity will oblige you to work with your dog more than one hour a day consistently. Travel is probably also involved (mainly to weekend events).
🐾🐾🐾🐾	This activity will require a large investment of time.
🐾🐾🐾🐾🐾	This activity must take a central place in your lifestyle. Lots of training, conditioning, and travel are necessary and should be expected.

Estimate of Expenses

These estimates do not include the cost of the dog. First, I am assuming you already have a devoted pooch and are looking for an adventure to explore. Second, the cost of a dog varies from free to thousands of dollars.

The estimates include the start-up cost of equipment and a typical one-year period of expenses.

$	This activity will cost you up to $100.
$$	This adventure will require that you spend between $100 and $500.
$$$	This one will cost you $500 to $1,000.
$$$$	This activity will run you between $1,000 and $3,000.
$$$$$	This expensive adventure will cost you more than $3,000.

Common Breed Participants

Some sports are specialized and demand a particular type of dog, but you can try nearly any activity for fun. For serious competition and to lower the risk of injury to your dog, find the adventures that favor your type of dog.

One more thing—for consistency, in this section of the book I refer to your dog as a male.

As you read this section, keep an open mind and an adventurous spirit. Read a quick peek; then sit back in your chair and pet your dog while you daydream about the two of you participating in the activity. How does it feel? Are you having fun? I promise you will find several of these activities that warrant your further investigation. I hope that these quick peeks will get your imagination and creativity soaring!

Hanging Out

Dog Camps

Level of Commitment	🐾 to 🐾🐾🐾
Training Level	🐾
Level of Physical Fitness	🐾
Time Investment	🐾 (Just a week out of your summer.)
Estimate of Expenses	$$$
Common Breed Participants	All breeds and types of dogs.

A BRIEF DESCRIPTION

How does spending a week or so with your dog swimming, canoeing, doing arts and crafts, eating gourmet food, tracking, running over agility obstacles, and learning tricks sound? How about lessons for you in canine behavior and care? Then maybe a vacation spent at a dog camp is just what you need to escape from your everyday world.

Several dog camps exist, and more are being started as this type of vacation for dog lovers becomes more popular. Set in beautiful environments with friendly and enthusiastic hosts, dog camps are truly luxury spas for people and their dogs.

You will come away from dog camp appreciating your dog like never before. All the praise and support you will receive from the campers and counselors and the successes you will have will strengthen your knowledge and appreciation of your dog's unique gifts.

OVERVIEW OF NECESSARY EQUIPMENT

Each camp is unique and, depending on the activities offered, requires a different packing list. Ask the director of the camp for specific information.

TRAINING SYNOPSIS

Before you attend a camp, you should assess your dog's manners. He should not be out of control, although he doesn't have to be a star in precision heeling. When you get to camp you will learn many games and skills to practice with your dog.

SPECIAL CONSIDERATIONS

Your dog will not be welcome if he is aggressive to dogs or to people.

ADVICE FOR FIRST-TIMERS

Be prepared to have the time of your life! Dog camp is addicting. You will want to go back again and again.

WHY YOU WILL ENJOY THIS ADVENTURE

Many dog lovers hate leaving their dogs behind while on vacation. Dog camps are a great way to solve this dilemma. Your dog will have as much fun as you will.

Attending a camp with your dog is an experience you will never forget, and it will be good for you and your dog's relationship in many ways. When you return home, you will feel a renewed bond with your dog.

SOURCES FOR INFORMATION AND ASSISTANCE

Internet

Camp Dances with Dogs
http://www.flyingdogpress.com/camp.html
Camp Gone to the Dogs
http://www.camp-gone-tothe-dogs.com:80/index.htm

Dog Parks

Level of Commitment	🐾
Training Level	🐾
Level of Physical Fitness	All
Time Investment	🐾 to 🐾🐾🐾
Estimate of Expenses	$
Common Breed Participants	All breeds and types of dogs.

A BRIEF DESCRIPTION

Since some parks do not allow dogs at all, a park that allows dogs is often considered a "dog park." This quick peek refers to specially designated dog parks that offer amenities unique to the desires and needs of dogs and their people.

Some dog parks are enclosed and some are not. They can also vary in size—some cover half a block while others encompass many acres.

Although dog parks are full of amusement for you and your dog, you do have one large responsibility—you must pick up after your dog. Some parks provide pooper-scooper bags as a courtesy. Bring your own anyway in case they run out. Sometimes when your dog is running about, you may miss one of his deposits. Remember this when you find a pile that hasn't been cleaned up, and clean up what you find.

OVERVIEW OF NECESSARY EQUIPMENT

You will need a leash, an extra in case the first one breaks, and a quick-release collar (in case your dog gets entangled in something). Your dog needs to be up to date on all vaccinations. He may come in contact with a dog that hasn't been cared for as well as you care for your dog.

Bring a collapsible bowl and a container of water from home. The less your dog drinks with other dogs from a common source, the less chance he has of getting sick.

TRAINING SYNOPSIS

Socialization is the most important element in your dog's training. It is even more significant if you are going to allow him to run free with a bunch of strange of dogs.

Although there is no requirement for Canine Good Citizen (CGC) certification for dogs who attend dog parks, getting a CGC certificate for your dog shows that you have taken the time to ensure your dog has good manners. (See page 256 for more information on CGC certification.)

SPECIAL CONSIDERATIONS

The wide expanses of groomed, green grass in a place where dogs are welcome is a seductive image for dog lovers. Do be cautious though. Dog fights are not unheard of in dog parks. No matter how well mannered your dog is, no matter how much effort you have made to socialize him and keep him under control, you may encounter someone who has taken no such responsibility.

Because there is usually no official peacekeeper on the grounds, user groups are often established to enforce the rules. If the park you use has an active user group, the rules regarding aggressive and dangerous dogs will be more strictly enforced. Accept your obligation to protect your dog as best you can. Keep aware of any interactions between your dog and other dogs and learn to read the signs of impending problems.

Another potentially big problem is the spread of disease, especially if your park is frequented by irresponsible dog owners who do not pick up after their dogs.

Bitches in heat should not be taken to a dog park.

Some parks charge a fee for use; others are free of charge. Contact your local parks and recreation department to find out. A fee may be required on a per-use or an annual basis.

ADVICE FOR FIRST-TIMERS

Keep your dog leashed until you have a feel for the other dogs in the park and have identified any dogs who cause you to be apprehensive.

Follow all rules so the park can be kept open and operating for our dogs.

WHY YOU WILL ENJOY THIS ADVENTURE

Watching your dog joyfully playing in an open space with other dogs is certainly one of the best reasons to enjoy a dog park. It is a good place for city-dwelling dogs to get the exercise they need. A dog park is also a place to socialize with other dog people and to safely practice obedience exercises over long distances.

SOURCES FOR INFORMATION AND ASSISTANCE

Organizations

Contact your local parks and recreation department.

Books

Barish, Eileen. *Vacationing with Your Pet*. Scottsdale, Ariz.: Pet Friendly Productions, 1997.

Walters, Heather MacLean. *Take Your Pet Too!* MCE, 1997. This book is available from Direct Book Service.

Internet

Free Play
http://www.freeplay.org
Public Open Space and Dogs
http://www.petnet.com.au/openspace/posindex.html
When can I let my dog off leash? by Perfect Paws
http://www.perfectpaws.com/offleash.html

Games

Level of Commitment	🐾
Training Level	🐾
Level of Physical Fitness	Can be adapted to any.
Estimate of Expenses	$
Common Breed Participants	All breeds and types of dogs.

A BRIEF DESCRIPTION

Playing with your pup is probably so natural you don't even think about it. You may not even realize the benefits of play—you are just having fun! Your dog does benefit from engaging you in some fun doggie games, and if you are aware that play serves other positive purposes, you may be more inclined to put down that book, turn off that television, get off that couch, and play!

Romping in the backyard together over fun, small obstacles always delights a dog. Playing a game of fetch or disc catching is enjoyment in its purest form. A game of hide and seek with your dog's nose as the tool of the search) gives your dog an opportunity to use his remarkable sense of smell.

OVERVIEW OF NECESSARY EQUIPMENT

You'll need toys and a desire to have fun.

TRAINING SYNOPSIS

Some general manners are important for your dog to know before you engage him in play. He should release objects from his mouth immediately at your first command. Teach him that your possessions are off-limits by giving him consistent reminders and offering him his own toys to play with. "Sit" and "stay" are important concepts for your dog to know. With these commands, you can keep general control of the games.

General obedience makes playing with your pooch more fun. Your enthusiasm for a game of fetch will diminish if your dog jumps up on you every time you try to throw the object.

If your dog doesn't seem interested in some basic dog games, pick up the book *Culture Clash* by Jean Donaldson. She shows how you can teach any dog how to play fetch and love it. She also has the best discussion I have ever read regarding the rules of game playing with your dog and how to teach and enforce them.

SPECIAL CONSIDERATIONS

Roughhouse games can be detrimental. Playing tug of war with your dominant, assertive dog and letting him win can fluff up his already inflated ego to a point where you will have difficulty dealing with his overbearing attitude. Your dog could even become aggressive.

Never, ever allow your dog to place his teeth on you. Human skin and canine teeth should not make contact. If he touches you with his teeth, even by accident, stop the game and calmly walk away. He should learn to play vigorously and excitedly without putting his teeth on you.

Take your dog's physical conditioning into consideration while playing. He may be so excited and wound up that he may not realize when he has pushed himself too far. You must know if your dog has had enough physically and give him a break.

Stop playing if your dog gets too rough or you start to lose control of his behavior.

ADVICE FOR FIRST-TIMERS

I doubt that anyone is truly a first-timer at playing with a dog. Start with a fun activity that your dog already loves to do and then build on that, teaching your dog new tricks or allowing him to teach you.

WHY YOU WILL ENJOY THIS ADVENTURE

You'll be spending time with your dog and having nothing but fun, fun, fun! Playing with your dog can be spontaneous, and you can squeeze playtime in between other responsibilities.

SOURCES FOR INFORMATION AND ASSISTANCE

Books

DeBitetto, James, D.V.M., and Sarah Hodgson. *You & Your Puppy: Training and Health Care for Puppy's First Year.* New York: Howell Book House, 1995.

Donaldson, Jean. *Culture Clash: A Revolutionary New Way of Understanding the Relationship between Humans and Domestic Dogs.* Berkeley, Calif.: James & Kenneth Publishers, 1996.

Ludwig, Gerd. *Fun and Games with Your Dog.* Hauppauge, N.Y.: Barron's Educational Series, 1996.

Equipment Suppliers

Discount Master
Humboldt Industrial Park
1 Maplewood Drive
Hazleton, PA 18201-9798
800-346-0749

J-B Wholesale Pet Supplies Inc.
5 Raritan Road
Oakland, NJ 07436
800-526-0388
800-788-5005 fax

Jake's Dog House
P.O. Box 3748
Cherry Hill, NJ 08034
800-734-5253

Pedigrees
1989 Transit Way
Box 905
Brockport, NY 14420-0905
800-528-4786

R.C. Steele
1989 Transit Way
Box 910
Brockport, NY 14420-0910
800-872-3773

That Pet Place
237 Centerville Road
Lancaster, PA 17603
800-733-3829 phone and fax

Valley Vet Supply
East Highway 36
P.O. Box 504
Marysville, KS 66508-0504
800-360-4838

Wholesale Pet USA
P.O. Box 325
Topsfield, MA 01983
1-800-4-PET-USA
800-329-6372 fax

Training and Service

Canine Good Citizen

Level of Commitment	🐾 🐾
Training Level	🐾 🐾
Level of Physical Fitness	🐾
Time Investment	🐾 🐾
Estimate of Expenses	$
Common Breed Participants	All dogs, except those with extreme temperament flaws.

A BRIEF DESCRIPTION

The CGC test was designed to promote responsibility in dog owners by creating a safe, tolerant doggie citizen. I believe this certificate should be earned by every dog. It isn't a formal requirement test like the AKC CD (American Kennel Club Companion Dog obedience title), but it does measure your dog's ability to handle a number of normal, daily situations. If your dog is going to be out in public, your first step might be to acquire a CGC certificate.

The CGC test evaluates your dog in ten different situations. The evaluator will lightly comb or brush your dog to make sure that he is clean, parasite free, and willing to accept the contact. The evaluator will then approach you and after greeting you, shake your hand. Because the purpose of the CGC test is to simulate real situations, you are allowed to talk to your dog and remind him to mind his manners. Your dog must not jump up on the stranger. He should hold his position and stay calm.

The evaluator will then ask you to walk your dog on a loose leash. You must be able to make turns in both directions, make about turns, and halt in an orderly manner with your dog staying close and paying attention. Your dog must be on your left side but does not need to walk in a formal heel position. The next exercise requires that your dog walk through a crowd of at least three people.

In the "sit for exam" portion of the test, the evaluator approaches your sitting dog and pets him. The evaluator then circles you and your dog. You will be asked to demonstrate your dog's ability to obey the control commands of sit and stay. You can take your time and repeat the commands as necessary. You will be asked to have your dog sit and stay as you walk 20 feet away and then return to him.

Your dog's ability to stay calm and in control of his excitement is further tested by adding distractions. The first is another handler and dog meeting you face to face. Your dog must stay at your side while you and the other dog-human team meet, shake hands, and then walk on. Your dog will then be tested using two other distractions. These are up to the evaluator and can include all sorts of interesting experiences, such as running children, a wheelchair, bicycles, or joggers passing by.

The final exercise to prove your dog's good citizenship measures how well he will do when you are away from him. You will tie your dog to a 15-foot line and leave the area for five minutes. Your dog must remain calm. He does not have to hold the position, but must be well behaved.

You can find an evaluator in your area by contacting local clubs and trainers. The evaluator may want to meet you and your dog before the actual test.

OVERVIEW OF NECESSARY EQUIPMENT

You will need a collar and leash.

TRAINING SYNOPSIS

The exercises requested in a CGC test are not the same rigid ones used in obedience competition. You have more leeway in your dog's behavior in CGC testing. The training is lower key, and more people and dogs are able to be successful.

You can to talk to your dog as necessary and can take your time when making requests of him. If you have good control of your dog in public situations and general control over his body position, you will have no problem passing this test.

The main training you will need to perform involves socialization (see part I). Get your dog out and about meeting as many people and other pets as possible. Putting your dog in a myriad of situations will ensure that when it comes time to test his reactions (either in the CGC test or in real life), you can be assured that he will be in control.

You may want to enroll in a companion dog training class that emphasizes basic good behavior rather than obedience competition.

SPECIAL CONSIDERATIONS

You may have a hard time finding a qualified evaluator in your area, depending on where you live. As CGC certification becomes more popular, then it will be easier to find an evaluator.

Aggressive dogs are a danger to everyone. If your dog is aggressive toward dogs or people, you may want to find a professional trainer to help you. If your dog doesn't seem to like the CGC evaluator for whatever reason or if any doubts or fears creep into your mind, postpone the test and try again later with a different evaluator. Never put anyone in jeopardy.

ADVICE FOR FIRST-TIMERS

Relax and take your time. If you are nervous, you will send all the wrong signals to your dog. If you have done your homework, you will both do just fine.

WHY YOU WILL ENJOY THIS ADVENTURE

A CGC certificate is something to be proud of. You can brag to people that your dog is a good citizen. You can assure leery strangers you meet that your dog has been certified and encourage other dog owners to earn this certification.

SOURCES FOR INFORMATION AND ASSISTANCE

Organizations

American Kennel Club (AKC)
51 Madison Avenue
New York, NY 10010
919-233-9767

Books

Volhard, Wendy. *Canine Good Citizen*. New York: Howell Book House, 1984.

Internet

Canine Good Citizenship Certificate
http://www.dog-play.com/cgc.html

Education

Level of Commitment	🐾 to 🐾🐾
Training Level	Any
Level of Physical Fitness	All
Time Investment	🐾 to 🐾🐾🐾🐾
Estimate of Expenses	$ to $$$$
Common Breed Participants	All breeds and types of dogs.

A BRIEF DESCRIPTION

What's going on in your dog's mind? How can you get him to do something? Why does your dog do that? By educating yourself on dog behavior and training, you can discover the answers to these and many more questions.

Opening one good book on training or behavior is the start of your education. (I recommend Karen Pryor's *Don't Shoot the Dog*.) This self-education can include an array of books (many, many books are devoted to dog training theory and practical application), videos, and practice and experience with your own dog. Attending workshops and seminars will give you a more in-depth education with the extra benefits of being able to ask the instructor questions and talking to other dog lovers.

If you truly love dog training, you may want to attend a dog training school or become an apprentice at a dog training facility. This will extend your dog training influence beyond your own dog to other people's dogs as well. This kind of work takes commitment, and you may find that the old adage is true—a dog trainer's dog is not always trained. Don't become so busy training other people's dogs that your dog takes a back seat.

OVERVIEW OF NECESSARY EQUIPMENT

Equipment specific to the activity you are teaching your dog will obviously be necessary. But to teach him simple commands or behaviors you need only a gentle heart, the ability to clearly make your requests, patience, knowledge about how dogs learn, a plan, flexibility, and tons of treats.

TRAINING SYNOPSIS

You may choose to take a group or private class where you train your own dog. If you attend a "college" or training facility that has a set curriculum, you may or may not be able to take your dog and use him during your education. Seminars and workshops generally do not invite dogs, but some hands-on workshops request dogs for demonstrations. Whether you bring your pooch or not is left up to you. These seminars will require you to take notes and are given in a traditional classroom setting.

SPECIAL CONSIDERATIONS

Be careful—you may become addicted!

The estimate of expenses depends on how much and what type of education you plan to pursue—from a basic obedience class to a full curriculum at a nationally known dog training school.

ADVICE FOR FIRST-TIMERS

Keep an open mind. Winnow the good advice from the unusable advice. Remember that there is probably a contradicting opinion for almost every training theory.

If you keep in mind the basic principles that guide all learning and how they specifically apply to dogs, you can decipher the best course of action in any situation, without hurting your dog.

WHY YOU WILL ENJOY THIS ADVENTURE

The challenging aspects of training dogs are a driving force for many people. Others are thrilled to be able to do something that involves dogs. You will never be bored because once you know the basics of training the canine mind, you can accomplish anything.

SOURCES FOR INFORMATION AND ASSISTANCE

Organizations

Association of Pet Dog Trainers
P.O. Box 385
Davis, CA 95617
800-738-3647
707-745-8310 fax
apdtbod@aol.com

National Association of Dog Obedience Instructors
(NADOI, Inc.)
P.O. Box 432
Landing, NJ 07850

Puppyworks Seminars
P.O. Box 385
Davis, CA 95617
800-PET DOGS
707-745-8310 fax
apdtbod@aol.com

Books

Burnham, Patricia Gail. *Playtraining Your Dog.* New York: St. Martin's Press, Inc., 1980.

Donaldson, Jean. *The Culture Clash: A Revolutionary New Way of Understanding the Relationship between Humans and Domestic Dogs.* Berkeley, Calif.: James & Kenneth Publishers, 1996.

Evans, Job Michael. *Training and Explaining: How to be the Dog Trainer You Want to Be.* New York: Howell Book House, 1995.

Fisher, John. *Dogwise: The Natural Way to Train Your Dog.* London: Souvenir Press, Ltd., 1992.

Pryor, Karen. *Don't Shoot the Dog: The New Art of Teaching and Training.* New York: Bantam Books, 1984.

Reid, Pamela J., Ph.D. *Excel-erated Learning.* Oakland, Calif.: James & Kenneth Publishers, 1996.

Weston, David. *Dog Training: The Gentle Modern Method.* New York: Howell Book House, 1990.

Periodicals

Off-Lead
204 Lewis Street
Canastota, NY 13032
315-697-2749

Forward (NADOI, Inc.)
P.O. Box 432
Landing, NJ 07850
Attn: Peggy Prudden, Secretary

Internet

Canine Good Citizenship Certificate
http://www.dog-play.com/cgc.html
Clicker Training
http://txk9cop.metronet.com/kathleen/clicker.html
Dog Seminars and Workshops
http://www.inch.com/~spectrum/topdog/
Dog Training—Fast and Simple
http://www.dog-play.com/fast.html
Dog Training Information
http://www.uwsp.edu/acad/psych/dog/library.htm
Puppyworks
http://www.puppyworks.com
Practical Obedience
http://csa.delta1.org/~greyhound/obeddog.html
Teaching and Training Articles by Suzanne Clothier
http://www.flyingdogpress.com/articles.htm

Search and Rescue

Level of Commitment	🐾🐾🐾🐾🐾
Training Level	🐾🐾🐾
Level of Physical Fitness	🐾🐾🐾🐾
Time Investment	🐾🐾🐾🐾🐾
Estimate of Expenses	$$$
Common Breed Participants	Hounds, German shepherds, Labrador retrievers

A BRIEF DESCRIPTION

Search and rescue (SAR) dogs are used in many different situations. SAR dogs may be associated primarily with a local law enforcement agency, trailing escaped convicts or at-large criminals. SAR dogs also search for victims of catastrophes such as an avalanche or collapse of a building. They may search for missing or lost persons in wilderness areas or even lost children in cities.

National and regional SAR organizations exist, and you can begin by ferreting out a known organization that is commonly called upon in times of need. Some organizations are actually formed by local law enforcement agencies (this does not necessarily preclude your participation), and others will have a close relationship with law enforcement. The different organizations will have their own certification and testing procedures, so find out their requirements. Many of these organizations will create mock disasters to test dogs and give them experience.

An SAR dog is required to do one of two things—track or trail. Tracking is following a person's exact trail. A Track Solid dog follows a trail, usually the freshest. "Tracking Solid" would include leading the handler to any human scent in rubble caused by a disaster. A Track Sure dog follows the trail associated with the first smell he is exposed to and will follow only that track, not veering off to follow a scent laid by another person. A Track Clean dog follows the scent he was asked to even if it crosses other scent trails and even if those other trails were laid at the same time (and so are as fresh) as the correct trail. A dog "Tracking Clean" leads the handler to a specific person by scent no matter how many scents are in the area.

Dogs who are searching for missing people in the wilderness, disaster dogs, or dogs searching for fugitives use "air scenting"—they search the air for a specific scent and follow the clues from there. And contrary to popular belief, dogs can follow a scent through water. Dogs are often used to find drowning victims.

The AKC (American Kennel Club) and the ABC (American Bloodhound Club) offer the following titles: TD (Tracking Dog), TDX (Tracking Dog Excellent), MT (Master Tracking Dog), and MTX (Master Tracking Dog Excellent).

OVERVIEW OF NECESSARY EQUIPMENT

You will need the equipment for tracking as outlined in the Tracking quick peek (see page 402). Once you begin advanced training, you will need specialized equipment. When you become involved with a local SAR group, you will be able to use its equipment for training.

TRAINING SYNOPSIS

Teaching a dog to track a clear-cut scent is fun and easy, but SAR dogs require specialized training in situations that are unique. The best way to train your dog is to have help from someone with experience. Contact your police department, dog trainers who train tracking or protection dogs, or your local bloodhound or German shepherd group.

SPECIAL CONSIDERATIONS

If you are going to take SAR seriously, then you will have to spend considerable time training your dog. You may have to travel. You must be able to remain calm in the middle of disasters, crises, and other traumatic situations. Your dog must be stable, hardworking, resilient, and dedicated.

In order to be an SAR dog, a dog must have the ability to discriminate between often minute amounts of scent. Some breeds are better at this than others, although all dogs have incredible olfactory power. Hounds are especially well equipped to handle SAR. Bloodhounds, with their stubborn temperaments, will follow a scent trail for miles with patience and unwavering dedication. Other popular breeds for SAR are German shepherds and Labrador retrievers. These breeds do better off leash than the hounds but don't do as well with long and old trails. All breeds enjoy tracking and it is a fun and easy skill to teach your dog.

ADVICE FOR FIRST-TIMERS

Get involved with a good professional organization that works with the local law enforcement agency.

SAR is difficult work. Your dog will be asked to work to the limits of his abilities, and you too will be physically and mentally exhausted.

WHY YOU WILL ENJOY THIS ADVENTURE

The joy of finding a lost or injured person and assisting officials in getting a person help is a truly glorious feeling.

Watching a dog work, seeing firsthand the power of his truly amazing ability to smell, and bearing witness to his devotion to his job and to the human race is overwhelming.

SOURCES FOR INFORMATION AND ASSISTANCE

Organizations

California Rescue Dog Association
1062 Metro Circle
Palo Alto, CA 94303
http://www.crc.ricoh.com/carda/

International Rescue Dog Organization
104 Ballantine Road
Bernardsville, NJ 07924
Attn: Caroline Hebard
908-766-7235

National Association of Search and Rescue
4500 Southgate Place, Suite #100
Chantilly, VA 20151
703-222-6277
703-222-6283 fax
nasar@nasar.org

North American Search Dog Network
RR2, Box 32
Urbana, IL 61801

SAR Dogs of the United States
P.O. Box 1411
Denver, CO 80211

SAR K-9 Service
P.O. Box 32621
Fridley, MN 55432

Books

Bryson, Sandy. *Search Dog Training*. Pacific Grove, Calif.: Boxwood Press, 1991. You can purchase this book from Direct Book Service as well as other catalogs.

Bulanda. *Ready! Training the Search and Rescue Dog*. Wilsonville, Oreg.: Doral Publishing, 1994. You can purchase this book from Direct Book Service as well as other catalogs.

Button, Lue. *Practical Scent Dog Training*. Loveland, Colo.: Alpine Publications Inc., 1990.

Davis, L. Wilson. *Go Find! Training Your Dog to Track*. New York: Howell Book House, Inc., 1984.

Pearsall, Milo D., and Hugo Vergruggen, M.D. *Scent: Training to Track, Search and Rescue.* Loveland, Colo.: Alpine Publications, Inc., 1982.

Videos

Stopper & Watts. *Search Dog Training: How to Get Started.* 1996. You can purchase this video from Direct Book Services as well as other catalogs.

Internet

Avalanche Search Dog Information
http://www.drizzle.com/~danc/avalanche.html
California Search Dog Association
http://www.crc.ricoh.com/carda/
Search and Recue Overview
http://www.k9web/dog.faqs/working.html

Equipment Suppliers

Search Gear
882 Bruce Lane
Chico, CA 95928
800-472-2612
530-899-2612
530-894-1416 fax
searchgr@sierra.net

Show Business

Level of Commitment	🐾 to 🐾🐾🐾
Training Level	🐾🐾🐾🐾
Level of Physical Fitness	🐾🐾 to 🐾🐾🐾🐾
Time Investment	🐾🐾🐾
Estimate of Expenses	🐾 (Factoring in an income from the work.)
Common Breed Participants	All breeds and types of dogs.

A BRIEF DESCRIPTION

Has anyone ever told you that your dog ought to be in pictures? Imagine seeing your dog each week on a sitcom. What a thrill it would be to perform with your dog live before a real audience of appreciative fans. Wouldn't it be wonderful to have your dog's sweet face forever recorded in an advertisement? It is possible. The need for animal actors, models, and performers is growing.

If you are not shy and have a dog who is a trainable ham, then this may be a fun activity to add to your life together. Your dog will also have to be healthy, fit, and energetic to succeed.

You can perform entertainment acts locally for parties and special events, or you can take educational shows into classrooms.

You don't have to live in a large metropolitan area. In smaller cities you will actually have more control over your pet's career as you will meet personally with many of the business owners/managers in your area. During these visits, you can expound on the benefits of using your dog in the businesses' marketing campaigns, for example.

You will probably want to sign up with an animal agency. If not, you will need a license from the U.S. Department of Agriculture (USDA). When you chose an agency, make sure it is licensed with the USDA.

You may have to do some marketing on your own, especially if you live in a less populated area. You may have to convince a potential client that a cute dog will greatly increase his or her sales. Know the business so that you can also convince your potential client that hiring you won't make his or her life any more complicated.

OVERVIEW OF NECESSARY EQUIPMENT

You'll need your trick-trained dog, dog training skills, knowledge of how show business works, and some enthusiasm and persistence. You may also need photos of your dog and a résumé.

TRAINING SYNOPSIS

The first consideration is that you must have complete control of your dog at all times. Your dog should look to you for direction and follow your commands.

In addition, you will need to teach your dog tricks to get him noticed and then be able to teach him the tricks that are needed for each particular job. To accomplish this, you should have a solid understanding of how dogs learn.

Your dog will have to respond to hand and body signals. On a television set or stage, you will not be able to use your voice to tell your dog what to do. Your dog should be able to pay attention to you in spite of any distractions.

SPECIAL CONSIDERATIONS

Your dog must be stable, happy, reliable, and calm. He will be surrounded by strange equipment and unfamiliar people who will touch him quite a bit.

He must also look good on camera, with a nice contrast of colors, and ooze personality.

ADVICE FOR FIRST-TIMERS

Show business is not as easy as you might think. You'll spend long, boring hours on a set and lots of time training and grooming your dog. You'll need to do plenty of research about show business.

WHY YOU WILL ENJOY THIS ADVENTURE

People get involved in show business with their dogs for many reasons. They want to show off their dogs and enjoy seeing them in print or on film. They want to earn more money. Some people hope they'll meet celebrities.

SOURCES FOR INFORMATION AND ASSISTANCE

Organizations

Actors Equity Association
165 West 46th Street
New York, NY 10036

American Guild of Variety Artists
164 Fifth Avenue
New York, NY 10019

Screen Actors Guild
5757 Wilshire Boulevard
Los Angeles, CA 90036

Books

Baer, Ted. *How to Teach Your Old Dog New Tricks*. Hauppauge, N.Y.: Barron's Educational Series, Inc., 1991.

Haggerty, Captain Arthur J. *How to Get Your Pet into Show Business*. New York: Howell Book House, 1994.

Zeigenfuse & Walker. *Dog Tricks: Step by Step*. 1997. You can purchase this book from Direct Book Services as well as other catalogs.

Videos

Broitman & Lippman. *Take a Bow . . . Wow! Fun and Functional Dog Tricks*. 1996.

Haggerty, Captain. *Dog Tricks with Captain Haggerty*. 1996.

Moore. *Dog Tricks*. You can purchase this video from Direct Book Services as well as other catalogs.

Winton. *Yes! You can Teach Your Dog Tricks and Have Fun, Too!* 1997. You can purchase this video from Direct Book Services as well as other catalogs.

Internet

Absolutely Wild Studios
http://aspenfil.com/wild/
Star Pets Animal Talent Agency
http://www.starpet.com/

Therapy

Level of Commitment	🐾🐾 to 🐾🐾🐾
Training Level	🐾🐾
Level of Physical Fitness	🐾
Time Investment	🐾 to 🐾🐾🐾
Estimate of Expenses	$
Common Breed Participants	All breeds and types of dogs.

A BRIEF DESCRIPTION

Therapy teams volunteer at children's hospitals, veterans' hospitals, rehabilitation centers, rest homes, convalescent hospitals, and social centers. The dogs offer unconditional love to the patients and residents of such facilities, giving them respite from the difficulties of their lives.

The dogs and the people visited often form special relationships that are important to both of them. The dogs also have a way of bringing previously withdrawn or hard-to-please people out of their shells and showing them they still have the ability to experience love.

If you decide to become a therapy team with your dog, you may want to think up some special way for your dog to entertain people. Tricks such as shaking hands or fetching a tissue from a box when someone sneezes are appropriate and appreciated. One therapy team in New York is very popular because the dog can gently pull people in their wheelchairs.

The rewards of this activity are great. Make sure that your dog fits the criteria described below, and give therapy a try.

OVERVIEW OF NECESSARY EQUIPMENT

You will need a collar and leash. Bring a brush if your dog is a big shedder. Therapy dogs may be invited to sit on furniture or beds and you should do your best not to leave hair behind. Bringing treats that people can feed your dog is a nice way to form relationships. Pack whatever you need for your dog's tricks or special activities. You may want to bring a blanket or towel to wipe off your dog in wet weather, to place on the furniture or bed before your dog gets on it, and to clean up any spills or accidents.

TRAINING SYNOPSIS

Becoming a therapy dog does not require any sort of official training other than general good manners. What may help you get your foot in the door is having a CGC certificate. In fact, some groups require this certification.

SPECIAL CONSIDERATIONS

You may need to be registered with one of the many organizations that arrange therapy visits. Being a part of an established entity is good in many ways. You will have the experience and support of other members and you will have more opportunities for service if you join an organization.

You must be dependable. People often form strong bonds with the visiting dogs. The patients or residents look forward to the visits and usually spring to life when they know dogs have arrived. Your dedication can make a difference in these people's lives.

Your dog must be clean and well groomed. He should be parasite free and have all his vaccinations. He will get lots of baths (one bath before every visit), so healthy skin is an advantage.

The breed is far less important than your dog's personality. Your dog must be friendly, calm, affectionate, gentle, well behaved, and loving. He must have an outgoing manner and be able to "read" people—not pushing himself on those who are reserved yet acting like a clown for those who need a lift. He must get along with other dogs and animals (there may be some visiting at the same time), and he must handle large groups with ease and not be afraid of the special equipment required by some patients.

ADVICE FOR FIRST-TIMERS

When just starting out, contact the director of recreation or volunteer services at a place you would like to visit. Set up an appointment to discuss the merits of beginning a therapy program. You'll probably leave your dog at home for this first meeting.

If your initial call reveals a therapy program already in place, ask if you can join it. Observe a therapy visit without your dog so that you will have a clear idea of what goes on during a visit.

WHY YOU WILL ENJOY THIS ADVENTURE

The relationships that are formed during regular visits are the reason many people commit to therapy visits. The joy that the patients or residents express when a dog enters their rooms is motivational for the handler and creates a special time in the handler's and dog's lives.

You can really make a difference in people's lives by participating in this activity. When your dog has comforted, stimulated, and brightened a person's day, you will see why people are committed to therapy dog programs.

SOURCES FOR INFORMATION AND ASSISTANCE

Organizations
Alpha Affiliates
103 Washington Street, Suite 362
Morristown, NJ 07960-6813
201-539-2770

Delta Society
289 Perimeter Road East
Renton, WA 98055
800-869-6898
206-235-1076 fax
DELTASOCIETY@CIS.COMPUSERVE.COM

Love on a Leash
P.O. Box 6308
Oceanside, CA 92058
619-724-8878
ekelley@cts.com

Therapet
P.O. Box 1696
Whitehouse, TX 75791
Therapet@Juno.com

Therapy Dogs Inc.
P.O. Box 2786
Cheyenne, WY 82003
307-638-3223

Therapy Dogs International
719 Darla Lane
Fallbrook, CA 92028-1505
tdi@gti.net

Books

Davis, Kathy Diamond. *Therapy Dogs*. New York: Howell Book House, 1992.

Internet

Therapy
http://www.uwsp.edu/acad/psych/dog/work.htm
Therapy Dogs
http://www.dog-play.com/index.shtml

On the Street

Bicycling

Level of Commitment	🐾 to 🐾🐾🐾
Training Level	🐾
Level of Physical Fitness	🐾🐾🐾
Time Investment	🐾 to 🐾🐾
Estimate of Expenses	$$ to $$$$ (Depending on the cost of your bike.)
Common Breed Participants	All breeds and fit dogs of any type.

A BRIEF DESCRIPTION

If your dog is very active and it seems you can never wear him out, then bicycling may be right for you. It is also a great choice for those people who are unable to exert the same energy that their dogs can.

Imagine casually riding your bicycle through your neighborhood as your dog, attached to your bike, trots alongside you. He will get the benefit of a thorough workout while you get to experience a leisurely ride. I say leisurely because you will have to be careful not to make him run too hard or too fast for too long.

OVERVIEW OF NECESSARY EQUIPMENT

You'll be more comfortable and have more fun with a good road bike, but unless you are investing in a bike you can also ride without your dog, you won't need anything too fancy.

You should also invest in a piece of equipment that attaches your dog to your bike. Stringing your dog along with a leash isn't safe. He could become tangled in the wheels, chain, or pedals. Contact the companies listed below and purchase the accessory that best fits your needs.

TRAINING SYNOPSIS

You may want to start training your dog with a buddy. While one of you rides a bike, the other can jog along with your dog at the side. This will get your dog accustomed to the sounds, movements, and presence of the bike without risk to either one of you. After your dog is used to this setup and appears to understand where he should stay to remain safe, then you are ready to attach him to your bike.

Keep a fast enough pace to maintain your dog's interest, but don't start speeding. Your dog is going to need time to adjust to this workout. As with other conditioning exercises, keep the F.I.T.T. principles in mind when designing a program of bicycling.

SPECIAL CONSIDERATIONS

If your dog is not well behaved, he could get you both hurt. Before deciding to roll along with your dog, make sure that he looks to you for direction and listens to you when you ask something of him.

The road may be hard on your dog's paws at first. Refer to the section on paw care and street sense in part I of this book.

This activity is open to any breed but is best for those dogs who are great endurance runners—long-legged, deep-chested individuals who have lots of energy and good health. It's an especially good way for sighthounds to get their exercise.

ADVICE FOR FIRST-TIMERS

Purchase a bike-mounted leash to take your dog bicycling. It may save you a lot of headaches and will keep you both safe.

Start out slowly and build up speed, duration, and frequency in small increments.

WHY YOU WILL ENJOY THIS ADVENTURE

This is a great way to exercise overly active dogs and those who are bred to run, run, run!

You don't have to work very hard to get your dog the exercise he deserves.

Dogs love to run, and this is a great adventure that allows your dog to run to his heart's content.

SOURCES FOR INFORMATION AND ASSISTANCE

Books

Kita, Joe, editor. *Bicycling Magazine's New Bike Owner's Guide*. Emmaus, Penn.: Rodale Press, 1990.

Periodicals

Bicycling Magazine
P.O. Box 7592
Red Oak, IA 51591-2592

Internet

Bicyclist
http://www.bicyclist.com/bicyclist.html

Equipment Suppliers

Alpine Outfitters
P.O. Box 245
Roy, WA 98580
253-843-2767

Black Ice
3620 Yancy Avenue
New Germany, MN 55367
320-485-4825

Dog Works
14297 Curvin Drive
Stewartstown, PA 17363-9432
800-787-2788
717-993-3698 fax
dogworks@cyberia.com
http://www.dogworks.com

K9-Cruiser
4640 DeSoto Street
San Diego, CA 92109
800-K9-Cruiser

Perry Greene
Route 1, 779 Atlantic Highway
Waldoboro, ME 04572
207-832-5227
207-832-6182 fax
PeryGreene@aol.com

Pet Supply Imports Inc.
P.O. Box 497
South Holland, IL 60473
708-596-1705
800-346-1369

Springer Bicycle Jogger
Springer USA Inc.
2995 Harbour Gates Drive, #49
Annapolis, MD 21401
800-835-DOGS

For bicycle equipment catalogs see the Mountain Biking quick
peek on page 315.

Cart Pulling/Drafting/Driving

Level of Commitment	🐾🐾🐾
Training Level	🐾🐾
Level of Physical Fitness	🐾🐾 to 🐾🐾🐾
Time Investment	🐾🐾
Estimate of Expenses	$$ to $$$$
Driving Carts (sulkies)	$1,250
Carts	$250 to 300
Common Breed Participants	All breeds and types of dogs.

A BRIEF DESCRIPTION

I grouped these activities together because they are so similar. Hitching your dog up to a cart or wagon is called drafting. If your dog is going to be pulling *you* around in the wagon or cart, this is called driving.

If you want to compete, you will have to turn to a breed organization for the rules and regulations. For example, the Bernese Mountain Dog Club of America, the Newfoundland Club of America, and the Saint Bernard Club each offer competitions. Some of these organizations will let other breeds participate, so if you are interested, contact them and ask for more information.

In a competition, you will need to prove your dog is under basic control with a series of exercises. These usually include heel work, sits, stays, and a recall exercise.

Your dog will be required to show his willingness to be harnessed and hitched to a wagon. He will be required to pull in different situations such as through and around obstacles or uphill and downhill, to change directions, and to ignore distractions. Your dog will be required to prove that he can carry weight. You must be able to load and unload the cart while your dog is attached.

You can also use your cart-trained dog in parades. Parades are stressful for some dogs. There is a lot of action all around and large parades especially require a lot from your dog both physically and mentally. If your dog can handle the extra requirements, parading is great fun and always a hit with the spectators.

A couple of helpful hints for parading will make your experience more enjoyable. Bring water for your dog as it often gets hot and you may be stuck in one place for quite a while. Bring your patience also. Most parades are pretty slow, casual affairs where no one is in much of a hurry. Wear comfortable shoes, make sure your dog is comfortable, bring a pooper scooper, and adopt a cute theme (possibly have a short routine ready for long stops).

OVERVIEW OF NECESSARY EQUIPMENT

You will need a cart or wagon. You can either buy one already manufactured or you can build your own. The quality varies from just good enough to high-tech. The one you select is up to you. If you are unsure about how your dog will handle a cart and whether you will enjoy this activity, then you may want to start out by making your own, purchasing a less expensive model, or trying to find a used one. If you want to make your own, contact the Newfoundland Club of America, which offers plans to do-it-yourselfers.

When choosing a cart or wagon, consider how heavy it is and whether or not your dog will be able to pull it. Also consider its transportability if you will be taking it to other places.

The driving cart, called a sulky, is more expensive than a simple wagon, but you get to go for a ride. If you have an extremely active dog who needs much exercise or if you have any physical limitations, this is a wonderful way for your dog to get his exercise. And it is great fun!

You will also need a harness. Many styles of harnesses suitable for carting await discerning harness buyers. The important criterion for the harness is that it should fit well so it does not cause abrasion or irritation to your dog. An ill-fitting harness will also distribute the weight of the cart badly, possibly causing injury to your dog or such discomfort that your dog will refuse to wear it.

TRAINING SYNOPSIS

Because you cannot know ahead of time whether your dog will like the harness and the act of pulling, you should start off slowly and let him get accustomed to the activity.

Introduce him to the harness step by step. First, show it to him and prove the harness is an innocent object. When he is used to it, you can have him wear it. He may be bothered by the new pressures he feels against his body. Encourage his calmness and acceptance with praise and treats.

Have your dog start pulling weight by tying a piece of wood to a 10- to 15-foot line tied to his harness. He should feel the weight, but he shouldn't strain at all to pull it around. Again, encourage his bravery and confidence and avoid coddling or babying him in any fashion.

Your dog will need to learn commands for left, right, slow down, speed up, and stop. If your canine companion is a shining example of obedience, he may have a little difficulty learning that it's okay to pull when you tell him to. He may also have difficulty working away from you since you will probably be behind him rather than at the heel position. As his confidence builds, he will understand that now is not the time to worry about the heel command.

Introduce him to the wagon apart from the harness. Pull the wagon around him to get him used to the sounds and movement. Run the wagon over different terrain so that your dog can hear the rattling, clanking, and bouncing noises it makes.

The first time you connect the wagon to the harness, your dog may take only a step or two, depending on how relaxed your dog is about the whole experience. Encouragement with praise and treats always helps.

Soon you will have your own drafting buddy to carry children, groceries, and all sorts of objects for you.

SPECIAL CONSIDERATIONS

Your dog will have to be tolerant of a wagon bouncing around behind him. This requires a steady temperament. Because he will be pulling the cart where there may be many distractions, he should also be stable, gentle, reliable, and tolerant.

Any dog can pull a cart for fun. Even small papillons can pull a tiny wagon.

Pulling carts has been part of the history of many breeds. The Rottweilers, Saint Bernards, Bernese mountain dogs, and Greater Swiss mountain dogs are examples.

ADVICE FOR FIRST-TIMERS

Your dog must be under control. He should know basic obedience and be responsive to your commands.

WHY YOU WILL ENJOY THIS ADVENTURE

Watching your dog doing something that he loves so much is always a rewarding experience. Dogs love to work, and this is a great way to have your dog work for you. It's fun for the whole family and can be as useful as it is enjoyable.

SOURCES FOR INFORMATION AND ASSISTANCE

Organizations

American Working Collie Association
c/o Linda C. Rorem
1548 Victoria Way
Pacifica, CA 94044

Bernese Mountain Dog Club of America
P.O. Box 956
Grantham, NH 03753-0956
603-795-2458
http://www.barney.org/webcover/cover.html

Newfoundland Club of America
5208 Olive Road
Raleigh, NC 27606

North American Working Bouvier Association
9101 Cresta Drive
Los Angeles, CA 90035

St. Bernard Club of America
7572 E 213 Street
Quenemo, KS 66528-8172
913-453-2363
913-453-2451 fax

Books

Powell, Consie. *Newfoundland Draft Work.*

Powell, Roger. *The Draft Equipment Guide.* Newfoundland Club of America Working Dog Committee.

Both of these books can be purchased from Dog Works (address below).

Videos

Dondino, Cheryl. *Carting.* Available from Harmony Enterprises, 20600 S.W. Johnson, Aloha, OR 97006, 503-591-9187.

Ostrander, Beth. *An Introduction to Canine Carting.* This video can be purchased from Dog Works (address below).

Internet

Carting
http://www.dog-play.com/
Carting
http://www.uwsp.edu/acad/psych/dog/work.htm

Equipment Suppliers

Alpine Outfitters
P.O. Box 245
Roy, WA 98580
253-843-2767

Black Ice
3620 Yancy Avenue
New Germany, MN 55367
320-485-4825

Dog Works
14297 Curvin Drive
Stewartstown, PA 17363-9432
800-787-2788
717-993-3698 fax
dogworks@cyberia.com
http://www.dogworks.com

Graham Carriage Works
4636 S.E. 30th
Portland, OR 97202
503-232-3745
http://www.pacifier.com/~carriage

K-9 Sulkies
P.O. Box 2746
Anaheim, CA 92814
714-621-7511
k-9sulkys@rott-n-chatter.com

Miniature Wagons
6 Charles Avenue
Westerly, RI 02891
Attn: Walter Neugent
401-596-7507
http://www.bond.net/~warrickw/minwagons/minwagons.html

New England Draft Adventures
456 Mt. Hermon Station Road
Northfield, MA 01360
413-498-4341

Nordkyn Outfitters
P.O. Box 1023
Graham, WA 98338-1023
253-847-4128
253-847-4108 fax
nordkyn@nordkyn.com
http://www.nordkyn.com

In-Line Skating

Level of Commitment	🐾🐾
Training Level	🐾🐾
Level of Physical Fitness	🐾🐾🐾
Time Investment	🐾 to 🐾🐾🐾
Estimate of Expenses	$$
Common Breed Participants	Breeds who enjoy pulling (see sled-dog racing, page 392, and weight pulling, page 411). Medium-sized, active, healthy dogs that love to pull make the best choice whether purebred or mixed breed.

A BRIEF DESCRIPTION

Are you a true adventure seeker? Does the thought of tearing down the street at breakneck speeds while you balance on eight little wheels thrill you? This is not an activity for the faint of heart. Your dog will probably love pulling you, and going slowly probably won't be part of his agenda, especially at first. If your dog has done many different types of activities, especially pulling activities, he will adapt quickly to this adventure. Remember, though, that not all dogs will pull. You may have worked so hard on achieving the perfect heel that your dog wouldn't dream of putting tension on the leash for all the doggie biscuits in the world. He can learn the difference—that the different equipment and commands mean two separate behaviors—but he may be a nervous wreck until he does.

OVERVIEW OF NECESSARY EQUIPMENT

You will need a pair of in-line skates. You may already have a dusty pair, but before you dig them out or go out and buy the cheapest pair you can find, remember this advice: Put comfort first. If your skates bind your feet, rub your toes so they blister, or make your instep ache from lack of support and poor fit, you won't want to use them. Depending on your feet, you may have to spend more than you planned on a pair of skates you can wear comfortably. Do it! You won't regret it for a minute and your feet will love you for it.

Always wear a helmet and crash gear. Knee pads, elbow pads, and wrist guards are a must for anyone who skates. This protection is especially important when you're being towed by 60 pounds of muscle pulling at the end of a line.

You will also need equipment for your dog. A simple collar and leash is not the best choice. A collar can choke your dog, so you need to purchase a harness—ideally an x-back harness (used for sledding and other pulling sports). An x-back harness is not too expensive, and it will fit your dog well without causing any sores or uneven pressures while he is pulling. A strong leash or line is then attached to the harness.

You can, if you are brave and know your dog well, use a skijoring belt. You wear this type of belt around your waist and attach the lead to the belt. This arrangement can prove dangerous if you don't have complete control of your dog.

TRAINING SYNOPSIS

The secret is to take the activity step by step. Even experienced skijor people are surprised at the speed that their dogs can pull them on skates. Have you run with your dog before? That experience will give you a clue as to how he may act in this activity. Does your dog listen to you well? You may want to teach him a "whoa" command before you get on your skates.

Don't attach your dog to yourself at first. Take him to an open area with no distractions. If he pulls you too fast or too hard, ask him to stop (whoa!). If he doesn't, then you can let go of the leash. You may want to attach a very long line to him so that you can catch him after you let him go, but you risk getting him or yourself tangled up in it. The best way to keep him safe if you must drop the leash is to make sure your dog responds reliably to a recall command.

Once you feel you have practiced enough times and your dog gets a sense of what you expect of him, you can cruise your neighborhood. Because your dog will always be more forceful at the beginning, pulling you faster and harder when he's "fresh," you should begin in an area with little pedestrian and automobile traffic.

SPECIAL CONSIDERATIONS

Skating with your dog can be a dangerous activity. Take it easy at first. If something unexpected happens, you could conceivably crash. Never become careless—pay attention and be alert.

Watch out for cars, bicycles, and other pedestrians.

ADVICE FOR FIRST-TIMERS

The most important piece of advice is *know how to skate first!* Practice skating before you even think about taking your dog along.

WHY YOU WILL ENJOY THIS ADVENTURE

This activity is a quick and interesting way to get around on your in-line skates. It's a great form of exercise for your dog that he will surely love. It is also a good way to keep him in condition for other pulling activities during the off-season.

SOURCES FOR INFORMATION AND ASSISTANCE

Organizations
International In-Line Skating Association
301-942-9770

Books
Feineman, Neil. *Wheel Excitement! The Official Rollerblade® Guide to In-Line Skating.* New York: Hearst Books, 1991.

Internet

In-Line Skating with Your Dog
http://www.dog-play.com/

Running

Level of Commitment	🐾🐾 to 🐾🐾🐾
Training Level	🐾
Level of Physical Fitness	🐾🐾🐾
Time Investment	🐾🐾 to 🐾🐾🐾
Estimate of Expenses	$ to $$
Common Breed Participants	Hunting breeds, sled dogs, sighthounds, and some working dogs. The most important considerations are your dog's temperament, structure, and health. Your dog must like the sport, and he needs to be trained and socialized. The most common participants are dogs from 30 to 75 pounds.

A BRIEF DESCRIPTION

Dogs are amazing runners. Some breeds and individuals are capable of covering more miles than you can imagine. A dog that runs 50 miles every day is not unheard of. Many dogs put in 35 to 40 miles a week.

You probably won't be asking this much from your dog, but having your companion join you for a run is a great way to spend time together. Once you have made running a habit, you will become as addicted to running as your dog did on the first day.

Running with your dog adds an extra measure of security to your workout. If you are a woman, this can be especially important. Although I often "check out" into my own little world when I run, I feel safe enough to do this only because I can tell by the way my dog behaves if someone else is on the road with me, if a car is coming, or if there is any other situation I should be aware of.

I don't like to run with other people because I don't want to concentrate on a conversation. When running with my dog, I can rattle off simple mantras of "good dog" and "you're running so well today." It is a way of telling myself I am doing a good job without feeling self-absorbed. In other words, it can be therapeutic to run with your dog.

OVERVIEW OF NECESSARY EQUIPMENT

You will need a collar for your dog. Once your dog learns not to pull on the leash, it will make no difference which kind of collar he wears. At first you may want a halter-style collar or a head collar so he doesn't choke himself.

Once you trust your dog not to pull you down the street the entire way, a hands-free leash is wonderful. The kind that looks like a thick bungee cord will give a little when you change directions. Your dog will feel a gentle tug rather than a harsh jerk when you make a turn.

Your dog may need a pair of booties if running on a rough trail or hot cement (see the first part of this book for a discussion on booties and paw care). You will need a good pair of running shoes. This is not the time to scrimp. Your shoes will have to be replaced every so often as they wear down.

TRAINING SYNOPSIS

Your dog should know commands such as heel (traditional left side), side (right side), stay (for crossing streets and approaching cross traffic), easy (don't pull on the leash), and leave it (ignore it).

Remember that if you have already been running regularly and you are adding your dog to your workouts, you must start at his level and work up.

SPECIAL CONSIDERATIONS

Some dogs are not good runners because of their structure or other physical limitations. Pay attention whenever your dog starts to drag behind you so that you can slow down and avoid working him beyond his personal limit.

ADVICE FOR FIRST-TIMERS

Have your dog checked by your veterinarian before you begin running with your dog.

It takes at least three weeks to make running a habit. People often give up on this form of exercise too soon. If you stick with it, you will come to enjoy the ease with which you can complete your desired mileage.

WHY YOU WILL ENJOY THIS ADVENTURE

Most runners run because of the freedom this activity offers. They like time alone and the escape from everyday life. It is also the best conditioning exercise you and your dog can engage in.

SOURCES FOR INFORMATION AND ASSISTANCE

Organizations

All American Trail Running Association
P.O. Box 9175
Colorado Springs, CO 80932
719-633-9740
719-633-3397 fax
TRLRUNNER@aol.com

Road Runners Club of America
1150 South Washington Street, Suite 250
Alexandria, VA 22314-4493
703-836-0558
office@rrca.org

Books

Gallup, Davia Anne. *Running with Man's Best Friend*. Loveland, Colo.: Alpine Publications, 1986.

Noakes, Timothy D. *Lore of Running.* Champaign, Ill.: Human Kinetics
Publishing, 1991.

Periodicals

Runner's World Magazine
P.O. Box 7307
Red Oak, IA 51591-0307
800-666-2828
runnerswdm@aol.com

Internet

Running
http://www.zebra.net/~distrunner

Walking

Level of Commitment	🐾
Training Level	🐾
Level of Physical Fitness	🐾
Time Investment	🐾 to 🐾🐾
Estimate of Expenses	$
Common Breed Participants	All breeds and types of dogs.

A BRIEF DESCRIPTION

What better way to enjoy the spring or early fall than taking your dog for a walk in your neighborhood? Whether you meet neighbors, stop for a visit, or just appreciate newly opened flowers in gardens or colorful leaves on the trees, walking is a good way to delight in the outdoors. You and your dog get exercise, and your dog gets a chance to explore an array of sights and smells. Getting out and about is good not only for your bodies but also for your minds. Walking is simultaneously meditative and energizing. It doesn't require any fancy equipment, and it can be done at any time and in any place.

Of course, there are times of the year that a walk isn't much fun. If walking is the only exercise your dog gets, you may want to stick to your exercise program despite bad weather. (Walking is often the only form of exercise that older, younger, injured, overweight, or disabled dogs can participate in.) If it isn't the only form of exercise your dog gets, however, you can wait and enjoy a walk with your dog only when you feel the urge or your dog needs sensory stimulation.

Your dog deserves an adventure in your neighborhood. The wonderful thing about a walk is that your dog *will* see it as an adventure each and every time. Walking is an easy gift to give your dog.

OVERVIEW OF NECESSARY EQUIPMENT

This adventure requires only the most basic equipment. You will need at least one collar and leash. (You must absolutely have a leash!) The collar type will depend on your dog, your trainer (if you have one), and your personal beliefs. Does your dog pull you so much that you change arms to keep both the same length? Then you should enroll your dog in an obedience class. You can, in the meantime, use a head collar. You will have much more control with one of these than with a collar that fits around your dog's neck. You can use a hands-free leash if your dog doesn't pull. A lot of walkers use retractable leashes. This handy invention allows your dog more freedom, if that's what you want. I suggest attaching the leash to your wrist (some brands have built-in attachment devices). If it is not attached, then the leash could retract quickly and strongly if you drop it and frighten your dog or even hit him.

See the section on booties in the first part of this book to determine whether or not you will need paw protection for your dog. You may need a doggie sweater in cold weather.

You will need a pair of walking shoes. If you are going to put in more than a few miles a week, then you should invest in a good pair of shoes specially designed for walking.

TRAINING SYNOPSIS

No formal training is needed unless your dog is a handful of energy, quite independent, or aggressive to dogs, people, or other animals. If the latter is the case with your dog, you should get help from a professional dog trainer before attempting to take your dog for a walk in your neighborhood. If you have problems with control, a basic obedience or companion training class would be a good idea. You can even read a book to get some basic guidelines if your dog's problems aren't too serious.

Your dog will need to understand that pulling on a leash is unacceptable. How much leeway you give him in this respect is up to you. He should also know how to sit and wait until you tell him it is okay to cross the street or continue on his way.

SPECIAL CONSIDERATIONS

When you are walking on the streets and sidewalks of your neighborhood, you must be respectful and follow the good-neighbor rules (see chapter 5 in the first part of this book). Set an example of responsible dog ownership. Pick up after your dog.

You should always be aware of other traffic, both on wheels and on foot. Watch for aggressive dogs—cross the street if you find yourself approaching a barking dog—and loose dogs. Both can be trouble.

If someone is obviously frightened by your dog, keep your dog close to you and under control; don't force your dog and the person to meet each other.

ADVICE FOR FIRST-TIMERS

Always take a pooper-scooper bag with you. You never know when you will need it.

Have control over your dog. A wild dog on a walk can get you into all sorts of mishaps.

WHY YOU WILL ENJOY THIS ADVENTURE

Taking your dog out and about is pure delight for him. For many people, that is reason enough to commit to a walking program.

The simplicity of walking and the physical and emotional benefits all add up to relaxed and healthy walkers.

SOURCES FOR INFORMATION AND ASSISTANCE

Periodicals
Walking
P.O. Box 5489
Harlan, IA 51593-2989

Internet

Ruth's Power Walking
http://members.aol.com/PowerWalkr/index.htm

Outdoor Adventures

Boating/White-Water Rafting

Level of Commitment	🐾 🐾
Training Level	🐾 🐾
Level of Physical Fitness	🐾 🐾
Time Investment	🐾 🐾 🐾
Estimate of Expenses	$$$ to $$$$$
Common Breed Participants	Those that excel in swimming (see page 319).

A BRIEF DESCRIPTION

This is a great example of including your dog in an activity that you already enjoy. If you spend your summers on the shore of a lake or river fishing, boating, skiing, or just romping in the water, bringing your dog along may seem like the natural next step. He can have fun in a boat as long as you take a few extra safety precautions listed below.

White-water rafting can also be fun for your dog as long as you keep him safe. He must be brave and stable (a dog running around while you are navigating white water can make for a dangerous situation) and a real adventurer. If your dog fits the bill and you are experienced in white-water rafting, then you and your four-legged friend will have a great adventure on the water.

OVERVIEW OF NECESSARY EQUIPMENT

Your dog must wear a life vest for these water activities, no matter how strong a swimmer he is. A life vest for you is a must also.

You may want to bring a towel, blanket, or other means of warming and drying off your dog for the trip home. If you expect to be boating at high speeds, then you may want to get some eye protection for your dog.

Although they may seem silly, a pair of sunglasses or goggles will protect his eyes from flying debris.

TRAINING SYNOPSIS

Get your dog accustomed to the water and swimming before you take him for rides in a boat or on a raft. See the swimming section below for more information.

You can teach your dog to grab onto a life preserver, either with his teeth or with his paws, so that you can throw one in and pull him out if he falls in the water.

SPECIAL CONSIDERATIONS

Going fast in a boat creates the same problem for your dog as riding in the back of a pickup truck or hanging his head out the window of a moving car—his face may be hit by airborne debris. Don't go too fast and put him at risk.

The footing will be slippery, so give your dog something stable to stand on. Don't attach him to the boat or raft with a leash. If you were to have an accident, he would be helpless. Have someone hold onto him instead.

If you are taking your dog white-water rafting, no matter how strong a swimmer he is, never exceed Class II rapids.

ADVICE FOR FIRST-TIMERS

Know what you are doing and build up your own experience before you take your dog along on one of these adventures.

Keep all safety considerations in mind.

Take it slow and easy until you find out for certain that your dog is comfortable and won't do anything to jeopardize you or your craft.

WHY YOU WILL ENJOY THIS ADVENTURE

You will be including your dog in an activity that you already enjoy.

Having your dog camp with you and spend the whole day by your side is rewarding.

SOURCES FOR INFORMATION AND ASSISTANCE

Equipment Suppliers

See the appendix for companies to contact to order a life vest for your dog.

For another water activity, see Water Rescue on page 407.

Hiking/Backpacking

Level of Commitment	🐾🐾🐾
Training Level	🐾
Level of Physical Fitness	🐾🐾🐾
Time Investment	🐾🐾🐾
Estimate of Expenses	$ to $$
Common Breed Participants	Working and hunting dogs as well as many mixed breeds.

A BRIEF DESCRIPTION

Beautiful scenery, fresh air, and time to reflect—what could be more awe-inspiring and refreshing in your busy world than this? Taking your dog with you, of course! Hiking and backpacking with your dog takes you out into nature and gives your dog's (and your own) mind and body healthy exercise.

Your dog will even enhance your experience if you are paying attention. He will smell, see, and hear things that are beyond your scope of ability. He can alert you to some of the wonders of the outdoors that you would probably miss without him. Whether you take him for easy nature walks that last an hour or two or more strenuous hikes that stretch on for a week, you will be glad you did not leave him at home.

You can even earn titles for your dog while you are spending this time with him. Some breed clubs, such as the Alaskan Malamute Club of America and the American Working Collie Association (AWCA) offer titling.

The AWCA offers two such titles to collies and other breeds. Your dog can earn a Back-Pack Dog (BPD) title on either natural terrain or city streets. The natural terrain option requires his finishing twenty miles that must be divided into two or more trips. The city terrain option requires twelve miles to be divided into four or more trips and must include one group walk (such as a community-sponsored event). Your time to accomplish this mileage is unlimited. You must have your dog examined by a veterinarian and obtain a dated letter stating your dog's good health before starting your program and then again yearly if you are still working on your mileage. Your mileage is reported on the honor system. You will need to keep all your maps, trail guides, and other proof of your route. This route will need to be highlighted on a map and then submitted, along with the vet's letter and a photo of your dog wearing his pack, to the AWCA.

AWCA also offers the Back-Pack Dog Excellent (BPDX) title. Your dog will have to earn both the BPD titles in order to earn this one. If the trail you choose is more strenuous and has more altitude gains, you can compensate for this extra challenge by subtracting one mile (from the total mileage required to earn your title) for every 1,000 feet in elevation gain.

For both titles, your dog must carry a minimum of 4 percent of his body weight and not more than 10 percent.

Of course, your trips hiking and backpacking with your dog don't have to focus primarily on earning titles. These activities are just plain fun! If you already backpack or hike on natural trails, taking your dog will add spice to your trips, and it will never be the same if you go alone.

See the outdoor section in the first part of this book for more information about the equipment you will need and basic information you should know about traveling outdoors with your dog.

OVERVIEW OF NECESSARY EQUIPMENT

You will need good shoes for you as well as a comfortable pack (either a backpack or fanny pack). Your dog will need a well-fitted backpack and possibly a pair of booties. A more extensive list of what you will need when hitting the trails is offered in the first part of this book.

TRAINING SYNOPSIS

Introducing your dog to a pack is explained in chapter 6. It is important to accustom your dog to hiking and backpacking in stages.

SPECIAL CONSIDERATIONS

Your dog must be able to handle this type of work. It seems logical to think that if your dog can handle walking around the neighborhood, he can handle a hike in the wilderness, but this is not true. Natural hiking trails demand much more strenuous physical exertion than streets require. Gains in elevation, uneven footing, and the twists and turns of a trail increase the difficulty.

Your first trip should be to an area and trail that you are already familiar with. You will know what to expect and can concentrate on enjoying your dog's company. You should be familiar with the length and difficulty of the trail and know if your dog can handle the requirements.

Dogs who don't do well in the wilderness are independent breeds and individuals or those who do not have the physical strength to walk and carry their own packs. Remember that little dogs will be putting in a lot more effort to go the same distance as you do.

ADVICE FOR FIRST-TIMERS

Start with an easy adventure. A short trip, close to home, on an easier trail will give you a good experience and you will be able to judge your dog's ability to handle more difficult hikes.

Be prepared. Bring plenty of water along with all the supplies you might possibly need. Even if you feel you're bringing too much at first, you will be prepared if something happens along the way. (See chapter 6 for more information.)

WHY YOU WILL ENJOY THIS ADVENTURE

Spending time outdoors with your dog is rewarding because you can experience his excitement as well as your own. You will appreciate his ability to use all his senses to explore an area.

SOURCES FOR INFORMATION AND ASSISTANCE

Organizations

Alaskan Malamute Club of America
8565 Hill Road
Pickerington, OH 43147-9661
614-837-7702

American Working Collie Association
c/o Linda C. Rorem
1548 Victoria Way
Pacifica, CA 94044

Books

LaBelle, Charlene. *A Guide to Backpacking with Your Dog.* Loveland, Colo.: Alpine Publications, 1993.

Lerner, Richard, D.V.M. *The Nuts 'n' Bolts Guide: Backpacking with Your Dog.* Birmingham, Ala.: Menasha Ridge Press, 1994.

Smith, Cheryl S. *On the Trail with Your Canine Companion: Getting the Most Out of Hiking and Camping with Your Dog.* New York: Howell Book House, 1996.

Internet

Hiking
http://www.uwsp.edu/acad/psych/dog/work.htm
Hiking
http://www.dog-play.com/

Equipment Suppliers

Alpine Outfitters
P.O. Box 245
Roy, WA 98580
253-843-2767

Black Ice
3620 Yancy Avenue
New Germany, MN 55367
320-485-4825

Dog Works
14297 Curvin Drive
Stewartstown, PA 17363-9432
800-787-2788
717-993-3698 fax
dogworks@cyberia.com
http://www.dogworks.com

Eagle Creek Travel Gear
1740 La Costa Meadows Drive
San Marcos, CA 92069
800-874-9925
619-471-7600
619-471-2536 fax
http://www.eaglecreek.com

Granite Gear
P.O. Box 278
Industrial Park
Two Harbors, MN 55616
218-834-6157
218-834-5545 fax

Mountain Smith Ltd.
Englewood Marketplace
209 West Hampden Avenue
Englewood, CO 80110-2401
800-426-4075

Nordkyn Outfitters
P.O. Box 1023
Graham, WA 98338-1023
253-847-4128
253-847-4108 fax
nordkyn@nordkyn.com
http://www.nordkyn.com

Perry Greene
Route 1, 779 Atlantic Highway
Waldoboro, ME 04572
207-832-5227
207-832-6182 fax
PeryGreene@aol.com

Ruffwear
P.O. Box 1363
Bend, OR 97709
541-388-1821

Sylmer Dogwear
22710 S.E. 23rd Place
Issaquah, WA 98029
206-557-8956

Wenaha Dog Packs
4518 Maltby Road
Bothell, WA 98012
206-488-2397
800-917-0707

Wolf Packs
755 Tyler Creek Road
Ashland, OR 97520-9408
541-482-7669

Horseback Riding

Level of Commitment	🐾 to 🐾🐾
Training Level	🐾🐾
Level of Physical Fitness	🐾🐾🐾
Time Investment	🐾🐾🐾
Estimate of Expenses	$ ($$$$$ if you include the cost of the horse.)
Common Breed Participants	Any dogs who have the energy to keep up with your horse and will stay close and be obedient. Dalmatians are the stars of this activity.

A BRIEF DESCRIPTION

Riding horseback is, of course, for you. Your dog gets the assignment of trotting along beside you and your horse, keeping you company, and enjoying the adventure.

Trail riding on horseback is a unique and wonderful experience, and those who have had the privilege know the incredible serenity and yet excitement that this brings. What could be more perfect than taking your dog along?

Some dog breeds have a history of joining humans and horses on trips through the countryside. Hunting hounds racing ahead of a horse and rider bring to mind a timeless image. Dalmatian fanciers even test dogs on their ability to run beside a horse and rider in events called Road Trials. These dogs must be able to maintain their position at the horse's hocks, keep up with the horse, and stay focused on the job at hand without wandering off or lagging behind. They are also tested on their ability to sit and stay while the handler goes off for a distance and leaves the dog.

Some groups hold long-distance races through the countryside with awards for the best-conditioned dog. A veterinarian is present to assess each dog's condition before, during, and after each race.

OVERVIEW OF NECESSARY EQUIPMENT

If you are considering this adventure, you probably already have a horse. But if not, I don't advocate renting an unknown horse. You need to know that your dog and horse will be tolerant and comfortable with each other on the trail.

You'll need to have a collar with identification for your dog to wear. If you are just beginning to train your dog, you may need a lightweight, long lead to offer you some control over your dog.

TRAINING SYNOPSIS

Start slowly. Introduce your dog and horse to each other. Let them spend plenty of time together at home forming a relationship.

The first stage in training your horse and dog to be trail buddies is to accustom them to the trail together. Have a friend bring your dog on a leash to hike along with you and your horse. Your friend can show your dog where he should be and how he should act. If this training doesn't go well, you will need to repeat it a few times. Dogs often fall right into the pace of the adventure and one session is enough.

The next stage is to take your dog along without having someone walk him. Attach a long, lightweight lead to him so you can hold onto him while on your horse. If your dog runs off, he may drag the lead behind him and get tangled and injured. Use a collar that will easily break if he were to get caught on something. The lead can also get tangled with the horse if you are not paying attention or something unexpected happens, so you need to keep a close eye on it.

The final stage is having your dog trot along at your horse's side. You may skip the previous stage and go right to this stage if your dog and horse are comfortable with each other and your dog is minding you consistently. Your dog has to remember his manners, and even when he graduates to this stage, you will still have to teach him a thing or two. This is why having a dog who is responsive and reliable is important in this venture. A dog who runs off constantly and won't come back when you call should probably not come along on this adventure.

SPECIAL CONSIDERATIONS

Your horse must know and tolerate your dog. A horse who shies from your dog all along the trail poses a danger to you. Your dog must be comfortable and relaxed around your horse as well. Not only must he be confident, but he must not chase or harass your horse in any way. Spend time with the two of them together before you head out on any trail.

If you are already involved in trail riding with your horse, you will be familiar with the trails in your area, but make sure that dogs are also allowed and that they can be off leash. Consider the safety of the trail, including the presence of predators and other dangers.

ADVICE FOR FIRST-TIMERS

Go with a buddy or in a group. This will keep you safer (you should never trail ride alone), and you can learn from the experience of your companions.

Trail ride without your dog so that you can become familiar with your horse's behavior on the trail. A dog who won't listen, runs in and out of your horse's legs, barks, or causes any commotion and a horse that is shy, stubborn, or unreliable on the trail is a dangerous combination.

WHY YOU WILL ENJOY THIS ADVENTURE

You get to experience nature with two of your best friends.

Both your horse and your dog will exercise their minds and bodies at the same time.

SOURCES FOR INFORMATION AND ASSISTANCE

Books

Bayley, Lesley, and Caroline Davis. *The Less-Than-Perfect Rider: Overcoming Common Riding Problems.* New York: Howell Book House, 1994.

Hatley, George. *Horse Camping.* Moscow, Idaho: The Appaloosa Museum, 1992.

Hill, Cherry. *Becoming an Effective Rider: Developing Your Mind and Body for Balance and Unity.* Pownal, Vt.: A Garden Way Publishing Book, 1991.

Periodicals

Chronicle of the Horse
P.O. Box 46
Middleburg, VA 22117

Equus
656 Quince Orchard Road
Gaithersburg, MD 44112

Horse & Rider
1060 Calle Cordillera, Suite 103
San Clemente, CA 92672

Practical Horseman
Gum Tree Corner
Unionville, PA 19375

Western Horseman
P.O. Box 7980
Colorado Springs, CO 80933

Internet

Equisearch
http://www.equisearch.com/
Equestrian Trails
http://www.eti.av.org/
Horse Lovers
http://www.javanet.com/~mermaid/horselover/zine.htm

Mountain Biking

Level of Commitment	🐾 to 🐾🐾🐾
Training Level	🐾🐾
Level of Physical Fitness	🐾🐾🐾🐾
Time Investment	🐾🐾🐾
Estimate of Expenses	$$ to $$$$ (Depending on which bike you choose.)
Common Breed Participants	Hunting dogs, herding dogs, mixed breeds, and terriers.

A BRIEF DESCRIPTION

Imagine what fun it would be to cruise down a rugged single track (a narrow trail that allows one bike at a time to pass through) over rocks, through creeks, and around fallen trees while having your trusty canine friend enthusiastically enjoying the adventure with you. This is one adventure that any dog will love!

It is difficult to traverse all but the most wide, level trails with your dog attached to you or your bicycle. Therefore, for this sport you must have a dog that you can trust when he is off leash.

Mountain biking is a challenging sport that usually includes a few falls, and nothing can make you feel better than having your best buddy lick your face after an embarrassing spill.

Your dog will tire quickly if he is in poor shape, and if you aren't attentive enough, he could push himself too hard. Before hitting the trail, make sure your dog is in good physical condition. To ride in varied terrain with a fit, energetic dog is pure pleasure. Climbing over rocks, jumping over fallen trees, and leaping through streams is doggie heaven.

OVERVIEW OF NECESSARY EQUIPMENT

Unlike bicycling on the street—where you can go much faster than your dog—when you go mountain biking on rough terrain, your dog has the advantage over you with his natural four-wheel drive. If you plan to mountain bike for very long, you'll want to purchase a technically advanced bike to keep up with your dog and be comfortable.

You will need a bell for your dog to wear around his neck to warn other trail users and animals of his presence as well as water bottle cages and bottles for you and your dog.

You will also need a quick-release collar for your dog in case his collar gets caught on something.

TRAINING SYNOPSIS

The first stage of training your dog in mountain biking is to train yourself. If you can, learn the basics from a friend who knows where and how to mountain bike. Once you feel comfortable on the trail, you can add your dog.

In the meanwhile, you can take your dog on the street, preferably attached to your bike (see the bicycling quick peek on page 278). This lesson in bike etiquette can be the beginning of your dog's education regarding the dangers of getting too near your tires and of cutting across your path. You should also teach him commands for right and left and for front and back and enforce your recall and down commands. The down command with a "stay" is useful when you must clear the trail for other users, especially horses.

The first time you take your dog on a full-fledged mountain biking adventure, choose a trail that you have explored before. The fewer unexpected conditions you have to worry about, the more you can concentrate on helping your dog. Once he is an old pro at this pastime you can both explore new trails together.

SPECIAL CONSIDERATIONS

You must have enough control over your dog's behavior that you can call him to your side when another trail user is passing and guarantee your and others' safety while using the trail. Sometimes, no matter how well behaved he is, your dog may give in to his instinct to chase something; but if it happens too often, you should consider leaving your dog behind. A loose dog is not safe to wildlife and other users of the area.

Mountain biking is generally not good for dogs who can't be trusted off leash in the wilderness. These include Nordic breeds, breeds that are closely related to wolves, sighthounds, and those individual dogs that are feisty and not trustworthy enough to stay with you.

ADVICE FOR FIRST-TIMERS

Your dog must know how to stay beside you yet out of the way of your tires.

Know the basics of mountain biking before you take your dog. It is difficult to teach your dog and keep track of him while he's learning if you are also a novice.

You may have to do some research to find a good trail. Begin by asking people at a local bicycle shop. You can also call the parks and recreation department. If you are fortunate enough to live in an area with many great trails, you may be able to buy a book describing the ones in the area. Find out how difficult the trails are, but most importantly, find out if dogs are allowed. The same type of investigation will help you find trails while vacationing.

WHY YOU WILL ENJOY THIS ADVENTURE

Mountain biking gives an energetic dog lots of exercise. You'll get a great workout yourself while having loads of fun.

SOURCES FOR INFORMATION AND ASSISTANCE

Books

Nealy, William. *Mountain Bike! A Manual of Beginning to Advanced Techniques*. Boulder, Colo.: VeloNews Books, 1992.

Periodicals

Mountain Bike Action
25233 Anza Drive
Valencia, CA 91355
805-295-1910
805-295-1278 fax

Internet

Mountain Bike Action
http://www.angelfire.com/de/mountainbike1
Mountain Bike Daily
http://www.mountainbike.com/
Mountain Biking Magazine
http://www.challengeweb.com/mtnbiking/
MTBinfo
http://www.mtbinfo.com/

Equipment Suppliers

Bike Nashbar
4111 Simon Road
Youngstown, OH 44512-1343
800-627-4227
http://www.nashbar.com/cat

Bike Pro
1599 Cleveland Avenue
Santa Rosa, CA 95401
800-245-3776
http://www.bikepro.com

Colorado Cyclist
3970 E. Bijou Street
Colorado Springs, CO 80909-9946
800-688-8600
http://www.colcyc.com

Swimming

Level of Commitment	🐾
Training Level	🐾
Level of Physical Fitness	🐾🐾
Time Investment	🐾 to 🐾🐾
Estimate of Expenses	$
Common Breed Participants	Natural swimmers, such as Labradors, retrievers, and Newfoundlands. Some dogs are not suited to swimming, such as bulldogs and others with short legs. Most dogs can be eased into the water. Their amount of enjoyment is based on their individual temperaments.

A BRIEF DESCRIPTION

Swimming is a non-weight-bearing activity. It strengthens the muscles and cardiovascular system of your dog without stressing bones and joints. It is great for dogs who have limiting conditions or who are extremely overweight. Dogs with dysplasia and arthritis especially benefit from this form of exercise.

However, swimming does not increase bone density—only weight-bearing activities can do that. It also doesn't burn as much fat or offer the weight resistance that other activities do. Swimming will help your dog's flexibility.

A swimming pool is by far the safest place to allow your dog to swim. You can walk around the edge of the pool and encourage your dog to get his exercise while you have a break. Natural sources, especially rivers, are more dangerous for your pooch. He can become tangled in floating debris, get swept away in a current, or get too tired to swim back to you.

OVERVIEW OF NECESSARY EQUIPMENT

When swimming in natural bodies of water, your dog should have a life jacket with a handle and a place to attach the leash, no matter how strong a swimmer he is.

Your dog should not swim with a regular collar on. The collar could become caught on an obstacle underwater and he could choke and drown. A halter collar will prevent him from choking himself if he becomes caught (although if he is caught underwater, he still risks drowning) and will allow you to lift him out of danger more easily if a mishap occurs.

A towel or blanket may be necessary to warm or dry off your dog for the trip home, especially on cooler days.

TRAINING SYNOPSIS

When training your dog to swim, think in terms of teaching your dog to enjoy the water. Even if he wades into the water only up to his knees, he is tolerating and possibly enjoying the water.

Get into the water yourself and coax your dog in by calling him. If your dog sees you having a good time, he will want to join you.

Be patient when training a dog to appreciate swimming. Begin in shallow, calm water. The first time, just get in the water and enjoy yourself. Don't even pay attention to your dog while you play around. This should encourage him to at least come close and investigate. You can encourage him farther into the water by throwing floating toys out a bit. Don't force your dog; let him proceed at his own pace.

If your dog will be swimming in a pool, you will have to teach him where the stairs are. Dogs must swim with their noses out of the water, so their eyes are tilted up and they can't see directly in front of them. Your dog will not be able to see the stairs while swimming. This is why you may witness your dog swimming frantically around the edge of the pool—he is looking for a place where he can put his feet down and get out. Place some kind of landmark near the stairs. A pole or sign of some sort that uses high-contrast colors (black and white are best) or an eye-catching decoration (such as a pinwheel) on the top of the pole will help your dog find a way out of your pool.

SPECIAL CONSIDERATIONS

If you have a pool in your own yard, you should keep a fence around it to protect your dog as you would protect small children. If your dog fell into the water when there was no one around, he could drown while trying to find his way out.

Depending on where you live, there could be danger lurking in natural bodies of water. Florida residents and visitors must be aware of alligators. Those in the South must watch for water moccasins.

If you take your dog swimming in the ocean, obey all hazard flags. If there are signs warning of rip currents, don't let your dog go in the water.

Be aware of water that is too cold. When a dog is wet and cold, he is more susceptible to hypothermia.

Finally, if your dog does a lot of swimming, make sure that his ears are free from hair. The drier and cleaner your dog's ears remain, the less chance of bacterial infections. Shave off excess hair around the ears and wipe them dry after swimming. If your dog has a chronic problem with ear infections, talk to your veterinarian about using an ear-drying solution after swimming.

ADVICE FOR FIRST-TIMERS

Gradually accustom your dog to swimming if he is not immediately thrilled with the idea.

The first few times you take your dog swimming, take him to a place where you have been and feel comfortable. Your being relaxed about the whole affair will help your dog relax also.

WHY YOU WILL ENJOY THIS ADVENTURE

Water-lovers enjoy bringing their pups with them during their favorite water-related activity.

Swimming is a great activity for those dogs who cannot perform weight-bearing exercises or who are healing from an injury.

Watching your water-loving pooch bouncing in the shallow water, splashing himself, and swimming with such confidence when he hits deep water is plain fun!

SOURCES FOR INFORMATION AND ASSISTANCE

Equipment Suppliers

See the appendix for companies to contact to mail-order a life vest for your dog.

Organized Sports

Agility

Level of Commitment	🐾 to 🐾🐾🐾🐾🐾
Training Level	🐾🐾🐾
Level of Physical Fitness	🐾🐾🐾🐾
Time Investment	🐾🐾🐾🐾
Estimate of Expenses	$$ to $$$$ (Depending on whether you purchase equipment.)
Common Breed Participants	All breeds and types of dogs. The stars of this sport are Border collies, Shetland sheepdogs, Australian shepherds, and mixed breeds.

A BRIEF DESCRIPTION

This is an activity that is enjoyed by both dogs and handlers. The sport is quickly growing in popularity as people experience the unadulterated thrill of running an agility course.

Agility combines color, speed, strength, and excitement: dogs run up and down A-frames as tall as the top of your head, soar over jumps, sprint through U-shaped tunnels, and fishtail through weave poles. The agility course is a big playground for your dog!

An agility course is patterned after a jumping course from the horse world. But because dogs are so agile and strong, many more interesting obstacles are used in proving a dog's talents.

Handlers are allowed in the ring with their dogs to direct the dogs over a predetermined course using verbal and body signals. In the top teams, each handler and dog pair has a relationship that is a marvel to witness. The two almost seem to read each other's minds, and some handlers can run their dogs through the course on subtle body language alone.

One dog at a time runs the course, attempting to finish in the shortest time with the fewest faults. Faults can include touching a jump, going off course, jumping off the side of an obstacle, or refusing an obstacle. Contact obstacles (dog walk, A-frame, and teeter) must be touched only in the designated contact area.

In the United States, four organizations govern the sport of agility. The USDAA (United States Dog Agility Association), NADAC (North American Agility Council), UKC (United Kennel Club), and AKC (American Kennel Club) all hold agility trials and give points and awards to the winning dogs. The NADAC concentrates on speed, the USDAA has the most challenging jumps, and the AKC and UKC use smaller obstacles and put less emphasis on speed. If you aren't sure which rules you would prefer to title under, train for the USDAA rules since they are the most stringent. If your dog isn't able to attain the level required of USDAA, train for the AKC (as long as he qualifies).

USDAA dogs can earn Agility Dog, Advanced Agility Dog, and Master Agility Dog titles. The AKC offers titles for Novice Agility Dog, Open Agility Dog, and Agility Dog Excellent. Write to the different organizations for their rules of competition and find out how your dog can earn his title. Specific games such as snookers, gambler's choice, team relay, and jumpers all have special titles. With games like those, you can tell that the emphasis in agility is on fun!

OVERVIEW OF NECESSARY EQUIPMENT

The amount of equipment you will need varies greatly in this activity. If you are a member of a club and use the club's equipment to train and practice, then you will need very little equipment. You will need a leash, a short tab (which is approximately four inches long and attached to your dog's collar for control if needed, but unlike a regular leash, won't get caught on any equipment), a quick-release collar, and treats.

One alternative to joining a club is making your own equipment out of objects in and around your home (for example, you can place a broomstick across two cement blocks) or using play equipment in local parks. This option can be quite easy and inexpensive and is limited only by your imagination (but remember to always keep safety in mind). You can also make your own regulation-style agility equipment.

If you aren't handy at building, you can purchase equipment already made. Although this is the most expensive of your choices, it is the most convenient. If your equipment is on hand, it is much simpler to step outside and train and so you may do it more often. Some of the equipment is quite heavy; you may need help setting it up and taking it down. Upkeep and storage may present problems.

Agility requires a lot of different equipment: A-frame; teeter; dog walk; tire jump; single, wing, long, and spread jumps; chute; pause table; tunnel; and weave poles. Everyone should have a set of weave poles at home. They are the most difficult obstacle to teach your dog to maneuver, and frequent, quick training sessions are the best way to make your dog comfortable and fast.

You will, of course, need all your normal show paraphernalia (chairs, snacks, and so on) and something to keep your dog safe and comfortable in between runs, such as a crate or exercise pen. You will need a leash and collar, but in the ring your dog must wear neither (everything is performed off leash).

TRAINING SYNOPSIS

Agility can be a physically demanding competitive sport. It is an activity that has a high potential for injury. For these reasons, you should consider joining a class to learn the basics if you plan to compete.

Agility is also a fun, positive sport and there is no place in the training for any reprimands or negative training methods. Even a "naw" should be avoided. Agility is a sport that emphasizes the handler's responsibility for showing the dog what is expected of him. If there is a mistake, it is the handler's fault.

Agility training allows a dog to be a dog. You have control, but it is a control that allows your dog to use his own brain. Your dog works in front of you, and you direct his actions by voice or signal controls without being too close to him. You are not allowed to touch your dog while he is running the course.

SPECIAL CONSIDERATIONS

If your dog has any physical limitations, you will have to take it easy and may not be able to use regulation equipment. Physical limitations include serious conditions such as arthritis, but agility can also be too strenuous if your dog is overweight, very large, or long-backed and short-legged.

If you are joining a club, remember that you have control over what your dog performs. If the trainers seem to be pushing your dog too fast, then you have the right to step in and request a slower approach.

ADVICE FOR FIRST-TIMERS

If you are considering competing, you should start in a class. If you are only going to play around and give your dog a fun activity, then you can read books and watch videos.

Beware! Agility is an addicting and time-consuming activity. The more serious you are about agility, the bigger the commitment you will need to make.

WHY YOU WILL ENJOY THIS ADVENTURE

The excitement and high energy of participating in agility is the sport's greatest reward.

Dogs absolutely love agility!

SOURCES FOR INFORMATION AND ASSISTANCE

Organizations

American Kennel Club
51 Madison Avenue
New York, NY 10010
919-233-9796
http://www.akc.org

Australian Shepherd Club of America
6091 East State Highway 21
Bryan, TX 77808-9652
409-778-1082
asca@myraid.net

National Committee for Dog Agility
c/o Bud Kramer
401 Bluemont Circle
Manhattan, KS 66052

North American Dog Agility Council
Box 277
St. Maries, ID 83861
208-689-3803

United Kennel Club
100 E. Kilgore Road
Kalamazoo, MI 49001-5598
616-343-9020

United States Dog Agility Association
P.O. Box 850955
Richardson, TX 78085-0955

Books

Clean Run Productions. *Introductory Agility Workbook.* Turners Falls, Mass.: Clean Run Productions, 1996. *Intermediate Agility Workbook* and *Advanced Agility Workbook* also available.

Clothier, Suzanne. *The Clothier Natural Jumping Method.* Stanton, N.J.: Flying Dog Press.

Daniels, Julie. *Enjoying Dog Agility from Backyard to Competition.* Wilsonville, Oreg.: Doral Publishing. 1991.

Hobday, Ruth. *Agility Is Fun!* Manchester, England: "Our Dogs" Publishing Co., 1989.

Simmons-Moake, Jane. *Agility Training: The Fun Sport for All Dogs.* New York: Howell Book House, 1991.

Tatsch, Kenneth A. *Construction Plans for Dog Agility Obstacles*. 1995. You can purchase this book through J and J Dog Supplies.

Zink, M. Christine, D.V.M., Ph.D., and Julie Daniels. *Jumping from A to Z: Teach Your Dog to Soar*. Luterville, Md.: Canine Sports Productions, 1996.

Periodicals

Agility Spotlight
SuperNova Productions
P.O. Box 2851
Santa Clara, CA 95055-2851

Clean Run
Clean Run Productions
35 Walnut Street
Turners Falls, MA 01376-2317
413-863-8303

The Contact Line
Cascade Publications
401 Bluebonnet Circle
Manhattan, KS 66502-4531

Videos

Simmons-Moake, Jane. *Competitive Agility Training*. Series: Tape One—*Agility Obstacle Training*; Tape Two—*Agility Sequence Training*; Tape Three—*Advanced Agility Skills Training*. Center for Studies in College, 1997.

Internet

Agility
http://www.uwsp.edu/acad/psych/dog/work.htm
Canine Activities: Agility
http://www.zmall.com/pet_talk/dog-faqs/activities/agility.html
Canis Major Agility Site
http://www.canismajor.com/dog/agility.html
Dog Agility
http://cust.iamerica.net/dsta1/DogAgility.html

The Dog Agility Page
http://www.dogpatch.org/agility.html
Dog Play
http://www.dog-play.com/
Flying Dog Press
http://www.flyingdogpress.com

Equipment Suppliers

Acme Machine Company
2901 Fremont Avenue South
Minneapolis, MN 55408
612-827-3571
800-332-2472

Action K9 Sports
27425 Cataluna Circle
Sun City, CA 92585
909-679-3699
909-679-9309 fax

EconoJumps
1517 N. Wilmont Road, #111
Tucson, AZ
520-751-1077

Flying Dog Press
P.O. Box 290
Stanton, NJ 08885
800-735-9364
908-689-9426
http://www.flyingdogpress.com

Flying Dog Press offers a helpful audio tape for agility participants (*Clear Mind, Clean Run*)

HOGA Agility
128 Chippewa Circle
Jackson, MS 32911
agilel@misnet.com

Max 200/Pipe Dreams
114 Beach Street Building 5
Rockaway, NJ 07866
800-446-2920
973-983-0450
973-983-1368 fax
http://www.max200.com

Woulf-Fab
N1750 Buchanan Road
Kaukauna, WI 54130
414-788-6706

Canine Freestyle

Level of Commitment	🐾🐾🐾
Training Level	🐾🐾🐾
Level of Physical Fitness	🐾🐾🐾 to 🐾🐾🐾🐾
Time Investment	🐾🐾 to 🐾🐾🐾
Estimate of Expenses	$
Common Breed Participants	All breeds and types of dogs.

A BRIEF DESCRIPTION

Canine freestyle is the perfect blend of showmanship, teamwork, dance, and obedience. This activity has great music, fun costumes (for the handlers only), and enthusiastic audiences—*and* you get to be with your dog!

The three- to five-minute routine danced by you and your dog is set to music of your choice. The stage (a marked-off area) is 40 by 80 feet, and as a team you will cover as much of this area as possible. Routines are judged on their creativity, artistic expression (choreography, musical interpretation, and movements to the music), and technical execution (your dog's quickness of response, difficulty of moves, and attitude).

Musical Canine Sports International (MCSI) has put into effect rules to assure the safety of the activity. Dogs are not allowed to carry props in their mouths. You cannot lift your dog higher than your shoulders. Risky moves are penalized, although safe routines with higher levels of difficulty are awarded more points.

You can compete in one of three different divisions: you and your dog in the individual competition, two dogs and two handlers in the brace division, or three or more handlers, each with a dog, in the team division. Three classes of performance are offered in each of the above divisions: on leash, off leash, and masters. To participate in the masters division, you and your dog must have received a score of 55 percent in an off-leash class.

MCSI offers three titles: MFD (Musical Freestyle Dog), MFX (Musical Freestyle Excellent), and MFM (Musical Freestyle Master).

This is a sport where your dog's personality can really shine through. Capitalize on his uniqueness by paying close attention to your dog's personal style and then basing your routine on it.

OVERVIEW OF NECESSARY EQUIPMENT

You will need to find music that you are willing to listen to again and again and again so you can keep the enthusiasm and showmanship high during practice and competition. You may have to get a music clearance release for the piece you choose. (Further information is given below.)

You will need an area to practice in. You will also need a costume for yourself that goes with the style and theme of your music.

A big smile and a happy dog top off a well-practiced routine and please audiences and judges alike.

TRAINING SYNOPSIS

For this activity, your dog will learn many interesting and original tricks and maneuvers. You can decide which ones you will use in your performance. Your timing will have to be perfected until you can easily move together and stay on the beat of the music. Other than the safety of your dog, your imagination is the only limiting factor.

Your obligation is to know enough about training your dog in a gentle and respectful manner to keep his interest keen and make this activity fun. You can search out someone who has competed in canine freestyle and ask about coaching, watch videos, attend workshops and seminars, and practice on your own, exploring your dog's capabilities.

If your dog is a quick learner and you are dedicated, you can create a routine in a few months with ease.

SPECIAL CONSIDERATIONS

Most handlers in this sport have a show-off side. You are an equal participant with your dog, performing for an audience and earning your half of the points.

Although some dance background would be helpful, it is definitely not mandatory. If you can keep a beat and have good showmanship, you will do fine.

Your dog should be an attentive student, a quick learner, and a ham.

It may be hard to find an event in your area. Musical canine freestyle is becoming more popular, but the competitions are still scarce. If you find a competition anywhere nearby, make it a priority to attend.

ADVICE FOR FIRST-TIMERS

Order some of the videotapes listed below and attend an actual event if you can before you begin working on your routine. The routines you will see vary according to the personalities of the dogs and their handlers, and no two teams are alike, but it is important to get a feel for what winning performances are like.

WHY YOU WILL ENJOY THIS ADVENTURE

This event is a definitive crowd pleaser! It is exciting for both the dogs and handlers to be the center of so much enthusiastic attention.

Although the concept of teamwork is mentioned again and again when discussing sports and activities for you and your dog, this is one adventure in which teamwork is truly taken to new heights.

SOURCES FOR INFORMATION AND ASSISTANCE

Organizations

American Society of Composers, Authors and Publishers (ASCAP)
1 Lincoln Plaza
New York, NY 10019
212-586-2000

You must contact ASCAP to see if the piece of music you plan to use is still collecting royalties. You can use music in the public domain or pay a "royalty direction" to the copyright owners of the music, or apply for an ASCAP or BMI performance license.

Musical Canine Sports International
c/o Sharon Tutt
16665 Parkview Place
Surrey, B.C.
Canada V4N 1Y8
604-581-3641

Pup-Peroni Canine Freestylers
Heinz Pet Products
Professional Services
One Riverfront Place
Newport, KY 41071
718-332-8336
718-646-2686
VENAD@AOL.COM

Videos

Cycle Canine Freestylers in Action. Freestyle Video, Ventre Advertising, Inc. P.O. Box 350122, Brooklyn, NY 11235, 718-332-8336 or 718-646-2686. Ventre Advertising offers several videos.

Internet

Canine Freestyle
http://www.uwsp.edu/acad/psych/dog/work.htm
Pup-Peroni Canine Freestyle
http://www.woofs.org

Conformation

Level of Commitment	🐾🐾🐾 to 🐾🐾🐾🐾🐾
Training Level	🐾
Level of Physical Fitness	🐾🐾
Time Investment	🐾🐾🐾
Estimate of Expenses	$$ to $$$$$ (Depending on what shows you participate in. Owners of Westminster Dog Show participants can often spend $10,000 to 20,000 a year showing their dogs.)
Common Breed Participants	Purebred dogs registered with one of the organizations that sanction dog shows.

A BRIEF DESCRIPTION

Conformation shows have often been compared to beauty pageants. The difference is that beauty in a dog show corresponds to the breed's standard. The standard describes the perfect dog of that breed—his height, weight, coat, and muscle, bone, and head structure, among many features. The dog that most closely fits this description will be declared the winner for the day. There really are no perfect dogs. Each dog will have his faults, but the judge strives to choose the dog who is the closest to perfect.

The class distinctions and titles can be quite confusing, especially for a beginner. All breeds are divided into seven groups for judging: herding dogs, working dogs, hounds, sporting dogs, toy dogs, non-sporting dogs, and terriers.

Males and females do not compete together. The males compete first.

Puppies are placed in classes divided by age groups. When it comes to adult dogs, however, the class divisions get more confusing. For example, the Novice class is for adult dogs who have not won three times in the Novice class or who have not won in any other class.

The other classes are Bred by Exhibitor (dogs who are owned and handled by the same person—you), American-bred (dogs whose parents were mated in the United States and who were born here), and Open (open to any dog, usually those with more experience). Some breeds are further broken down into classes by color, size, or coat.

The judge chooses a first, second, third, and fourth place dog in each class. The first place dogs from all the classes in each breed compete against each other for the title of Winners Dog. This routine is then repeated for the females, resulting in the Winners Bitch. The judge also chooses Reserve Winners (second place) in both the dog and bitch classes.

The Winners Dog and the Winners Bitch then receive points toward their championship titles. The points are awarded based on how many dogs are competing in the breed's male and female classes that day and where the show is being held. Dogs may be awarded from 1 to 5 points. The goal is to reach 15 points. The catch is that the 15 points must be from at least three wins under three different judges. Two of those wins must be majors (an awarding of 3 to 5 points).

Once your dog has earned his championship (Ch), then he can compete in the Best of Breed (BOB) class. The Winners Dog and the Winners Bitch may also participate in the BOB class on the day they win. Between the Winners Dog and Winners Bitch, one will be chosen as the Winners Dog. The BOB winner is chosen. If it is a dog (male), then the judge chooses a female to be Best of Opposite Sex.

The BOB dogs compete against all other BOBs in their group (herding, working, terrier, toy, nonsporting, sporting, or hounds). The dog who wins best of his group joins the other six dogs (who have won best in their respective groups) to compete for Best in Show (BIS). This is the dog who typifies his breed standard better than any other dog that day.

The UKC runs its shows by age categories: Puppies (six months to under one year), Junior (one year to under two years), Senior (two years to under three, and Veteran (three years and over). The dogs earn 10 points for a class win, 15 for best male or best female, and 10 for the best of the winners. UKC dogs need 100 points to win their championship titles. Once your dog becomes a champion, he will compete in the Champion of Champions class. If your dog wins in this class five times when the class has at least three dogs, he is given the title Grand Champion.

A specialty show is a show put on by one breed group solely for that breed. Groups often work together with one or two other breeds or hold a group specialty such as the Terrier Specialty.

The various organizations that sponsor and regulate dog shows have their own rules. If you are interested in a particular club's events, you should understand their specific rules and regulations.

Dogs who compete in conformation usually must not be spayed or neutered because the reason for choosing the best representatives of a breed is to find the best dogs for breeding. If you can't breed the dog, then there is no reason to compare him conformationally with other dogs.

Shows are held almost every weekend during peak show season (spring through fall, depending on where you live) all over the country. Once you start competing, you will receive information on upcoming shows. Refer to the section on finding shows and events in the first part of this book for help.

OVERVIEW OF NECESSARY EQUIPMENT

Depending on your breed, the grooming equipment alone can make for an interesting and long list of equipment. You should consult breed books, breeders, or groomers for advice.

You will need a show collar and leash (while in the ring) and treats. Your dog will also need a crate or exercise pen at the show while he waits his turn.

TRAINING SYNOPSIS

Here is what goes on in the ring. The handlers and dogs come into the ring and line up side by side. The judge gets an overall look at all the dogs. The judge then asks the handlers to "circle" their dogs and watches as they trot around the ring as a group. The judge then looks at each dog individually and makes a hands-on inspection. He or she will ask each handler to perform a gait pattern of choice, usually a trot at a diagonal, out and back. After the judge has finished with each dog, he or she will ask for the dogs to take one last jaunt around the ring. The dogs will then be placed first, second, third, and fourth.

This description gives you a general idea of what your dog should be able to do. What it doesn't describe is the *art* of conformation showing—showing your dog in the best possible manner to impress the judge. Winning dogs have sparkle. They exude confidence, even cockiness, and they have an aura about them. The handler must be able to control the dog, keep his pace, keep his attention on his performance, and make him stand still in the alert manner the judge expects from him.

You can learn this art through your own experience and through the experiences of others. Ask others for help or enroll in a class if you are serious about winning. Learning how to impress the judge can make the difference between placing and not placing.

SPECIAL CONSIDERATIONS

If your dog has any noticeable faults, then he probably won't do well in this activity. You can still show him just for fun and not worry about winning.

ADVICE FOR FIRST-TIMERS

Conformation showing looks easy, but there is an art to it. Attend matches first to get some experience for both you and your dog. Matches are fun get-togethers to give you experience. They do not offer points or titles.

Listen carefully to the judge and do exactly as he or she says.

It is best to learn conformation showing from an experienced handler. Ask your breeder to show you the details. There may be classes in your area; ask around at shows and matches.

WHY YOU WILL ENJOY THIS ADVENTURE

Showing off your dog is definitely enjoyable. It is also fun to see the same people from your area again and again at shows. Great friendships can develop and last for years or even a lifetime.

At dog shows, vendors often feature one-of-a-kind items at booths, and these are fun places to shop for dog stuff.

SOURCES FOR INFORMATION AND ASSISTANCE

Organizations

American Kennel Club
5580 Centerview Drive, Suite 200
Raleigh, NC 27606
919-233-9767

American Rare Breed Association
9921 Frank Tippett Road
Cheltenham, MD 20623
301-868-5718
arba@erols.com
http://www.arba.org

United Kennel Club
100 E. Kilgore Road
Kalamazoo, MI 49001-5598
616-343-9020

Books

Alston, George, and Connie Vanacore. *The Winning Edge: Show Ring Secrets*. New York: Howell Book House, 1992.

Buechting, LaVerne. *Beginning Conformation Training*. St. Louis: Kennelwood Village, 1989.

Coile, Caroline D. *Show Me! A Dog Show Primer*. Hauppauge, N.Y.: Barron's Educational Series, 1997.

Fraser, Jacqueline, and Amy Ammen. *Dual Ring Dog: Successful Training for Both Conformation & Obedience Competition.* New York: Howell Book House, 1991.

Hall, Lynn. *Dog Showing for Beginners.* New York: Howell Book House, 1994.

Periodicals

American Kennel Club Gazette
American Kennel Club
51 Madison Avenue
New York, NY 10010

Dog Fancy Magazine
P.O. Box 6050
Mission Viejo, CA 92690

Dog World Magazine
Maclean Hunter Publishing Corp.
300 W. Adams Street
Chicago, IL 60606

Videos

Brucker, Jeffrey. *Show Dogs.*

Kemp, Michael. *Handling I, Basic.* 1993.

Kemp, Michael. *Handling II, Advanced.* 1993.

The above videos can be purchased from Direct Book Services.

Internet

The Actual Dog Show
http://users.neca.com/szeder/dogshoh.html
American Kennel Club
http://www.akc.org
Showing in Conformation
http://www.k9web.com/dog-faq/activities/conformation.html
United Kennel Club
http://www.ukcdogs.com/

Disc Catching (Frisbee)

Level of Commitment	🐾🐾🐾
Training Level	🐾🐾 to 🐾🐾🐾
Level of Physical Fitness	🐾🐾🐾🐾
Time Investment	🐾🐾🐾
Estimate of Expenses	$
Common Breed Participants	Any dog who is physically fit, medium sized, reliable around other dogs and people. The stars are Border collies, whippets, and mixed breeds.

A BRIEF DESCRIPTION

This is one of the most loved activities in backyards and parks for both dogs and their owners. But you can take disc catching to a competitive level if you are so inclined and your dog is physically capable.

The Catch and Retrieve or Mini-Distance is a timed event where the dog and handler have one minute to complete as many throws and catches as possible. Only one disc can be used, and more points are awarded for throws and catches that are of longer distances.

Freestyle or Freeflight is the most exciting event for dog and handler, as well as spectators. The routine is usually set to music and is a sensational presentation of tricks. The imagination of the handler and the physical ability of the dog are the only limits in this event. Flips, jumps, twists, and more exciting tricks are performed to everyone's delight. Guidelines have been put into place limiting some tricks to protect the dogs, but the routines are still filled with impressive maneuvers. Each dog and handler team is judged in four categories, each worth 1 to 10 points. The categories are degree of difficulty, execution, leaping agility, and showmanship. The team can be awarded up to two bonus points for innovation or extra-spectacular moves.

OVERVIEW OF NECESSARY EQUIPMENT

You will need a disc that flies accurately yet is easy on your dog. When you begin training, you should have a disc that is soft enough to not harm your dog's mouth. As you become more involved in the sport and discover your own personal style and tricks, then you can get a disc that is geared to your type of performance. During the Friskies/ALPO-sponsored contest, you can use only the official Frisbee flying disc supplied to you.

To practice distance throwing, purchase a set of cones to mark various measurements. To measure the distances accurately, you will need a crank-type measuring tape that extends 30 yards. You can find one of these at a hardware store.

Later you may need protection on various parts of your body as your dog leaps off of you to perform some of his tricks. Neoprene body wear is often used to protect abused areas.

TRAINING SYNOPSIS

As with so many of the activities mentioned in this book, basic obedience is the cornerstone of a great Frisbee dog. The specific training involved in teaching a dog to catch a disc are done step by step.

First, get your dog to chase the disc by rolling it on the ground. In the beginning, don't worry if he doesn't bring it back to you. After he chases the disc on the ground, you can try some short, gentle passes through the air. Don't expect your dog to catch the disc at first. If he does catch one of these gentle throws, then make a celebration out of the event. He will quickly realize that the goal is to catch the disc. As your dog demonstrates more confidence, you can increase his skills by tossing the disc farther, higher, and at different angles.

Some dogs are naturals, and you don't have to teach them much. If this is the case with your dog, make sure not to ask more of him than he is physically ready to give.

SPECIAL CONSIDERATIONS

Some people cite the dangers of disc catching, and it is true that there are some inherent risks associated with this sport. After a catch, a dog will often land only on his hind legs, overstressing his knees (which aren't meant to be used in this way) and his spine. The dogs are often twisted and unbalanced, which means a risk of immediate or long-term injury. Have your dog checked by your veterinarian before participating in this sport. Your dog should be lean, not too large, and physically fit to reduce the possibility of problems. Teaching your dog to land on all four legs at the same time will save him from experiencing too much concussion on his rear legs.

As these events become more competitive, the tricks get trickier. The handler must possess many athletic skills. You will have to be in shape as well as your dog.

Practicing this sport (because you will need the large space of a park or field) will attract spectators. Can you handle the spotlight?

ADVICE FOR FIRST-TIMERS

Spend time watching competitions. You will learn a lot and understand what some of the tricks are.

Try to find someone who participates to show you the basics.

Don't get discouraged if your dog can't leap like the pros right away, and don't attempt to push him too far, too fast. Remember the potential for injury, and get your dog's body and mind into disc-catching shape slowly.

WHY YOU WILL ENJOY THIS ADVENTURE

Who wouldn't want to watch his or her dog gleefully and intensely fetching a flying disc for hours upon hours during all that training time? How could a dog be any happier?

SOURCES FOR INFORMATION AND ASSISTANCE

Organizations

Friskies/ALPO Canine Frisbee Disc Championships
4060-D Peachtree Road, Suite 326
Atlanta, GA 30319
800-786-9240

National Capital Air Canines
William Linne, Director
2830 Meadow Lane
Falls Church, VA 22042
703-532-0709
ncac@discdog.com

Books

Ashley Whippet® Catch a Flying Disc Dog Training System®. Send a self-addressed, stamped envelope to: Friskies Training Manual, P.O. Box 2092, Young America, MN. 55553-2902 for this free booklet.

Bloeme, Peter. *Frisbee Dog: How to Raise, Train and Compete.* Atlanta, Ga.: PRB & Associates, 1994.

Pryor, Karen. *How to Teach Your Dog to Play Frisbee.* New York: Simon & Schuster, 1985.

Videos

Bloeme, Peter. *Peter Bloeme's Frisbee Dogs: Training Video.* Skyhoundz, 1994.

Bloeme, Peter. *Peter Bloeme's Frisbee Dogs: Throwing Video.* Skyhoundz, 1996.

Internet

Disc Catching
http://www.uwsp.edu/acad/psych/dog/work.htm
DogDisc
http://www.DogDisc.com/
Freestyle Frisbee® Page
http://www.frisbee.com/
Frisbee Dog FAQ
http://www.discdog.com//FAQ.htm
Mary Jo's Frisbee Dog Page
http://dogpatch.org/frisbee.html
Skyhoundz™
http://www.skyhoundz.com

Earthdog Trials

Level of Commitment	🐾 🐾
Training Level	🐾
Level of Physical Fitness	🐾 🐾
Time Investment	🐾
Estimate of Expenses	$
Common Breed Participants	The American Working Terrier Association (AWTA) recognizes these breeds: Australian terriers, Bedlington terriers, Border terriers, cairn terriers, dachshunds, Dandie Dinmont terriers, smooth and wire fox terriers, Lakeland terriers, Norwich terriers, Norfolk terriers, Scottish terriers, Sealyham terriers, Jack Russell terriers, Patterdale terriers, and Jadgeterriers.

AKC recognizes most of the above plus Manchester terriers, miniature bull terriers, and miniature schnauzers. It excludes Jack Russell terriers, Patterdale terriers, and Jadgeterriers.

A BRIEF DESCRIPTION

Earthdog trials are simulated hunting events. Dachshunds and small terriers were bred to catch vermin such as rats. The dogs often followed the vermin into a tunnel in the ground and cornered them. The earthdog trials reenact this with manmade tunnels of a predetermined length and shape that your feisty terrier must make his way through.

Wooden liners are inserted into the tunnels, and the path is scented with rat scent. A live rat is then placed in a cage at the end of a tunnel. The dogs cannot actually touch the rat, but they must "work" (bark at) the rat until they are removed from the tunnel. The people who work in earthdog trials claim that the rat is not bothered at all by the dog and remains calm. Some people (usually outsiders) do not believe this, and there has been some controversy regarding the use of live rats.

Two main organizations now hold earthdog trials. One is the AWTA and the other is the AKC. Each differs in its rules and titling.

The AWTA uses a 9-by-9-inch tunnel. The Novice Class uses a 9-foot-long tunnel with a 90-degree (right-angle) turn. The dog is released 10 feet away from the entrance and the handler can issue one command. The dog has 1 minute to enter the tunnel find the quarry (rat) and work it for 30 seconds. He either passes or fails. If he passes, he moves on to the Certificate of Gameness (CG).

To earn a CG title, your dog must enter the tunnel and travel 30 feet to reach the quarry within 30 seconds. This is worth 50 percent of his score. He must then work the quarry for one continuous minute (another 50 percent). If he passes both these tests, he earns his CG.

The Working Certificate (WC) is awarded to a terrier or dachshund who follows a woodchuck, fox, raccoon, or badger. This is not a set-up event; it is worked in natural earth.

The Hunting Certificate (HC) is awarded to a dog who actually hunts rabbits, squirrels, opossums, rats, raccoons, or muskrats. The quarry must be shot by the handler or the dog must kill it. The dog must hunt an entire season before being given an HC title.

AKC offers three titles for your dog to earn as well as a beginning class called an introduction to quarry. The introduction to quarry event does not offer a title. The tunnel is 10 feet long with one 90-degree turn. The starting point is 10 feet from the entrance. The dog has 2 minutes to reach the quarry and must work it for 30 seconds.

The Junior Earthdog (JE) class tunnel is 30 feet long with three 90-degree turns. No commands are allowed. Your dog has 30 seconds to reach the quarry and must work it continuously for 1 minute. Your dog must qualify at two tests with two different judges to earn a JE title.

The Senior Earthdog (SE) class has the starting point set at 20 feet; the tunnel is 30 feet long and has three 90-degree turns, a false exit, and a false den. Your dog must reach the quarry within 90 seconds and work it for the same amount of time. The quarry is then removed, the handler calls the dog, and he must return in 90 seconds. Your dog must be successful in three tests with two different judges to obtain the title.

The tunnel layout for the Master Earthdog (ME) class is basically the same as for the Senior Earthdog class but includes many additional difficulties. The entrance is not visible but is scented. There is a false entrance that is visible. The tunnel is constricted to 6 inches at one point, and a pipe forms an obstruction at another point. Dogs are worked in pairs, which are selected at random. Dogs are released 100 feet from the entrance and must enter the tunnel within 1 minute. The working dog of the pair (the one that reaches the tunnel first) has 90 seconds to find the quarry and must work it for the same length of time. The judge will distract the dog working the quarry. Your dog must pass the test at least four times under two different judges.

OVERVIEW OF NECESSARY EQUIPMENT

You must supply your own basic equipment (leash and collar), but it would be difficult to purchase or make your own earthdog trial equipment. (You would have to dig up a substantial part of your yard.)

TRAINING SYNOPSIS

Because of the logistical difficulties of producing your own tunnel and quarry situation, training is basically built on experience. That is one reason why the introduction to quarry class is offered. Even though the "hunt" should be instinctive, some dogs can take a year or more to understand what is expected of them. The time your dog takes to learn will depend on how much experience he gets, where you live, and how much time you are willing to invest.

SPECIAL CONSIDERATIONS

Some people are sensitive about the use of live animals as quarry. Consider your own views.

ADVICE FOR FIRST-TIMERS

Be patient while your dog is learning. Give him time to figure out what to do.

WHY YOU WILL ENJOY THIS ADVENTURE

You will love watching the excitement of your dog as he performs the task he was bred for.

SOURCES FOR INFORMATION AND ASSISTANCE

Organizations

American Kennel Club
51 Madison Avenue
New York NY 10010
212-696-8200

American Working Terrier Association
503 NC 55 West
Mt. Olive, NC 28465
Attn: Patricia Adams Lent
919-658-0929

Field Rep for AKC
Gordon Heldebrant
2406 Watson Street
Sacramento, CA 95864
916-485-5950

Books

Migliorini, Mario. *Dig In! Earthdog Training Made Easy*. New York: Howell Book House, 1997.

Internet

AKC Earthdog Regulations
http://www.akc.org/earthdr.html
Dachshund Field Trials
http://www1.mhv.net/~dca/Field/fieldtrials.html
The Earthdog and Squirrel Dog Hunting Homepage
http://www.k9web.com/dog-faqs/activities/edsdhp.html
Earthdogs
http://www.k9web.com/dog-faqs/activities/earthdogs.html

Flyball

Level of Commitment	🐾🐾🐾
Training Level	🐾🐾
Level of Physical Fitness	🐾🐾🐾🐾
Time Investment	🐾🐾🐾
Estimate of Expenses	$$
Common Breed Participants	Any dog who is highly energetic, enthusiastic about retrieving, focused, dog friendly, and physically healthy.

A BRIEF DESCRIPTION

A dog bursts from his handler's grip and soars over jumps at an all-out sprint. Four jumps and he's at the flyball box. With a pounce on the box, a tennis ball is practically stuffed into the dog's mouth. A quick turn and he is back again through the jumps. The next of the four dogs on a team scrambles from his handler and is off.

Flyball is a relay race with four dogs per team. Each team can have two alternates in case one dog needs a rest. A lane is provided for each team, and lanes can be as close as 10 feet apart. Four jumps are placed in each lane. The jumps are 4 inches taller than the shortest dog's shoulder height with the jumps set at a minimum of 8 inches and a maximum of 16 inches. This makes having a short dog on your team advantageous. The jumps are placed at 10-foot intervals. The team that finishes the race the quickest wins.

Each dog needs to have his own handler, and an additional person places the balls in the flyball box. If you participate in this sport, you will see how difficult it is to hold your dog back at the gate. This is a very exciting sport for dogs.

The North American Flyball Association (NAFA) offers titles to competing dogs: Flyball Dog (FD), Flyball Dog Excellent (FDX), and Flyball Dog Champion (FDCh). The titles are earned on the basis of points. All the dogs on a team get the same number of points. To earn an FD title, your dog needs 20 points. FDX dogs need 100 points. To earn an FDCh title, your dog must earn 500 points. The other titles that NAFA offers are Flyball Master (5,000 points), Flyball Master Excellent (10,000 points), and Flyball Master Champion (15,000 points). Extreme athletes can also earn the Onyx Award (20,000 points) and the Flyball Grand Champion (30,000 points).

The points are awarded according to the speed of the dogs. If the team finishes in less than 32 seconds, each dog on the team is awarded 1 point. For less than 28 seconds, the dogs each earn 5 points. If the team finishes in less than 24 seconds, each dog earns 25 points.

OVERVIEW OF NECESSARY EQUIPMENT

A flyball box is easy to build. Only a few criteria must be met. The box cannot be wider than three feet and must shoot the tennis ball at an arc with a height of two feet. A pedal of some sort that the dog can push with his front paws is all that is needed.

TRAINING SYNOPSIS

Start with basic obedience. Your dog will need a reliable recall off leash because he will be working at a distance from you. Look for a flyball group in your area to learn the intricacies of training your flyball hopeful. If you can't find anyone who trains flyball dogs, find a book or video to help you.

Even though this sport looks less complicated than other sports, it involves many small steps that only look simple when done expertly by an experienced dog. Don't expect too much too soon. One step builds on another, so be patient. Your dog will absolutely love this activity if you keep it fun.

SPECIAL CONSIDERATIONS

You must find at least three other dog-handler teams in order to put a relay team together for competition.

An aggressive dog cannot participate in this sport. There are too many dogs running off leash at once.

ADVICE FOR FIRST-TIMERS

Find as many people as you can to train and play with so you can figure out which four dogs make the best team together. A large group will also give your dog more practice participating around many dogs. You'll both be more prepared for competition if you can invest in this preparatory time.

WHY YOU WILL ENJOY THIS ADVENTURE

This sport is absolute, pure excitement for your dog and the spectators!

SOURCES FOR INFORMATION AND ASSISTANCE

Organizations

North American Flyball Association
P.O. Box 8
Mt. Hope, Ontario LOR 11W0
Canada

Books

Parkin, Jacqueline. *Flyball Training . . . Start to Finish.* You can purchase this book from Direct Book Services as well as other catalogs.

Payne, Joan. *Flying High: The Complete Book of Flyball.* You can purchase this book from Direct Book Services as well as other catalogs.

Periodicals

The Finish Line
1002 E. Samuel Avenue
Peoria Heights, IL 61614
Attn: Melanie McAvoy
309-682-7617
mel.davidson@worldnet.att.net

Internet

Flyball
http://www.uwsp.edu/acad/psych/dog/work.htm
Flyball Home Page
http://muskie.fishnet.com/~flyball

Equipment Suppliers

Al Champlain
4204 Goldenrod Lane
Plymouth, MN 55441
612-559-0880
sprig@worldnet.att.net or Ian Hogg at ijh@ces.com

Burnett Designs
206-644-1288

Derrel West
9715 Orangevale Drive
Spring, TX 77379
713-376-9061

Dog Works
14297 Curvin Drive
Stewartstown, PA 17363-9432
800-787-2788
717-993-3698 fax
dogworks@cyberia.com
http://www.dogworks.com

J and J Dog Supplies
P.O. Box 1517
Galesburg, IL 61402-1517
800-642-2050
http://www.jandjdog.com

Jim Michel
1714 Edgement
Maplewood, MN 55117
612-774-9682

Max 200
114 Beach Street
Rockaway, NJ 07866
800-446-2920

Mike Smith
12302 Knigge Road
Cypress, TX 77429
713-469-0105

Herding

Level of Commitment	🐾🐾🐾 to 🐾🐾🐾🐾
Training Level	🐾🐾🐾
Level of Physical Fitness	🐾🐾🐾
Time Investment	🐾🐾🐾 to 🐾🐾🐾🐾
Estimate of Expenses	$$
Common Breed Participants	Herding breeds such as the Border collie and Australian shepherd. Individuals of any breed or mixed breed can learn to herd, and most herding trainers will accept any breed.

A BRIEF DESCRIPTION

While watching the Westminster Dog Show on television, you may have noticed that the herding group is a diverse group of dogs.

Herding involves several different skills (boundary and fetching/gathering, for instance), and each breed has developed its own specialized style. Some dogs use their eyes to stare down the sheep, intimidating them into cooperation. Border collies are considered a strong-eyed breed. Old English sheepdogs do not use their eyes in the same manner and so are considered a soft-eyed breed. The Bouvier des Flandres and Rottweiler are called drovers; they butt up against the animals to herd them. Some dogs, such as corgis, nip the heels of the stock and bark to get them moving.

What are often called the British herding dogs (for example, collies, Old English sheepdogs, Shetland sheepdogs, and Border collies) had to work quite differently than the continental breeds (for example, German shepherds, Bouviers, belgian Sheepdogs, and Rottweilers). Britain had shy sheep that only rarely had to be brought in for shearing or other care. The British-style dogs had to go wide around the group so as not to startle the sheep and then "fetch" or "gather" them. The dogs did not need to protect the sheep, just bring them in. The continental dogs, on the other hand, would patrol the "boundary" of the fields to protect the sheep from predators (human and animal) and keep them in the boundary. The sheep were much more tame than in Britain. They were herded into a barn at night and to the fields during the day. The dogs could be more assertive in their style and often needed to be to get their job done.

The ASCA (Australian Shepherd Club of America) offers the following Stockdog titles: Started Trial Dog (STD), Open Trial Dog (OTD), Advanced Trial Dog (ATD), Post Advanced Trial Dog (PATD), Ranch Dog (RD), Ranch Trial Dog (RTD), and Working Trial Champion (WTCh). For each title, a dog must work three classes of stock (ducks, sheep, and cattle).

Started dogs may have no experience but must be under the handlers' control and yet have control of the stock at all times. Open dogs must know more commands, such as right, left, walk on, and stop. They should be able to work the stock at a farther distance from their handlers. Advanced dogs should be confident, able to work at any distance, able to make decisions on their own for the good of the stock, and responsive to the handler. Post Advanced dogs should be able to work at any distance without the benefit of a fenced area and should inflict little stress on stock of any type or size.

There are also novice classes that concentrate on the handler; no matter how experienced or inexperienced the dog, the judges watch to see how well the handler controls his or her dog. Junior classes judge handlers up to 17 years old on their handling ability.

OVERVIEW OF NECESSARY EQUIPMENT

You will need something to herd and a place to herd in. You're not a cattle rancher? There are no herds of sheep around? That's okay. Most herding trainers have all the necessary "gear," and you may not even have to travel to the country. It's possible to find herding trainers in some cities if you search thoroughly enough.

If you live in the country and can take care of some stock, you may eventually want to get your own little herd. But wait until you know that you are serious about herding.

TRAINING SYNOPSIS

Some dogs are natural herders and the only thing that you have to do is direct their energy. Others take a while longer to learn some of the basics.

If you have no experience training herding dogs, then you will need to find a trainer who will teach you. I also suggest attending clinics that are routinely held for herding dog training.

You will start off with ducks or geese and a small pen. You will be directing your dog while he does the work. Here are some of the directions you and your dog will learn:

- Away to me—run counterclockwise behind the herd and drive them to the handler

- Drive—move a group away from the handler to a predetermined area

- Fetch—bring the herd in a direct line to the handler, sometimes over hurdles

- Go bye—run clockwise behind the herd and drive them to the handler

- Outrun—run wide to gather the herd

- Penning—drive the animals into a pen through an open gate

- Shed—separate a particular animal from the herd

- That will do—stop the herding

- Wearing—use a weaving motion to keep the herd together

SPECIAL CONSIDERATIONS

If you become addicted, you'll be looking for a home in the country in no time.

If you want to do this only for fun, go ahead! Don't be intimidated by all those high-powered Border collies and Australian shepherds.

ADVICE FOR FIRST-TIMERS

Don't be frustrated if your dog is not a natural. You can still teach him what he needs to know. If your dog is a natural and you are not experienced, you'll have to work hard to learn the skills so you can catch up to him (maybe!).

WHY YOU WILL ENJOY THIS ADVENTURE

True teamwork is needed for this activity. You will enjoy the experience of seeing your dog make confident decisions on his own yet rely on you for guidance.

SOURCES FOR INFORMATION AND ASSISTANCE

Organizations

American Border Collie Association
Route 4, Box 255
Perkinston, MS 39573
Attn: Patty A. Rogers, Secretary-Treasurer

American Herding Breed Association
1548 Victoria Way
Pacifica, CA 94044
650-355-9563
Sheltyherd@aol.com

American Working Collie Association
c/o Linda C. Rorem
1548 Victoria Way
Pacifica, CA 94044

Australian Shepherd Club of America
6091 E. State Highway 21
Bryan, TX 77808-9652
409-778-1082
asca@myriad.net

Border Collie Club of America
c/o Ms. Janet E. Larson, Secretary
6 Pinecrest Lane
Durham, NH 03824

Livestock Guarding Dog Association
Hampshire College
Amherst, MA 01002

North American Sheep Dog Society
c/o Rossine Kirsh
Route 3
McLeansboro, IL 92859

U.S. Border Collie Club
Sunnybrook Farm, Rt. 1 Box 23
White Post, VA 22663
Attn: Ethel B. Conrad, President

U.S. Border Collie Handler's Association
2915 Anderson Lane
Crawford, TX 76638
Attn: Rancis Raley

Working Kelpies Inc.
4047 Sheridan S
Minneapolis, MN 55410

Books

Holland, Vergil S. *Herding Dogs—Progressive Training*. New York: Howell Book House, 1994.

Holmes, John. *The Farmer's Dog*. London: Popular Dogs Publishing Co. Ltd. Available through Jeffers pet supply catalog.

Lithgow, Scott. *Training and Working Dogs for Quiet, Confident Control of Stock*. Manchester, N.H.: University of Queensland Press, 1991.

Taggart, Mari. *Sheepdog Training—An All Breed Approach*. Loveland, Colo.: Alpine Publications, 1991.

Templeton, John, with Matt Mundell. *Working Sheepdogs Management and Training*. New York: Howell Book House.

Videos

Lithgow, Scott. *How to Get the Most from Your Working Dog*. 1991. This video can be purchased through Direct Book Service.

Winn, Steve. *Stock Dog Training*. Barker Photography & Video. 3711 E. 29th Street, Bryan, TX 77802, 800-635-6144.

Periodicals

The Ranch Dog Trainer
P.O. Box 599
Ellendale, TN 38029-0599

Sheep! Magazine
Route 1
Helenville, WI 53137

The Shepherd's Dogge
The Quarterly Journal of the Border Collie
Box 843
Ithaca, NY 14851-0843
607-659-5868

The Working Border Collie
14933 Kirkwood Road
Sidney, OH 45365
513-492-2215

Internet

Herding
http://www.dogpatch.org/herding.html

Herding
http://www.uwsp.edu/acad/psych/dog/work.htm
Herding on the Web
http://www.glassprotal.com/herding/herding.htm
Information on a Herding Camp and Lessons
http://www.moberlymo.com/mkc/herding.htm
Stockdog Resources
http://net.indra.com/~jmccrils/Herders/resrc.htm

Hunting and Field Trials

Level of Commitment	🐾🐾🐾🐾 to 🐾🐾🐾🐾🐾
Training Level	🐾🐾
Level of Physical Fitness	🐾🐾🐾🐾
Time Investment	🐾🐾🐾🐾
Estimate of Expenses	$$$
Common Breed Participants	Gun dogs and sporting breeds. UKC does not limit the trials to only UKC dogs if there are still spaces available at the competition. UKC also offers a limited privilege program where mixed-breed dogs may be registered. These dogs must be spayed or neutered. They may enter agility, field trial, and obedience trial events.

A BRIEF DESCRIPTION

A hunter and his or her hunting dog share an intense partnership. They spend hours upon hours with each other, and hunters take great pride in their dogs' abilities. Hunting dogs can be tested on their talents by participating in organized sports for titles and awards.

A myriad of events and competitions are held throughout the United States every year. They include events such as water retrieving tests, squirrel tests, and flushing tests. In order to find out what kind of events take place in your area, contact a local field trial club or one of the breeds' local clubs. It is easier to find trainers and events when the sport or activity is popular where you live.

The UKC and AKC both hold many different and specialized events. Trailing hound trials (with different classes for dachshunds, basset hounds, and beagles), hunting tests for pointers, retriever and water retriever trials, and spaniel trials are all part of the AKC's offerings. The UKC also holds hunting retriever tests as well as an array of coonhound events with night hunts, water races, and field trials.

OVERVIEW OF NECESSARY EQUIPMENT

Each of the different activities requires its own special equipment. Generally, the list of required equipment is short. Contact your local trainer or club for more information.

TRAINING SYNOPSIS

The training styles for the different trials and tests are unique to each event. Some tests, such as the trailing hound tests, rely heavily on your dog's natural ability, and little training is necessary. Other activities require that you take your dog's natural instincts and guide them to fit the requirements of the tests.

The best way to start is to locate a club, group, or organization that can assist you in understanding the sport and the training necessary for your dog.

SPECIAL CONSIDERATIONS

These events are held outdoors, often in treacherous weather conditions. You must be able to rise early in the morning, as most of the events start at daybreak.

Field and hunting trials are physically demanding of your dog and you. You should be in good physical condition and have good stamina, just like your hunting pooch.

ADVICE FOR FIRST-TIMERS

Find someone who has experience in the sport. The firsthand knowledge you can absorb from an accomplished handler is the best education you can get.

WHY YOU WILL ENJOY THIS ADVENTURE

Being outdoors with your dog, especially in the early morning, and spending the day together venturing in the rugged countryside is like a short vacation from your workaday world.

SOURCES FOR INFORMATION AND ASSISTANCE

Organizations

The Hunting Retriever Club
United Kennel Club, Inc.
100 E. Kilgore Road
Kalamazoo, MI 49002-5584
616-343-9020

or

Multi-Breed Field Operations
616-343-9020

National Beagle Club
Rover Road
Bedminster, NJ 07921
Attn: Joseph B. Wiley, Secretary

National Kennel Club
Rt. 6, Box 174
Logansport, IN 46947
219-722-9604

Professional Retriever Trainer Association
4670 Harbour Hills Drive
Manhattan, KS 66502
Attn: Jane Laman, Secretary

United Coon Hunters of America, Inc.
Route 4, Box 677
Paoli, IN 47454

Books

Bailey, Joan. *How to Help Gun Dogs Train Themselves: Taking Advantage of Early Training*. Hillsboro, Oreg.: Swan Valley Press, 1992.

Bennet, Bill. *Beagle Training Basics: The Care, Training and Hunting of the Beagle*. Wilsonville, Oreg.: Doral Publishing, 1995.

Boggs, Bernard. *Succeeding with Pointing Dogs, Field Trials and Hunting Tests*. Dogs Unlimited, 1989.

Falk, John R. *Gun Dogs: Master Training Series*. Stillwater, Minn.: Voyageur Press, 1997.

Mason, Robert L. *The Ultimate Beagle: The Natural Born Rabbit Dog*. Centreville, Ala.: OTR Publications, 1997.

Mulak, Steven J. *Pointing Dogs Made Easy: How to Train, Nurture, and Appreciate Your Bird Dog*. Country Sport Press, 1995.

Powell, Mark. *Qualify! A Guide to Successful Handling in AKC Pointing Breed Hunting Tests*. Houston, Tex.: Attwater Publishing, 1995.

Tarrant, Bill. *Gun Dogs: Humane Way to Get Top Results*. Stockpole Books, 1989.

————. *Gun Dog Training: New Strategies from Today's Top Trainers*. Stillwater, Minn.: Voyageur Press, 1996.

Periodicals

AKC Hunting Test Herald
372 Wildwood Avenue
Worcester, MA 01603
508-798-2386

Full Cry
P.O. Box 10
Boody, IL 62514
217-865-2332
217-865-2334 fax
fullcry@compuser.com

Gun Dog
P.O. Box 343
Mt. Morris, IL 61054-0343
800-435-0715

Hunting Retriever
United Kennel Club
100 E. Kilgore Road
Kalamazoo, MI 49002-5584
616-343-9020
http://www.hrc_ukc.com/

The Pointing Dog Journal
P.O. Box 936
Manitowoc, WI 54221-0936
800-333-7646

Internet
AKC
http://akc.org/regs.htm
All About Hunting Retrievers
http://www.i1.net/~dogman/fieldtr1.htm
The Bird Dog
http://www.weber.edu/library/htmls/spw96/wayments/title.htm
Hunting and Retriever Trials
http.//www.uwsp.edu/acad/psych/dog/work.htm
Hunting Dogs
http://www.ool.com/hunting/birddogs.html
Working Retriever Central!
http://working_retriever.com

Equipment Suppliers
Hallmark Dog Training Supplies
3054 Beechwood Court
Hubertus, WI 53033
414-628-2500

Sylmar Dogwear
22710 S.E. 23rd Place
Issaquah, WA 98029
206-557-8956

Lure Coursing

Level of Commitment	🐾🐾🐾
Training Level	🐾🐾
Level of Physical Fitness	🐾🐾🐾🐾
Time Investment	🐾🐾🐾
Estimate of Expenses	$$ (Because there may be extended travel.)
Common Breed Participants	Greyhounds, Salukis, Afghan hounds, Basenjis, borzois, Ibizan hounds, Irish wolfhounds, pharaoh hounds, Rhodesian ridgebacks, Scottish deerhounds, and whippets. Other breeds are welcome to give it a try for fun.

A BRIEF DESCRIPTION

Sighthounds, one of the oldest recorded types of dogs, were developed to spot prey—primarily rabbits and hares—from great distances and then run it down at lightning speeds. Lure coursing was created to keep this keen talent and instinct alive in these breeds.

At the beginning of each competition, the dogs are given brightly colored coursing blankets to wear that make it easy for the judge or judges to identify them. An artificial lure (often rabbit skins or fake fur) is attached to a line that is then attached to a lure machine. The line is wrapped around pulleys staked into the ground in a large (five-acre minimum) field. When activated, the lure machine reels the line in ahead of the running dogs at around 40 miles per hour. Under AKC rules, the dogs receive a possible 10 points each for their ability in these areas: following the lure, speed, agility, endurance, and overall ability. This gives the dogs the chance to earn a perfect score of 50. If they receive a score of 25, it is considered a successful run.

The AKC Junior Courser title requires that the dog succeed in two competitions on at least a 600-yard course that contains at least four turns. If your dog completes the same type of course four more times, he will earn his Senior Courser title. Then if your talented pooch completes the same type of course a total of 31 times, he will earn the title of Master Courser. Further, if your dog consistently earns high points during the competitions, he can earn a Field Championship award. These are given on a breed-by-breed basis for the top scorers.

The American Sighthound Field Association (ASFA) also offers titles: the Field Champion (FCh) and the Lure Courser of Merit (LCM). These prestigious titles are more difficult to earn than the AKC titles. The FCh title requires that your dog earn 100 points and two first places or one first and two second places. To be successful, your dog must earn a minimum of 50 points during each run. The LCM title is awarded to dogs who earn 300 points and four first places. But it gets more complicated. Your dog must earn these points by beating dogs of his own breed. His score will count only if he places over a dog who receives a qualifying score or is dismissed, not over one who does not receive a qualifying score. If your dog is the only one of his breed, then he may earn the BIF (Best in Field) award over the best of the other breeds and this will count as a first place. Your dog can earn as many LCM awards as he is able to.

The ASFA point system is based on five criteria. Speed earns a maximum of 25 points; agility, 25 points; endurance, 20 points; enthusiasm, 15 points; and following the lure, 15 points.

ASFA also offers first, second, third, fourth, and NBQ (Next Best Qualifying) awards. The dogs are run in Open, Field Champion, or Veteran groups, and these awards are chosen from each group. These winners then compete in a runoff for BOB (Best of Breed). The dogs earn points for these placements, and these points are added up and count toward an ASFA Championship.

OVERVIEW OF NECESSARY EQUIPMENT

You will need a collar and leash to keep your dog under control at all times at an event. Your hound should not wear a buckle-type collar to these events. With their muscular necks and slender heads, sighthounds can easily maneuver out of a buckle collar in their excitement to chase a lure. A martingale or choke collar is a better choice.

Later, if you become devoted to competing in lure coursing events, you will need some specialized pieces of equipment. You will need one coursing blanket in each of these three colors: bright yellow, hot pink, and hot blue. You will also need a slip lead, which will save your fingers and hands from being wrenched and possibly broken when your dog flies from your grasp to chase after the lure. The collar is an inch or two shorter than the circumference of your dog's neck and has a three-inch ring at each end. A special leash threads through these two rings to hold the dog in place until you have official permission to release him to chase. The leash simply releases and frees the dog from the collar.

If you don't have these pieces of equipment, they will be supplied by the organizing club for your use on the day of the competition.

Because these events are held outside, you will need to provide a safe, secure place for your dog to rest between runs. These events take an entire day, so you will need all the normal show amenities for comfort.

TRAINING SYNOPSIS

Dogs who have never participated in lure coursing are not welcome to compete at sanctioned events, so you must find some way to practice with your dog before competing. This can be difficult, but it's not impossible. Call your local dog club to begin your search, and try to find other interested sighthound handlers in your area.

SPECIAL CONSIDERATIONS

Your dog will need to be in good cardiovascular condition before beginning lure coursing. Get him in shape gradually by engaging him in a fitness program at home.

ADVICE FOR FIRST-TIMERS

Each organization has slightly different rules. Contact the club that you are interested in and learn its specific rules and regulations.

Because so few lure coursing events are held, participate in any event put on by either club.

WHY YOU WILL ENJOY THIS ADVENTURE

The beauty and grace, along with the incredible speed, of these dogs is awe-inspiring.

Your beloved sighthound will thrill at the chance to use his racing instincts.

SOURCES FOR INFORMATION AND ASSISTANCE

Organizations

American Kennel Club
51 Madison Avenue
New York, NY 10010

American Sighthound Field Association
P.O. Box 1293-M
Woodstock, GA 30188

Greyhound Pets of America
800-366-1472

National Open Field Coursing Association
P.O. Box 68
Glenrock, WY 82637
Attn: Susan Loop-Stanley, Registrar

Books

ASFA offers many free informational booklets. Write to Denise Scanlan, 1517 Virginia Avenue, Rockford, IL 61103. She can send you one each of the following:

The Sport of Lure Coursing

Guidelines for Judges

Guidelines for Lure Coursing Practice

Guidelines for Course Design (This one is not free.)

Beaman, Arthur S. *Lure Coursing: Field Trialing for Sighthounds and How to Take Part.* New York: Howell Book House, 1994.

Branigan, Cynthia. *Adopting the Racing Greyhound.* New York: Howell Book House, 1992.

Periodicals

AKC Coursing News
5580 Centerview Drive
Raleigh, NC 27690-0643

Field Advisory News
P.O. Box 399
Alpaugh, CA 93201
Attn: Vicky Clarke, Editor

Internet

Coursing and Racing
http://www.k9web.com/dog-faqs/activities/lurecoursing.html
Lure Coursing
http://www.dog-play/index.shtml
Lure Coursing
http://www.uwsp.edu/acad/psych/dog/work.htm
The Lure Coursing Home Page
http://www.clark.net/pub/bdalzell/lure/lureinfo.html

Obedience

Level of Commitment	🐾🐾🐾 to 🐾🐾🐾🐾
Training Level	🐾🐾 to 🐾🐾🐾
Level of Physical Fitness	🐾🐾🐾
Time Investment	🐾🐾 to 🐾🐾🐾🐾
Estimate of Expenses	$$ (local shows) to $$$$ (national shows)
Common Breed Participants	All breeds and types of dogs. Unlike conformation dogs, obedience dogs may be spayed or neutered. Many organizations will allow mixed-breed dogs or dogs from other breeds to participate.

A BRIEF DESCRIPTION

The object of obedience trials is to prove that the dog is under the complete control of the handler. Sometimes frowned upon as being too military, the precision of obedience tests requires a commitment to practice and training. Even the most subtle of movements can lower your score and keep you from earning a title.

The AKC offers five title certifications: Companion Dog (CD), Companion Dog Excellent (CDX), Utility Dog (UD), Utility Dog Excellent (UDX), and Obedience Trial Championship (OTCh). To earn a title, a team must complete three "legs" with a qualifying score of 170 (200 being perfect) under three different judges. The tests for the different titles have progressively more difficult tasks for the dog, such as retrieve, scent discrimination, and jumping.

You will start each competition with 200 points. Each exercise of the competition is given a point value, and the judge will deduct points if you or your dog makes errors in an exercise. You and your dog must earn at least half of the points assigned to each specific exercise in order to pass that exercise. You must also score 170 or more overall to pass the entire test.

The CD title is earned in the Novice class at a trial. Your dog must heel on and off leash; sit when you stop; stand and stay while the judge touches his head, shoulders, and hips; pass the recall test off leash while you are 50 feet away; and sit-stay for one minute and down-stay for three minutes with you in the ring.

The CDX title is earned in the Open class at a trial. Your dog will be off leash for these exercises. You dog will be required to "drop." During the recall, you will ask your dog to "down" before he reaches you. Your dog will be required to retrieve a wood or plastic dumbbell first on the flat ground, and then he must clear a high jump to retrieve the dumb-bell that you throw over the obstacle. Your dog will also be expected to perform a broad jump. The sit-stay for three minutes and the down-stay for five minutes will be performed while you are absent from the ring and out of sight of your dog.

The UD title is earned in the Utility class at a trial. Your dog will be off leash throughout the exercises. You must perform a series of exercises (heel, stand, stay, down, come, and finish) using hand signals only. Two scent-discrimination exercises are part of the challenge of the UD title. Your dog must choose the dumbbell with your scent on it. The directed retrieve requires your dog to retrieve a glove by your direction from three placed on the ground. Your dog will be handled by the judge as in the CD title, but you will walk away and your dog must stay while the judge tests his willingness to accept being handled by a stranger. You will be required to send your dog away to the other side of the ring and have him turn around and sit. The ring has two jumps, and you will call your dog to you over one of the jumps and repeat the directed retrieve exercise for the other jump.

When you are competing, it is important to listen carefully to the judge's instructions and follow them closely. Avoid beginning an exercise too soon; wait until the judge has finished giving you directions. I witnessed a wonderful obedience team that failed to earn the high scores they deserved because although the dog's eyes were on his handler, he listened to the judge. The dog would do whatever the judge said, but he lost points because he was only supposed to do what his handler told him to do.

Obedience trials were created to demonstrate dogs' abilities to be orderly, useful companions to people. The trials have evolved into what many trainers refer to as "the unrealistic world of the obedience ring," meaning that the precision demanded in the obedience ring is hardly necessary in day-to-day life. But once you witness a team in the ring trying their best, listening to each other in an almost psychic way, you will appreciate the competitors for their hard work and the trust they have in one another.

OVERVIEW OF NECESSARY EQUIPMENT

Your training equipment will depend on your personal beliefs on dog training or those of your training school. Theoretically, you should be able to train your dog without any equipment except patience, praise, and treats. Most people train their dog with the communication aids of a collar and leash.

Which kind of collar you need is determined by your training style, but a simple buckle collar is really all that is necessary. If you feel you need help training your dog, talk to a professional trainer who uses positive-reinforcement techniques. If you need to eventually progress to negative-reinforcement equipment, such as a choke collar, a professional trainer can demonstrate the correct way to use it. Used in the wrong manner, some of these devices can harm your dog.

TRAINING SYNOPSIS

It is best to start training for obedience with a club or at a training facility. Many idiosyncrasies exist in obedience trials that you may as well learn while you are teaching your dog the first time. Small position shifts and attitude changes will be tougher to teach later after you have already taught him one way.

Starting early, when your dog is still a pup, is also beneficial. Taking your dog to shows to experience the hubbub of show activity will help him learn to take it in stride. Attending trials as a spectator is also good for you. It will help you to relax when you feel more comfortable with the atmosphere, learn how events are run, and see many dog-human teams competing in the ring.

SPECIAL CONSIDERATIONS

It is always true that if your dog makes an error, it is your fault. The problem is with your training or communication. Can you handle this humbling experience?

ADVICE FOR FIRST-TIMERS

Contact the sanctioning club that you are interested in for its complete rules and regulations. Slight differences in the rules can make a big difference in your scores.

Participate in as many fun matches as possible. These events do not offer points for titles but give you the opportunity to practice for trials. The more experience you get in the matches, the more prepared you and your dog will be for the real thing.

WHY YOU WILL ENJOY THIS ADVENTURE

Most people enjoy obedience because of the close companionship they have when working with their dogs in such a dedicated manner. The feeling of satisfaction one gets from completing a high-scoring test after hours of work is incredible.

SOURCES FOR INFORMATION AND ASSISTANCE

Organizations

American Kennel Club
51 Madison Avenue
New York, NY 10010
212-696-8200

American Mixed Breed Obedience Registry
10236 Topanga Boulevard, Suite 205
Chatsworth, CA 91311
ambor@aborusa.org

Australian Shepherd Club of America
6091 E. State Highway 21
Bryan, TX 77808-9652
409-778-1082
asca@myriad.net

Mixed Breed Dog Club of America
100 Acacia Avenue
San Bruno, CA 94066

States Kennel Club
P.O. Box 389
Hattiesburg, MS 39403-0389
601-583-8345

United Kennel Club
100 East Kilgore Road
Kalamazoo, MI 49001
616-343-9020

Books

Arnold, Terri. *Steppin' Up to Success: Book 1—Theory, Footwork, Handling and Attention; Book 2—Novice; Book 3—Open and Utility.* Freetown, Mass.: Steppin' Up, 1996.

Bauman, Diane L. *Beyond Basic Dog Training.* New York: Howell Book House, 1991.

Benjamin, Carol Lea. *Mother Knows Best: The Natural Way to Train Your Dog.* New York: Howell Book House, 1985.

Burnham, Patricia Gail. *Playtraining Your Dog.* New York: St. Martin's Press, 1980.

Fisher, John. Dogwise: The Natural Way to Train Your Dog. London: Souvenir Press, Ltd., 1992.

Pryor, Karen. *Don't Shoot the Dog: The New Art of Teaching and Training.* New York: Bantam, 1985.

Periodicals

AKC Gazette
5580 Centerview Drive, Suite 200
Raleigh, NC 27606-0643
919-233-9780

Bloodlines
100 E. Kilgore Road
Kalamazoo, MI 49001
616-343-9020

Forward
National Association of Dog Obedience Instructors (NADOI)
P.O. Box 432
Landing, NJ 07850

Front and Finish
P.O. Box 333
Galesburg, IL 61402-0333
309-344-1333

Off-Lead
204 Lewis Street
Canastota, NY 13032
315-697-2749
104501.1527@Compuserve.com

Videos

American Kennel Club. *200?* Available from AKC, 5580 Centerview Drive, Suite 200, Raleigh, NC 76706; 919-233-9767.

Handler, Barbara. *Successful Obedience Handling: The NEW Best Foot Forward.* Loveland, CO: Alpine Publishing, 1995.

Pryor, Karen. *Clicker Magic.* 1997.

Wilkes, Gary. *On Target!* 1993.

The two tapes above are available from Publisher's Book Distributors at 800-47-CLICK as well as from other catalogs.

Internet

Dog Training
http://www.dog-play.com/index/shtml
Obedience
http://www.k9web.com/dog-faq/activities/obedience.html
Obedience
http://www.dogpatch.org/obed.html
Obedience
http://www.uwsp.edu/acad/psych/dog/obed.htm
The Obedience Home Page
http://www.princeton.edu/~nadelman/obed/obed.html
Also see the quick peek Education on page 260.

Equipment Suppliers

ACME Machine Company
2901 Freemont Avenue South
Minneapolis, MN 55408
800-332-2472, 612-827-3571
612-827-98905 fax

Max 200
Dog Obedience Equipment Company
114 Beach Street Building 5
Rockaway, NJ 07866
800-446-2920, 201-983-0451
201-983-1368 fax
mlucas@skipjack.bluecrab.org
http://pages.bluecrab.org/max200

Paul's Obedience Shop
P.O. Box 767
Hanover, PA 17331
800-367-7285, 717-630-8474
717-630-8072 fax

Ray Allen Manufacturing Co. Inc.
P.O. Box 9281
Colorado Springs, CO 80932-0281
800-444-0404 orders
719-633-0404 customer service

Schutzhund

Level of Commitment	🐾🐾🐾🐾🐾
Training Level	🐾🐾🐾
Level of Physical Fitness	🐾🐾🐾🐾
Time Investment	🐾🐾🐾🐾🐾
Estimate of Expenses	$$$ to $$$$
Common Breed Participants	German shepherds, Rottweilers, Belgian Malinois, Tervurens, boxers, Doberman pinschers, Bouvier des Flandres, and giant schnauzers. Other dogs also participate. This sport was originally designed for the German shepherd in Germany in 1901, so some isolated groups prefer that the sport remain a test of the working abilities of the German shepherd.

A BRIEF DESCRIPTION

Schutzhund means "protection dog" in German. People participate in Schutzhund events as a sideline to whatever their dogs do otherwise, such as police and protection work, or for the enjoyment of the sport itself and to prove the working ability of their dogs' lineage. In Germany a German shepherd must have a title in Schutzhund in order to be used in a breeding program.

Schutzhund training involves obedience and tracking as well as protection work. All these areas are given equal importance.

There are three levels of proficiency, called degrees: Schutzhund Examination I, II, and III (SchH I, II, and III). The IPO (International Pruefungsordnung) rules also offer the Begleithunde (Companion Dog) title, Faehrtenhundpruefung (Advanced Tracking Dog Test),

Ausdauerpruefung (Endurance Test), and SchH A (Schutzhund Examination A).

The SchH I title requires an obedience demonstration much like the AKC obedience classes, partly on leash. Each level requires a gun test to test the steadiness of the dog when a gun is shot. The protection test at the SchH I level requires your dog go to a blind and bark and guard the man that he finds there. During an off-lead exercise, your dog will be "attacked" by a man and he must bite the man without hesitation and persist as he is struck twice with a bamboo stick on his back. When the agitator stops and the dog is commanded by his handler to release the man, the dog must do so immediately. The handler holds the dog by the collar while the agitator runs away until the judge gives the handler permission to let the dog go to chase the agitator. The agitator then turns and threatens the dog with the stick. The handler calls off the dog, and the team returns with the agitator to the judge.

In contrast, the SchH III requires the dog to make five bites and take two blows from the stick. The obedience tests are harder and all off leash, the distances are greater, and the agitator is aggressive and intimidating.

The SchH I through III tests increase in difficulty with the SchH III tests requiring an extremely high degree of skill and courage. Only a minority of dogs will be able to acheive the SchH I degree, and only a handful of those will make it all the way up to a SchH III degree.

OVERVIEW OF NECESSARY EQUIPMENT

The equipment needed for the tests will be provided by the club or organization during competition and training. The equipment list is long and specialized and includes blinds, special sleeves, and other outerwear that protects the agitator from an actual bite, as well as jumps for the obedience portion and scent tracks established for the tracking section.

TRAINING SYNOPSIS

Those breeders who breed for a Schutzhund dog train their pups from birth. The training consists of various techniques that a person raising a dog for companionship would avoid. The pup is encouraged to be tough and confident. This training never includes encouragement of inappropriate aggression, anything that hurts the dog, or negative treatment (this would only undermine the dog's confidence and stability). The puppy is encouraged to have control, to be brave, to develop his prey and defense drives more fully, and to use his intelligence.

It is best to get actual training from an experienced trainer. You can practice the obedience and tracking skills on your own, but the protection work needs the cooperation of many people and the knowledge to ensure it is done correctly and under control.

SPECIAL CONSIDERATIONS

This is an intense, specialized activity that only experienced handlers working with experienced trainers should participate in. With a dog of sound temperament, a confident and in-control handler, and a trainer of high quality, this sport enhances the dog's personality by teaching control, confidence, and gentleness. In the wrong hands, training in this adventure can produce chaos and possible danger.

A responsible trainer at a dedicated club will test your dog for a stable personality and the ability to remain trustworthy and comfortable around people and strange situations. The importance of carefully choosing a trainer cannot be overstated.

If your dog is aggressive and dominant, you may be attracted to this activity thinking that you will at least get control of his behavior and let him express it in a meaningful way. This is not wise. An overly aggressive dog will only become more uncontrollable and unpredictable. The same is true of a shy or nervous dog. Schutzhund training will not bring out hidden bravery. Shy and nervous dogs and Schutzhund could be a lethal mix. A Schutzhund dog is required to show extreme reliability, confidence, and discipline. Schutzhund training, or any protection work, will not make a good dog mean. Only a dog with an inappropriate temperament will become mean.

Many people start training in this activity to feel safer with a protection dog around. However, this is not always the best solution for protection. Most people do not understand the responsibility of caring for a dog who has this type of training.

A well-trained Schutzhund dog is a wonder to behold. For a dog to be in mid-attack and to back off with one command from his handler is the epitome of training. It also demands unwavering devotion on your part, a thorough understanding of your dog's mind and his training, and a high level of responsibility.

ADVICE FOR FIRST-TIMERS

It is undeniably important to get a great instructor. Don't risk going with a mediocre instructor because that person is nearby. Search out only the best.

Expect your dog to be evaluated for his abilities, trainability, and stability. If your dog is not tested, find another instructor.

This activity is intense, and you must take it seriously. You must be dedicated to it and be willing to spend the time and energy to keep your dog sound and responsive.

WHY YOU WILL ENJOY THIS ADVENTURE

This sport is a challenge that gives people an extraordinary sense of accomplishment. Many people thrive on the large amount of education required for themselves and their dogs.

Testing the ability of your dog to do the job he was created to do is satisfying and rewarding.

SOURCES FOR INFORMATION AND ASSISTANCE

Organizations

Independent Work and Sport Dog Association
P.O. Box 7272
Olympia, WA 98507

Landesverband DVG America
113 Vickie Drive
Del City, OK 73115
Attn: Sandi Nethercutt, Secretary
http://webusers.anet-stl.com/~dvgamer

United Schutzhund Clubs of America
3810 Paule Avenue
St. Louis, MO 63125-1718
http://www.dogzone.com/usa/usa.htm

Books

Barwig, Susan, and Stewart Hilliard. *Schutzhund: Theory and Training Methods*. New York: Howell Books, 1991.

Booth, Shiela. *Schutzhund Obedience: Training in Drive with Gottfied Dildei*. Ridgefield, Conn.: Podium Publications, 1995.

Periodicals

Dog Sports Magazine
32 Cherokee Trail
Douglas, WY 82633-9232
307-358-3487
307-358-3487 fax
dsm@coffey.com

Internet

Q & A on Schutzhund
http://leerburg.com/gasch.htm
Schutzhund
http://www. net.connect.net/~linda/sport.htm
Schutzhund

http://www.k9web/faq/activities/schutzhund
Schutzhund.Com
http://www.schutzhund.com
Schutzhund and Ring Sport
http://www.uwsp.edu/acad/psych/dog/protect.htm
United Schutzhund Clubs of America
http://www.germanshepherddog.com/

Equipment Suppliers

Ray Allen Manufacturing Co. Inc.
P.O. Box 9281
Colorado Springs, CO 80932-0281
800-444-0404 order
719-633-0404 customer service

Skijoring

Level of Commitment	🐾🐾 to 🐾🐾🐾
Training Level	🐾🐾🐾
Level of Physical Fitness	🐾🐾🐾🐾
Time Investment	🐾🐾 to 🐾🐾🐾
Estimate of Expenses	$$$ to $$$$ (Depending on your skis.)
Common Breed Participants	Same as those listed under the Sledding section below.

A BRIEF DESCRIPTION

Do you like to cross-country ski? Do you want to go faster and farther than ever before? Let your dog do some of the work for you! Skijoring also appeals to those who have a fondness for dog sledding but want to do their snow travel at a smidgen of the price and without keeping a team of dogs.

This emerging sport is rapidly attracting a number of enthusiasts. Although skijoring has been a means of transportation throughout arctic regions for ages, it is becoming a favorite activity for people all over the United States. It is a thrilling way to spend time outdoors during winter and, most importantly, spend time with your dog.

Your dog is attached to you by a line between his harness and a special belt around your waist. As you are pulled behind him on skis, your dog experiences the exhilarating experience of running through the snow on a crisp day. As long as you can train your dog to pull and he has the energy and physical fitness to run at this intensity, you two will make quite the team in a winter wonderland.

Aside from just having fun with this activity, you can participate in skijoring competitions held during sled dog races. The competitions are broken into classes by the number of dogs in your team (most commonly one to four dogs).

OVERVIEW OF NECESSARY EQUIPMENT

You will need an x-back harness as described in the dog sledding quick peek. You will need a padded belt that you wear around your lower waist. A towline then attaches your dog's harness to your belt. Some people use a handle to hold onto rather than a belt. A handle is easy to let go of if trouble arises, but a dog dragging a loose towline and handle can be endangered if he gets caught on something.

Cross-country skis are best but not mandatory; downhill skis will also work. Wrist straps are important to keep your ski poles with you. To prevent your poles from going too deep into the snow, you may want to equip your poles with funnel sleeves. You will need a pair of comfortable, well-insulated, well-fitting boots. You'll be going fast, so the wind chill factor can make a difference in your comfort. You should also have a pack of some sort to keep emergency supplies, snacks, and water for you and your dog.

TRAINING SYNOPSIS

The training begins with you. You must be an experienced cross-country skier. You will be traveling at breakneck speeds so you should feel comfortable and be safe on your skis first. Learning to fall is very important. You may need to execute a controlled fall in order to stop your dog and regain control.

Your dog will need to know the commands listed in the sledding section below. Begin by teaching them on the ground without skis.

When you finally move onto the snow, begin with short training sessions and build up your time and distance gradually. Although your dog could pull you for up to 25 miles a day, start with sessions of 15 to 20 minutes the first few times.

SPECIAL CONSIDERATIONS

You will be going faster in skijoring than in regular cross-country skiing. Be prepared. Skijoring is not the time to learn to ski.

ADVICE FOR FIRST-TIMERS

Start with just one dog. You will be surprised at how fast you can go with a dog pulling you. After you get more experience and have the desire to go faster still, you can add another dog, or maybe two, but begin with your own beloved pooch by himself.

Dress warmly. At the speeds you will be traveling, you'll need extra protection to stay comfortable.

WHY YOU WILL ENJOY THIS ADVENTURE

You'll get to go really fast!

You'll enjoy being with your dog in a snow-covered winter wonderland.

SOURCES FOR INFORMATION AND ASSISTANCE

Organizations

Alaska Skijoring and Pulk Association
3126 E. 88th Avenue
Anchorage, AK 99507
907-248-7344

International Federation of Sled Dog Sports Inc.
7118 N. Beehive Road
Pocatello, ID 83201
Attn: Glenda Walling
208-232-5130

Books

Hoe-Raitto, Mari, and Carol Kaynor. *Skijor with Your Dog*. Fairbanks, Alaska: OK Publishing, 1991.

Kaynor, Carol, and Mari Hoe-Raitto. *Skijoring: An Introduction to the Sport*. Fairbanks, Alaska: OK Publishing, 1992.

Periodicals
Mushing
P.O. Box 149
Ester, AK 99725
907-479-0454

Internet
How to Get Started in Skijoring
http://fytqm.uafadm.alaska.edu/dogs/skijoring.html
Skijoring
http://www.nmsr.labmed.umn.edu/~john/skijor/
Skijoring
http://www.uwsp.edu/acad/psych/dog/work.htm

Equipment Suppliers
See the sledding section below.

Sledding

Level of Commitment	🐾 🐾
Training Level	🐾 🐾 🐾
Level of Physical Fitness	🐾 🐾 🐾 🐾 to 🐾 🐾 🐾 🐾 🐾
Time Investment	🐾 🐾 🐾
Estimate of Expenses	$$ to $$$ (Depending on how much traveling you will have to do.)
Common Breed Participants	Alaskan malamutes, Siberian Huskies, Alaskan Huskies, and Samoyeds. Other breeds such as Australian shepherds, Dalmatians, golden retrievers, Irish setters, and other hunting dogs also participate.
	Of the two most common sled dogs, the Alaskan malamutes are stockier and stronger and are used for pulling heavier weights for shorter distances. Siberian Huskies are more commonly used for lighter weights, and they have a higher endurance ability.

A BRIEF DESCRIPTION

Sled dogs are some of the most elite canine athletes. Dogs running the 1,000-mile Iditarod race average 9 to 10 miles per hour, pulling sleds that weigh between 300 and 400 pounds (at the beginning of the race) and running through extreme weather conditions. The top racers will average 20 to 22 miles an hour during shorter races!

Races are held on groomed trails, usually with the start and finish lines being the same. The races are run in heats, sometimes spanning three days. The team with the best overall time is the winner. The racers start at predetermined intervals and race against the clock.

The International Sled Dog Racing Association (ISDRA) governs the actual sled dog races. Men, women, and children may all compete equally. The races are broken into 10 classes.

- Unlimited—teams of not less than 7 and usually from 12 to 16 dogs racing between 12 and 30 miles

- Ten Dog—not more than 10 dogs or less than 7 on a 10-mile minimum trail

- Eight Dog—5 to 8 dogs on an 8-mile minimum trail

- Six Dog—3 to 6 dogs on a 6-mile minimum trail

- Four Dog—3 to 4 dogs on a 4-mile trail

- Three Dog—2 to 3 dogs on a 3-mile minimum trail

- Distance—a 50- to 1,000-mile race

- Freight—three classes of team sizes; the trail lengths vary and the sleds are weighted with approximately 50 pounds per team

- Junior—for younger children with small teams

- Pee Wee—for children as young as three years old with a single dog, on a 100-yard to 1/4-mile course under heavy supervision

Unless you go to a very large event, you won't see all of the classes being run. The organizers distribute the teams fairly into appropriate categories.

OVERVIEW OF NECESSARY EQUIPMENT

Since the minimum number of dogs you can race with is two, you must live with and train at least two dogs.

You will, of course, need a sled. Actually, you will probably need two sleds—one for snow and one for training during the off-season.

There are two types of sleds for the snow: the basket sled and the toboggan sled. Basket sleds are about eight feet long and lightweight.

They do best on groomed, hard-packed, icy snow. They are used for racing and are a popular choice for mushers who are participating just for fun. The basket sled is also cheaper and more forgiving for the beginner.

If you will be traveling for longer distances and need to bring larger loads, then the toboggan sled may be best. Toboggan sleds are more rigid and ride two inches above the snow. They are not as easy as the basket sled to maneuver but are stable, durable, and better in soft snow.

Either sled you choose will come equipped with a brake—a necessary piece of equipment. Pushing down on the brake activates a hook that plows into the snow and brings you to a slow stop. It is also useful to hold the sled in place when it is stopped.

A driver steers a sled by directing the lead dog with his or her voice, leaning to the left or right, and dragging one heel. It takes balance to learn to ride the runners while steering and directing the dogs.

Training carts are used for training before the snow season. In areas where there is not enough snow, they are also used for competitions. These carts can be incredibly fast, so start off slowly and cautiously.

Your dog will need one of two different kinds of harnesses: the x-back and the weight-pulling harness. The x-back harness (sometimes referred to as a racing harness) is preferred by most mushers. The harness must fit well and be padded on the front to keep the weight of the load from putting pressure on sensitive parts of your dog's musculoskeletal system.

The weight-pulling harness is necessary when pulling heavier loads. This type of harness distributes the weight of the load differently and allows different movement from the x-back harness. The weight-pulling harness has a "spacer" behind the dog, away from his rear legs. It is usually made of wood and is as long as the dog is wide.

The equipment and dogs are connected by a gang line, which consists of the towline, tug lines, and neck line. The towline runs between the dogs with the dogs attached to either side of the line, side by side, then attaches to the sled. Tug lines are usually braided into the towline and attached to the harnesses. The neck line is then braided into the tug line and attached to the dog's collar. It is meant to keep the dogs close to the towline. You'll need an extra gang line in case yours breaks.

You will also need a sled bag and dog booties. The sled bags are required in races and are used to carry gear or an injured dog.

TRAINING SYNOPSIS

Training sled dogs, as with so many canine activities, is best when the dogs are younger and in their impressionable period, but you can teach an older dog new tricks.

The first order of business is to accustom your puppy or dog to the harness. Getting your dog used to dragging something behind him is also important. The object should be light, especially if your dog is a puppy. Let him have fun dragging it around the yard.

The dog needs to learn to keep the towline tightly drawn. He should learn to lean into the harness. Most dogs will do this naturally; others will have difficulty. If you keep the training fun, your dog will eventually get used to it. Consider obtaining a copy of one or more of the books and videos listed at the end of this quick peek, or subscribe to a sledding magazine. The best advice is to get help from an experienced musher.

In addition to training and working with the whole team, you will have to train your lead dog. If you are working with only one dog, then you will train him as your lead dog. Lead dogs must understand the commands for right, left, speed up, and take it easy. Working with a lead dog requires your being able to judge the terrain early enough to issue the command in time for your dog to be able to execute it. To build a dog's trust in you, you cannot wait until you are on top of an obstacle before calling out a turn command. Give your dog time to respond.

Start training your lead dog young and begin on bare ground rather than snow. You can then graduate to skijoring with him so that you can concentrate solely on *his* behavior before adding a team of dogs behind him. A well-trained lead dog will be worth his weight in gold. Beginners may find it worth their while to buy a lead dog who is already trained. A trained lead dog will be more expensive, but this is a less frustrating way to get into the sport of mushing.

Each dog must be trained independently and with the team. Other activities (as mentioned in the cross-training section in the first part of this book) in the off-season will help keep your dog in good athletic condition.

Conditioning a sled dog team involves a concentration in endurance, speed, and strength for pulling the weight. Remember your F. I.T.T. principles and increase one area of fitness at a time. You can travel short distances with intense speeds for one session. Then try long distances with light loads and short distances with increasingly heavier loads. You will probably have to train two or three days during the week to keep your team in top condition.

These are some of the common terms used in sledding that you will need to train your dog to follow:

- Mush—Although most people think this is the command for the dogs to head out and begin pulling, "mushing" is actually the action of driving the sled dogs. It is what the "musher" does. If you are sitting in the driver's seat of a sled pulled by a team of dogs, your title is "musher."

- Hike—This is the term you use when you want your dogs to get to work. It means "let's go!"

- Gee—Turn right.

- Haw—Turn left.

- Easy—Slow down.

SPECIAL CONSIDERATIONS

You are going to get a good workout, so you had better be in shape before heading out with your dogs. You are required to "pedal" the sled, meaning you help push the sled forward with one foot while riding on the runners of the sled. Many times, the musher will get off the runners and run alongside the dogs, giving them a break if they are tired. You must have the physical and emotional endurance necessary to guide, control, and encourage your team.

You may fall off the sled and have to get back on while the team is running full force. If your team gets away from you when you fall, you'll have to chase them down. Another consideration is possible injury to yourself. Depending on your experience and the terrain, you may run into trees or large berms that send you flying. Until you see it for yourself, you may not realize how fast the dogs can pull the sled.

If you get serious about racing sled dogs, you may want to increase the number of dogs on your team. If you do this, you will need to understand kennel management and the transportation needs of your dogs. You will also have to spend extra money for a truck and dog boxes, as well as camping equipment, because you will have to travel more.

You may find it hard to find an area where you can run your dogs. By asking other mushers, you should be able to find a long enough trail, not too far away, that you can work on.

ADVICE FOR FIRST-TIMERS

If you want to experience a sled dog adventure to see if you like it without making a big investment, there are places, usually around ski resorts, where you can pay for the experience.

Make friends with a driver and attend a race with him or her, helping where needed. Ask if you can visit the driver's home/kennels and see what a typical day and training session look like.

WHY YOU WILL ENJOY THIS ADVENTURE

You will experience the joy of seeing dogs run. They love it!
Both you and your dogs will get in good physical shape.
The air is clean and the scenery is beautiful!

SOURCES FOR INFORMATION AND ASSISTANCE

Organizations

International Council for Sled Dog Sports
P.O. Box 149
Ester, AK 99725
907-479-0454

International Sled Dog Racing Association (ISDRA)
HC 86 Box 3380
Merrifield, MN 56465
Attn: Dave Steele, Executive Director
dsteele@brainerd.net
218-765-4297

or

P.O. Box 446
Nordman, ID 83848-0446
208-443-3453

Books

Collins, Miki, and Julie Collins. *Dog Driver: A Guide for the Serious Musher*. Loveland, Colo.: Alpine Publications, 1991.

Fishback, Lee, and Mel Fishback. *Novice Sled Dog Training*. Lynwood, Wash.: Raymond Thomson Company, 1989. Other related titles are also available.

Fishback, Lee. *Training Lead Dogs*. Tun-Dra. This book is available in the Black Ice catalog.

Flanders, Noel K. *The Joy of Running Sled Dogs*. Loveland, Colo.: Alpine Publications, 1989.

Levorsen, Bella, ed. *Mush! A Beginner's Manual of Sled Dog Training*. Sierra Nevada Dog Drivers, Inc. Canastota, N.Y.: Arner Publications, 1976.

Periodicals

INFO
See ISDRA address above

Mushing
P.O. Box 149
Ester, AK 99725
907-479-0454

Team and Trail
P.O. Box 128
Center Harbor, NH 03226

Internet

Alaska Dog Musher's Association
http://ww.polarnet.com/
ISDRA
http://uslink.net/~isdra/
Mush!
http://dogbreeds.miningco.com/library/weekly/
Sledding
http://www.uwsp.edu/acad/psych/dog/work.htm

Equipment Suppliers

Alpine Outfitters
P.O. Box 245
Roy, WA 98580
253-843-2767

Black Ice
3620 Yancy Avenue
New Germany, MN 55367
320-485-4825

Dog Works
14297 Curvin Drive
Stewartstown, PA 17363-9432
800-787-2788
717-993-3698 fax
dogworks@cyberia.com
http://www.dogworks.com

Hall's Sleds and Equipment
5875 McCrum Road
Jackson, MI 49201
517-782-1786

Kaleb's Kart Company
W5770 Wildwood Road
Neillsville, WI 54456
715-743-3864

Nordkyn Outfitters
P.O. Box 1023
Graham, WA 98338-1023
253-847-4128
253-847-4108 fax
nordkyn@nordkyn.com
http://www.nordkyn.com

Perry Greene Kennels
U.S. Route One
Waldoboro, ME 04572
207-832-5227
207-832-6182 fax
info@mainely-dogs.com
http://www.mainely-dogs.com

Sylmar Dogwear
22710 S.E. 23rd Place
Issaquah, WA 98029
206-557-8956

Tun-Dra Outfitters
16438 96th Avenue
Nunica, MI 49448
616-837-9726
616-837-9517 fax

Tracking

Level of Commitment	🐾 🐾
Training Level	🐾 🐾 🐾
Level of Physical Fitness	🐾 🐾 🐾
Time Investment	🐾 🐾 to 🐾 🐾 🐾
Estimate of Expenses	$ or $$ (Depending on travel.)
Common Breed Participants	AKC-registered dogs. Dogs can be spayed or neutered or have unacceptable coloration or markings. Unregistered dogs may participate but cannot earn titles.

A BRIEF DESCRIPTION

The canine nose is an incredible organ. You can train your dog, no matter what breed or mix of breeds he is, to follow a scent trail.

AKC offers three tracking titles: Tracking Dog (TD), Tracking Dog Excellent (TDX), and the newest award, Variable Surface Tracking (VST). If your dog earns each of these titles, he will be honored with the initials TCh before his name.

The AKC tracking tests are pass/fail events. As your dog works the trail, you and your dog will be followed by two judges. If your dog wanders 50 feet off the track, becomes lost and does not regain the scent trail within a reasonable period, or just stops following the trail, then the judges will blow a whistle and your dog will have failed the test for that day.

In order to participate in the TD event, your dog must first complete a certification test. This is held on a course similar to the TD course and must be witnessed by an approved judge. Once you have completed this test successfully, you will be given four original certificates. One of these must be turned in with your dog's entry in a TD test. The certificates are good for one year only, and if your dog does not pass the TD test in four tries, he must be recertified. After your dog passes the TD test, you don't have to worry about these certificates anymore.

The TD test involves a field that is between a quarter mile and 500 yards long. The scent is laid 30 minutes to two hours before the test. A total of three to five turns are added after the first 60 yards. At least two of the turns will be 90 degrees. The field must be open with no gates or flags to mark the turns for the dogs. Your dog must show that he has clearly found the article at the end of the trail.

The TDX trail is at least 800 and not more than 1,000 yards long and is more varied than the TD trail. The scent is three to five hours old. In the TD test, a flag 30 yards from the start helps you identify the direction of the scent, but there is no such indicator in the TDX test. The trail will have between five and seven turns with three being 90-degree turns. Three false objects are placed along the trail. If the dog finds one of these articles, he must indicate the article, and the handler is required to carry it to the end of the trail. The test is made more challenging by the addition of cross-tracks (two tracks other than the one the dog is to follow) and obstacles. This test takes quite a bit of patience and can last from 30 minutes to an hour.

The VST is the most difficult track and the one that most resembles a true tracking situation. These tests are held in urban environments. Your dog does not have to be TDX titled; only a TD is necessary. The main difference between the TDX and the VST trials is that the VST requires at least three different surfaces, including concrete, asphalt, gravel, or sand. If the trail is contaminated, the test is still held (unlike the TDX test, where contamination renders a trail unusable).

OVERVIEW OF NECESSARY EQUIPMENT

Your dog will need a tracking harness and a 20- to 40-foot lead. The lead must be marked at the 20-foot measurement, and the handler must stay 20 feet back from the dog. You will also need a few scent articles (personal items such as gloves or socks), treats, and markers (such as flags) to mark starts and turns.

TRAINING SYNOPSIS

The most optimum training starts with a young pup as early as 12 weeks old. Scent discrimination and tracking are natural and generally easy to teach a young pup. Having him find something around the living room is a great start. Begin with an article of food that is especially appealing.

Later, as your dog finds less intense scents in more difficult hiding places, you can take him outside and lay a scent trail in your yard and then possibly in a park or field. There will be days when your dog is able to track with ease and other days when he may not stay on the trail or he gives up. Many factors are at work here including weather conditions, wind, terrain, and contamination of the trail. As your dog gains experience and learns that it is rewarding to keep searching no matter what, he will be ready to try for his TD title.

SPECIAL CONSIDERATIONS

Every dog can be taught to track. It is a fun way to put your dog's nose to work and spend time together. You can even teach your dog to use his ability to search out members of the family, playing hide and seek. Don't avoid expanding on your dog's natural abilities because his breed isn't a recognized "scent" breed.

ADVICE FOR FIRST-TIMERS

If you and your dog fail to pass a test again and again, don't give up. Your dog will get better with practice. The TDX can easily take five tries to pass.

WHY YOU WILL ENJOY THIS ADVENTURE

You'll be encouraging your dog to use his strongest natural instinct while you spend time together. Your dog will truly enjoy himself.

The tests are challenging and the excitement builds with each attempt.

SOURCES FOR INFORMATION AND ASSISTANCE

Organizations

American Kennel Club
51 Madison Avenue
New York, NY 10010
212-696-8200

American Mixed Breed Obedience Registry
P.O. Box 7841
Rockford, IL 61126-7841

Australian Shepherd Club of America
6091 E. State Highway 21
Bryan, TX 77808-9652
409-778-1082
asca@myriad.net

Independent Work and Sport Dog Association
P.O. Box 7272
Olympia, WA 98507

Landesverband DVG America
5718 Watson Circle
Dallas, TX 75225
Attn: Sandi Nethercutt, Secretary
http://webusers.anet-stl.com/~dvgamer

United Schutzhund Clubs of America
3810 Paule Avenue
St. Louis, MO 63125-1718
http://www.dogzone.com/usa/usa.htm

Books

Button, Lue. *Practical Scent Dog Training*. Loveland, Colo.: Alpine Publishing, 1990.

Ganz, Sandy, and Susan Boyd. *Tracking from the Ground Up*. Show-Me Publications.

Hogan, Julie, and Donna Thompson. *Practical Tracking for Practically Everyone*.

Hunter, Roy. *Fun Nosework for Dogs*. Eliot, Maine: Howln Moon Press, 1995. This book, and the above books, are available from Direct Book Service.

Johnson, Glen. *Tracking Dog: Theory and Methods*. Arner Publications, 1975.

Internet

Tracking
http://www.uwsp.edu/acad/psych/dog/work2.htm
Tracking
http://www.dog-play.com/
Tracking
http://www.cfw.com/~dtratnac/

Water Rescue

Level of Commitment	🐾 🐾 🐾
Training Level	🐾 🐾 🐾
Level of Physical Fitness	🐾 🐾 🐾 🐾
Time Investment	🐾 🐾 to 🐾 🐾 🐾
Estimate of Expenses	$$
Common Breed Participants	Newfoundlands

A BRIEF DESCRIPTION

The Newfoundland Club of America offers two titles: Water Dog for junior handlers and Water Rescue Dog for senior handlers. The tests have two judges present and consist of six exercises each. The judges must pass the dog and handler in each exercise.

The handler must first demonstrate "basic control." The exercise is held in a fenced area and the dog is off leash. The handler is not allowed to touch the dog but can talk to and signal the dog. The exercises are similar to obedience trials but allow for more flexibility in guiding the dog with voice and hand signals. The dog must heel at fast and slow paces with turns and stops. He must prove his reliability with a recall; the dog must move after one command, but after that, the handler may call the dog as much as he or she wants. A three-minute down-stay as a group exercise, with the handlers in the ring, finishes off the test. If the dog already has a CD title, the team does not have to do this exercise.

The "single retrieve" exercise is next. The handler throws a boat bumper into the water a minimum of 30 feet out. The dog must retrieve the bumper and take it to his handler. In the "drop retrieve," a steward drops an article from a boat 50 feet from shore on the far side of the boat. The boat leaves and the handler sends the dog for the article.

The next exercise is called the "take a line" exercise. A steward enters the water and goes out 50 feet. The steward then calls the dog, who is on the shore. The dog carries a boat bumper attached to a 75-foot line. The dog must swim to the steward and allow him or her to grab the line.

In the "tow the boat" exercise, the dog grabs a boat bumper attached to a 14-foot empty boat. The handler and dog are in wading-depth water for this test. (In all previous exercises, the handler cannot enter the water.) The dog must then pull the boat parallel with the shoreline for 50 feet. He must pull the boat back out into the water if it gets caught on the shore and must pick up the bumper and continue if it is dropped.

The final exercise is "swim with the handler." The handler and dog both enter the water. They must swim at least 20 feet from the shore. The dog must in no way interfere with the handler but must stay close. When the steward blows the whistle (when the team reaches 20 feet), the handler must grab the dog, usually by the hair on his sides or back, and be towed back to shore, keeping his or her feet out of the water to prove the dog is towing.

The senior exercises are different. The first exercise is the "directed retrieve." At 50 feet from shore, the steward drops two articles. The judge then directs the handler which article his or her dog should retrieve, first one and then the other. The "drop retrieve" exercise requires the handler and dog to be on a boat that is rowed 75 feet from shore. The handler then tosses an oar into the water and directs the dog to retrieve it. The dog must bring it to the boat. The handler may either jump into the water and swim to shore with the dog or bring the dog into the boat.

The next exercise tests the dog's ability to retrieve objects from under the water. The dog and handler wade into the water until it is chest high on the dog. The handler then throws a nonfloating article three feet from the dog. The dog must retrieve it from there or paw it closer to shore and retrieve it.

The rescue part of the test is included in the "directed rescue" exercise. Three stewards enter the water and swim 75 feet out. The judge determines which steward will be rescued, and the handler gives the dog a life ring with a line attached. The dog swims to the "drowning" person and gets close enough for the steward to grab the life ring. The dog then tows the steward to wading-depth water. The stewards keep their feet above water to prove they are being towed.

During the "take a line, tow a boat" exercise, the boat is rowed with two stewards out to 75 feet. One steward calls the dog and the handler (on shore) gives the dog a line with a boat bumper attached. The dog swims out, the steward grabs the line, and the dog tows the boat back to shore.

The last exercise is the "rescue off boat." The handler and dog are in the boat 75 feet from shore. The handler falls in and calls the dog, and the dog must jump off the boat and rescue the handler, towing him or her to shore.

During the senior exercises, the dog's name is not used. Terms such as "help" or "dog" are used.

OVERVIEW OF NECESSARY EQUIPMENT

In order to train your dog for water rescue, you will need a good water source in which to practice. You will also need a boat, a line, a boat bumper, and an oar.

TRAINING SYNOPSIS

Contact a local Newfoundland club and inquire about the training offered. You can learn about training basics by yourself, but you will need the assistance of another person for some of the more advanced training.

Training your Newfoundland to work in the water shouldn't be too difficult since Newfies love water. The challenging part will be showing him what you want him to do and when. Most will be eager and willing students.

SPECIAL CONSIDERATIONS

To participate in the contests and to train your dog, you will have to get in the water. You should be a strong swimmer. While learning, your dog may awkwardly bump you in the water; you must be able to keep yourself out of danger.

ADVICE FOR FIRST-TIMERS

Have patience—you are asking a lot of your dog. He will perform as soon as he understands what you want.

WHY YOU WILL ENJOY THIS ADVENTURE

It's a great excuse for getting your water-loving dog into the water!

SOURCES FOR INFORMATION AND ASSISTANCE

Organizations

Newfoundland Club of America
5208 Olive Road
Raleigh, NC 27606

Books

Adler. *Water Work, Water Play.* You can purchase this book from Dog Works as well as from other catalogs.

Bendure, Joan C. *The Newfoundland: Companion Dog—Water Dog.* New York: Howell Book House, 1994.

NCA Water Test Training Manual. Newfoundland Club Working Dog Committee.

Equipment Suppliers

Dog Works
14297 Curvin Drive
Stewartstown, PA 17363-9432
800-787-2788
717-993-3698 fax
dogworks@cyberia.com
http://www.dogworks.com
Ask for the Water Work catalog.

Weight Pulling

Level of Commitment	🐾 🐾
Training Level	🐾
Level of Physical Fitness	🐾 🐾 🐾 🐾
Time Investment (Depending on travel.)	🐾 to 🐾 🐾
Estimate of Expenses	$
Common Breed Participants	All dogs, mixed or purebred. The stars are the malamutes and the Siberian Huskies. Others that do well in competition are Newfoundlands, mastiffs, and other large, strong breeds.

A BRIEF DESCRIPTION

The purpose of weight pulling is to test your dog's working heritage and to keep your dog in good physical condition.

Canine participants can pull as much as 20 times their own weight. This event relies heavily on the dogs' willingness to pull. The handlers can have no contact with the dogs and can only provide encouragement.

Weight pulling is reminiscent of tractor pulls. The dog must pull either a wheeled cart on a dirt surface or a sled on the snow. The objective is to see which dog can pull the most weight over a distance of 16 feet. The dogs are divided into different classes based on their weight.

The dog begins at the starting line and is attached to the towline of a wagon. The handler positions himself or herself at the finish line. The only incentive for the dog to pull is the handler's encouragement. The dog must start his pull within one minute. Once the minute is over, as long as he is still moving steadily, it is a good pull. If he stops before he reaches the finish line, the pull is no good. The dogs all start out with

900 pounds of weight. The 900-pound pull is a sort of warm-up and con-fidence builder.

The International Weight Pull Association (IWPA) is one govern-ing body of sanctioned events. Although it is an international organiza-tion, there is as yet little interest outside North America. The IWPA takes the dogs' safety seriously and has a good record of safe events.

The winner in each weight class is the dog who pulls the most weight for 16 feet. In the IWPA events, there are six weight classes of dogs: up to 35 pounds, 36 to 60 pounds, 61 to 80 pounds, 81 to 100 pounds, 101 to 120 pounds, and 121 pounds and over.

The dogs earn points based on what place they finish in and how many dogs they compete against. The five best pulls are totaled at the end of the season for each dog's point standing. At the end of the sea-son, the three best dogs are invited to a pull-off.

Working Dog certificates are offered for dogs pulling a certain per-centage of their weight. This certificate is offered at three different lev-els. There are currently ten regions in North America; the dogs and han-dlers must compete in their own region to earn points, although they can pull in any region.

Some areas of the country have no pulling activities. Often a team must travel a few thousand miles during the competition season (September through March).

OVERVIEW OF NECESSARY EQUIPMENT

Some organizers of events will work with novices. They will loan equipment and give you and your dog some basic training. This would be a great way to make sure this activity is right for you and your dog.

Most of the equipment for the pulls is supplied by the organizer.

You will need a weight-pulling harness. These harnesses have side lines that connect to a bar behind the dog.

TRAINING SYNOPSIS

Begin by training your dog to pull as you would for dog sledding. See the sledding quick peek for more information.

SPECIAL CONSIDERATIONS

You must be sensitive to your dog's efforts. If you feel that additional weight or even the weight he is currently trying to pull is too much for him, you should stop the pull. Weight-pulling events have a great reputation for being extremely conscientious of the dogs' well-being. The object is to see how much your dog is willing and able to pull. In fact, if a dog is having difficulty pulling a weight, people will jump in behind and help push so that the dog feels successful and good about himself.

ADVICE FOR FIRST-TIMERS

Start with a light weight and gradually build up the amount, giving your dog's muscles and mind the opportunity to keep up with the demands being placed on them.

Keep a good attitude. This is a friendly competition and all dogs are winners.

WHY YOU WILL ENJOY THIS ADVENTURE

Watching these dogs pull the massive loads behind them—loads that often tower over them in height—is amazing. The animals really put their hearts into their work as they use their powerful bodies to pull such loads.

SOURCES FOR INFORMATION AND ASSISTANCE

Organizations

International Weight Pulling Association
570 Timber Trail
Stevensville, MT 59870
Attn: Mark Johnson

Books

Most books on sled dog training will contain a section on training your
dog to pull weight.

Internet

Weight Pulling
http://www.uwsp.edu/acad/psych/dog/work.htm

Appendix

As of the time that this book went to press, the following information was accurate. Many of the smaller organizations and companies frequently change contact information. Every effort will be made to keep this information as up to date as possible in future editions.

Alternative Veterinary Care

Academy for Veterinary Homeopathy
1283 Lincoln Street
Eugene, OR 97401
541-342-7665

American Canine Sports Medicine Association
12062 SW 117th Court, Suite 146
Miami, FL 33186
Attn: Dr. Ronald Stone, Secretary
305-633-2402

American Holistic Veterinary Medical Association
2214 Old Emmorton Road
Bel Air, MD 21015
410-569-0795

American Veterinary Chiropractic Association
623 Main Street
Hillsdale, IL 61257
309-658-2920

Center for Veterinary Acupuncture
1405 West Silver Spring Drive
Glendale, WI 53209
414-352-0201

Flying Dog Press
P.O. Box 290
Stanton, NJ 08885
800-735-9364
908-689-9426
http://www.flyingdogpress.com
Flying Dog Press offers information regarding BioMagnetics for dogs.

International Association for Veterinary Homeopathy
334 Knollwood Lane
Woodstock, GA 30188
404-516-5954

International Veterinary Acupuncture Society
P.O. Box 2074
Nederland, CO 80466
303-258-3767

Organizations

Actors Equity Association
165 West 46th Street
New York, NY 10036

Alaska Skijoring and Pulk Association
3126 E. 88th Avenue
Anchorage, AK 99507
907-248-7344

Alaskan Malamute Club of America
8565 Hill Road
Pickerington, OH 43147-9661
614-837-7702

All American Trail Running Association
P.O. Box 9175
Colorado Springs, CO 80932
719-633-9740
719-633-3397 fax
TRLRUNNER@aol.com

Alpha Affiliates
103 Washington Street, Suite 362
Morristown, NJ 07960-6813
201-539-2770

American Border Collie Association
Route 4, Box 255
Perkinston, MS 39573
Attn: Patty A. Rogers, Secretary-Treasurer

American Dog Owners Association
1654 Columbia Turnpike
Castleton, NY 12033
518-477-8469

American Guild of Variety Artists
164 Fifth Avenue
New York, NY 10019

American Herding Breed Association
1548 Victoria Way
Pacifica, CA 94044
650-355-9563
Sheltyherd@aol.com

American Kennel Club (AKC)
5580 Centerview Drive, Suite 200
Raleigh, NC 27606
919-233-9767

or

American Kennel Club (AKC)
51 Madison Avenue
New York, NY 10010-1686
212-696-8260
212-696-8299 fax
http://www.akc.org

American Mixed Breed Obedience Registry
10236 Topanga Boulevard, Suite 205
Chatsworth, CA 91311
ambor@aborusa.org

American Rare Breed Association
9921 Frank Tippett Road
Cheltenham, MD 20623
301-868-5718
arba@erols.com
http://www.arba.org

American Sighthound Field Association
P.O. Box 1293-M
Woodstock, GA 30188
(for general information)

American Sighthound Field Association
1517 Virginia Avenue
Rockford, IL 61103
Attn: Denise Scanlan
(to order pamphlets)

American Society of Composers, Authors and Publishers
(ASCAP)
1 Lincoln Plaza
New York, NY 10019
212-586-2000

American Working Collie Association
c/o Linda C. Rorem
1548 Victoria Way
Pacifica, CA 94044

American Working Terrier Association
503 NC 55 West
Mt. Olive, NC 28465
Attn: Patricia Adams Lent
919-658-0929

Association of Pet Dog Trainers
P.O. Box 385
Davis, CA 95617
800-738-3647
707-745-8310 fax
apdtbod@aol.com

Australian Shepherd Club of America
6091 East State Highway 21
Bryan, TX 77808-9652
409-778-1082
asca@myraid.net

Bernese Mountain Dog Club of America
P.O. Box 956
Grantham, NH 03753-0956
603-795-2458
http://www.barney.org/webcover/cover.html

Border Collie Club of America
c/o Ms. Janet E. Larson, Secretary
6 Pinecrest Lane
Durham, NH 03824

California Rescue Dog Association
1062 Metro Circle
Palo Alto, CA 94303
http://www.crc.ricoh.com/carda/

Delta Society
289 Perimeter Road East
Renton, WA 98055
800-869-6898
206-235-1076 fax
DELTASOCIETY@CIS.COMPUSERVE.COM

Field Representative for AKC
Gordon Heldebrant
2406 Watson Street
Sacramento, CA 95864
916-485-5950

Friskies/ALPO Canine Frisbee Disc Championships
4060-D Peachtree Road, Suite 326
Atlanta, GA 30319
800-786-9240

Greyhound Pets of America
800-366-1472

The Hunting Retriever Club
United Kennel Club, Inc.
100 E. Kilgore Road
Kalamazoo, MI 49002-5584
616-343-9020
or
Multi-Breed Field Operations
616-343-9020

Independent Work and Sport Dog Association
P.O. Box 7272
Olympia, WA 98507

International Council for Sled Dog Sports
P.O. Box 149
Ester, AK 99725
907-479-0454

International Federation of Sled Dog Sports Inc.
7118 N. Beehive Road
Pocatello, ID 83201
Attn: Glenda Walling
208-232-5130

International In-Line Skating Association
301-942-9770

International Rescue Dog Organization
104 Ballantine Road
Bernardsville, NJ 07924
Attn: Caroline Hebard
908-766-7235

International Sled Dog Racing Association (ISDRA)
HC 86 Box 3380
Merrifield, MN 56465
Attn: Dave Steele, Executive Director
dsteele@brainerd.net
218-765-4297
(for membership information)

International Sled Dog Racing Association (ISDRA)
P.O. Box 446
Nordman, ID 83848-0446
208-443-3453
http://uslink.net/~isdra/
(for general information)

International Weight Pulling Association
570 Timber Trail
Stevensville, MT 59870
Attn: Mark Johnson

Landesverband DVG America
5718 Watson Circle
Dallas, TX 75225
Attn: Sandi Purdy, Secretary
http://webusers.anet-stl.com/~dvgamer

Livestock Guarding Dog Association
Hampshire College
Amherst, MA 01002

Love on a Leash
P.O. Box 6308
Oceanside, CA 92058
619-724-8878
ekelley@cts.com

Mixed Breed Dog Club of America
100 Acacia Avenue
San Bruno, CA 94066

Musical Canine Sports International
c/o Sharon Tutt
16665 Parkview Place
Surrey, B.C.
Canada V4N 1Y8
604-581-3641

National Association of Dog Obedience Instructors (NADOI, Inc.)
P.O. Box 432
Landing, NJ 07850

National Association of Search and Rescue
4500 Southgate Place, Suite 100
Chantilly, VA 20151
703-222-6277
703-222-6283 fax
nasar@nasar.org

National Beagle Club
Rover Road
Bedminster, NJ 07921
Attn: Joseph B. Wiley, Secretary

National Capital Air Canines
William Linne, Director
2830 Meadow Lane
Falls Church, VA 22042
703-532-0709
ncac@discdog.com

National Committee for Dog Agility
c/o Bud Kramer
401 Bluemont Circle
Manhattan, KS 66052

National Kennel Club
Route 6, Box 174
Logansport, IN 46947
219-722-9604

National Open Field Coursing Association
P.O. Box 68
Glenrock, WY 82637
Attn: Susan Loop-Stanley, Registrar

Newfoundland Club of America
5208 Olive Road
Raleigh, NC 27606

North American Dog Agility Council
Box 277
St. Maries, ID 83861
208-689-3803

North American Flyball Association
P.O. Box 8
Mt. Hope, Ontario LOR 11W0
Canada

North American Search Dog Network
RR2, Box 32
Urbana, IL 61801

North American Sheep Dog Society
c/o Rossine Kirsh
Route 3
McLeansboro, IL 92859

North American Working Bouvier Association
9101 Cresta Drive
Los Angeles, CA 90035

Professional Retriever Trainer Association
4670 Harbour Hills Drive
Manhattan, KS 66502
Attn: Jane Laman, Secretary

Pup-Peroni Canine Freestylers
Heinz Pet Products
Professional Services
One Riverfront Place
Newport, KY 41071
718-332-8336
718-646-2686
VENAD@AOL.COM

Puppyworks Seminars
P.O. Box 385
Davis, CA 95617
800-PET DOGS
707-745-8310 fax
apdtbod@aol.com

Road Runners Club of America
1150 South Washington Street, Suite 250
Alexandria, VA 22314-4493
703-836-0558
office@rrca.org

St. Bernard Club of America
7572 E 213 Street
Quenemo, KS 66528-8172
913-453-2363
913-453-2451 fax

Screen Actors Guild
5757 Wilshire Boulevard
Los Angeles, CA 90036

SAR Dogs of the United States
P.O. Box 1411
Denver, CO 80211

SAR K-9 Service
P.O. Box 32621
Fridley, MN 55432

States Kennel Club
P.O. Box 389
Hattiesburg, MS 39403-0389
601-583-8345

Therapet
P.O. Box 1696
Whitehouse, TX 75791
Therapet@Juno.com

Therapy Dogs Inc.
P.O. Box 2786
Cheyenne, WY 82003
307-638-3223

Therapy Dogs International
719 Darla Lane
Fallbrook, CA 92028-1505
tdi@gti.net

United Coon Hunters of America, Inc.
Route 4, Box 677
Paoli, IN 47454

United Kennel Club
100 E. Kilgore Road
Kalamazoo, MI 49001-5598
616-343-9020
http://www.ukcdogs.com/

U.S. Border Collie Club
Sunnybrook Farm, Rt. 1 Box 23
White Post, VA 22663
Attn: Ethel B. Conrad, President

U.S. Border Collie Handler's Association
2915 Anderson Lane
Crawford, TX 76638
Attn: Rancis Raley

United States Dog Agility Association
P.O. Box 850955
Richardson, TX 78085-0955

United Schutzhund Clubs of America
3810 Paule Avenue
St. Louis, MO 63125-1718
http://www.dogzone.com/usa/usa.htm

Working Kelpies Inc.
4047 Sheridan S
Minneapolis, MN 55410

Periodicals

Agility Spotlight
SuperNova Productions
P.O. Box 2851
Santa Clara, CA 95055-2851

AKC Coursing News
5580 Centerview Drive
Raleigh, NC 27690-0643

AKC Gazette
American Kennel Club
5580 Centerview Drive, Suite 200
Raleigh, NC 27606-0643
919-233-9780

AKC Hunting Test Herald
372 Wildwood Avenue
Worcester, MA 01603
508-798-2386

Bicycling Magazine
P.O. Box 7592
Red Oak, IA 51591-2592

Bloodlines
100 E. Kilgore Road
Kalamazoo, MI 49001
616-343-9020

Canine Chronicles
Court Square Tower
605 Second Avenue N, Suite 203
Columbus, MS 39701
601-327-1124
601-327-9750 fax

Canine Sports Medicine Update
P.O. Box 351
Newmarket, NH 03857
Attn: Geoffrey N. Clark, D.V.M.

Chronicle of the Horse
P.O. Box 46
Middleburg, VA 22117

Clean Run
Clean Run Productions
35 Walnut Street
Turners Falls, MA 01376-2317
413-863-8303

The Contact Line
Cascade Publications
401 Bluebonnet Circle
Manhattan, KS 66502-4531

Dog Fancy
Fancy Publications
P.O. Box 6050
Mission Viejo, CA 90690
714-855-8822
714-855-3045 fax

DogGone
P.O. Box 651155
Vero Beach, FL 32965-1155
561-569-8434
doggonenl@aol.com

Dog Sports Magazine
32 Cherokee Trail
Douglas, WY 82633-9232
307-358-3487
307-358-3487 fax
dsm@coffey.com

Dog World Magazine
Maclean Hunter Publishing Co.
29 North Wacker Drive
Chicago, IL 60606-3298
312-726-2802
312-726-4103 fax

Equus
656 Quince Orchard Road
Gaithersburg, MD 44112

Field Advisory News
P.O. Box 399
Alpaugh, CA 93201
Attn: Vicky Clarke, Editor

The Finish Line
1002 E. Samuel Avenue
Peoria Heights, IL 61614
Attn: Melanie McAvoy
309-682-7617
mel.davidson@worldnet.att.net

Forward (NADOI, Inc.)
P.O. Box 432
Landing, NJ 07850
Attn: Peggy Prudden, Secretary

Front and Finish
P.O. Box 333
Galesburg, IL 61402-0333
309-344-1333

Full Cry
P.O. Box 10
Boody, IL 62514
217-865-2332
217-865-2334 fax
75701.3464@compuser.com

Good Dog!
Good Communications, Inc.
P.O. Box 31292
Charleston, SC 29417
803-795-9555
803-795-2930 fax

Gun Dog
P.O. Box 343
Mt. Morris, IL 61054-0343
800-435-0715

Horse & Rider
1060 Calle Cordillera, Suite 103
San Clemente, CA 92672

Hunting Retriever
United Kennel Club
100 E. Kilgore Road
Kalamazoo, MI 49002-5584
616-343-9020
http://www.hrc_ukc.com/

INFO
International Sled Dog Racing Association
HC 86 Box 3380
Merrifield, MN 56465
Attn: Dave Steele, Executive Director
dsteele@brainerd.net
218-765-4297
or (continued on next page)

INFO
P.O. Box 446
Nordman, ID 83848-0046
208-443-3453

Mountain Bike Action
25233 Anza Drive
Valencia, CA 91355
805-295-1910
805-295-1278 fax

Mushing
P.O. Box 149
Ester, AK 99725
907-479-0454

Off-Lead
204 Lewis Street
Canastota, NY 13032
315-697-2749
104501.1527@compuserve.com

The Pointing Dog Journal
P.O. Box 936
Manitowoc, WI 54221-0936
800-333-7646

Practical Horseman
Gum Tree Corner
Unionville, PA 19375

The Ranch Dog Trainer
P.O. Box 599
Ellendale, TN 38029-0599

Runner's World Magazine
P.O. Box 7307
Red Oak, IA 51591-0307
800-666-2828
runnerswdm@aol.com

Sheep! Magazine
Route 1
Helenville, WI 53137

The Shepherd's Dogge
The Quarterly Journal of the Border Collie
Box 843
Ithaca, NY 14851-0843
607-659-5868

Team and Trail
P.O. Box 128
Center Harbor, NH 03226

Walking
P.O. Box 5489
Harlan, IA 51593-2989

Western Horseman
P.O. Box 7980
Colorado Springs, CO 80933

The Working Border Collie
14933 Kirkwood Road
Sidney, OH 45365
513-492-2215

Resources: Books

4-M Enterprises
1280 Pacific Street
Union City, CA 94587
800-487-9867
510-489-8331 fax

Alpine Publications, Inc.
214 19th Street SE
Loveland, CO 80537
800-777-7257

Cherrybrook
Route 57, P.O. Box 15
Broadway, NJ 08808
800-524-0820
201-689-7979
201-689-7988 fax

Direct Book Service
Dog & Cat Catalog
P.O. Box 2778
Wenatchee, WA 98897-2778
800-776-2665
509-662-7233 fax

Dog Lovers Bookshop
http://www.dogbooks.com

Flying Dog Press
P.O. Box 290
Stanton, NJ 08885
800-735-9364
908-689-9426
http://www.flyingdogpress.com

Howell Book House
866 Third Avenue
New York, NY 10022
800-257-5755
212-702-3424 fax

OK Publications
P.O. Box 84302
Fairbanks, AK 99507
907-488-6854

Publisher's Book Distributors
800-47-CLICK

Raymond Thompson Co.
15815 Second Place, West
Lynwood, WA 98036

Resources: General

Care-A-Lot
Pet Supply Warehouse
1617 Diamond Springs Road
Virginia Beach, VA 23455
800-343-7680
804-460-0317 fax

Cool Paw Productions
708 E. Solana Drive
Tempe, AZ 85281
800-650-PAWS

Discount Master
Humboldt Industrial Park
1 Maplewood Drive
Hazleton, PA 18201-9798
800-346-0749

Drs. Foster & Smith Inc.
P.O. Box 100
Rhinelander, WI 54501-0100
800-826-7206

Dog Power
Power Bone
505-822-8432
888-364-7693

Doggie-Sox
P.O. Box 669
Green Lake, WI 54941
920-294-6719

Endo
Extreme HPD dog running shoes
801-281-1331

J-B Wholesale Pet Supplies Inc.
5 Raritan Road
Oakland, NJ 07436
800-526-0388
800-788-5005 fax

Jake's Dog House
P.O. Box 3748
Cherry Hill, NJ 08034
800-734-5253

Jeffers Vet Supply
P.O. Box 948
West Plains, MO 65775
800-533-3377

Kosica Enterprises
Bo-Boots
P.O. Box 10834
Marrillville, IN 46411
219-942-0500

Lewis Dog Boot
P.O. Box 10572
Enid, OK 73706
405-237-1292

My Dog Book
Mr. Woofey's
P.O. Box 368
Ahwahnee, CA 93601-0368
888-672-6364
woofey@woofeys.com
http://www.woofey.com

Pedigrees
1989 Transit Way
Box 905
Brockport, NY 14420-0905
800-528-4786

Pet Warehouse
P.O. Box 310
Xenia, OH 4542
800-443-1160

Premier Pet Products
2406 Krossridge Road
Richmond, VA 23236
800-933-5595

R.C. Steele
1989 Transit Way
Box 910
Brockport, NY 14420-0910
800-872-3773

Show Quality Pet Products
601 Excelsior Avenue East
Hopkins, MN 55343
612-933-7758

Sylmar Dogwear
22710 S.E. 23rd Place
Issaquah, WA 98027
800-592-6996

That Pet Place
237 Centerville Road
Lancaster, PA 17603
800-733-3829 phone and fax

UPCO
P.O. Box 969
St. Joseph, MO 64502
800-444-8651

Valley Vet Supply
East Highway 36
P.O. Box 504
Marysville, KS 66508-0504
800-360-4838

Wholesale Pet USA
P.O. Box 325
Topsfield, MA 01983
800-4-PET-USA
800-329-6372 fax

Videos

Some of the following listings do not contain complete information. Every effort was made to list all the pertinent information for each book. However, if your bookstore or library does not have these items, all are available either through the above-mentioned book resources, general dog-related catalogs, or through the publishers.

American Kennel Club. *200?* Available from AKC, 5580 Centerview Drive, Suite 200, Raleigh, NC 27606; 919-233-9767.

Bloeme, Peter. *Peter Bloeme's Frisbee Dogs: Training Video.* Skyhoundz, 1994.

————. *Peter Bloeme's Frisbee Dogs: Throwing Video.* Skyhoundz, 1996.

Broitman & Lippman. *Take a Bow . . . Wow! Fun and Functional Dog Tricks.* 1996.

Brucker, Jeffrey. *Show Dogs.*

Cycle Canine Freestylers in Action. Freestyle Video, Ventre Advertising, Inc. P.O. Box 350122, Brooklyn, NY 11235, 718-332-8336 or 718-646-2686. Ventre Advertising offers several videos.

Dondino, Cheryl. *Carting.* Available from Harmony Enterprises, 20600 S.W. Johnson, Aloha, OR 97006, 503-591-9187.

Haggerty, Captain. *Dog Tricks with Captain Haggerty.* 1996.

Handler, Barbara. *Successful Obedience Handling: The NEW Best Foot Forward.* Loveland, CO: Alpine Publishing, 1995.

Kemp, Michael. *Handling I, Basic.* 1993.

———. *Handling II, Advanced.* 1993.

Lithgow, Scott. *How to Get the Most from Your Working Dog.* 1991.

Moore. *Dog Tricks.*

Ostrander, Beth. *An Introduction to Canine Carting.*

Pryor, Karen. *Clicker Magic.* 1997.

Simmons-Moake, Jane. *Competitive Agility Training—Agility Obstacle Training.* Center for Studies in College, 1997.

———. *Competitive Agility Training—Agility Sequence Training.* Center for Studies in College, 1997.

———. *Competitive Agility Training—Advanced Agility Skills Training.* Center for Studies in College, 1997.

Stopper & Watts. *Search Dog Training: How to Get Started.* 1996.

Wilkes, Gary. *On Target!* 1993.

Winn, Steve. *Stock Dog Training.* Barker Photography & Video. 3711 E. 29th Street, Bryan, TX 77802, 800-635-6144.

Winton. *Yes! You can Teach Your Dog Tricks and Have Fun, Too!* 1997.

Bibliography

Some of the following listings do not contain complete information. Every effort was made to list all the pertinent information for each book. However, if your bookstore or library does not have these items, all are available either through the above-mentioned book resources, general dog-related catalogs, or through the publishers.

Acker, Randy, and Jim Fergus. *Field Guide: Dog First Aid Emergency Care for the Hunting, Working and Outdoor Dog*. Wilderness Adventure Press, 1997.

Alston, George, and Connie Vanacore. *The Winning Edge: Show Ring Secrets*. New York: Howell Book House, 1992.

American Sighthound Field Association. *The Sport of Lure Coursing*. Rockford, IL: ASFA. (free)

———. *Guidelines for Judges*. Rockford, IL: ASFA. (free)

———. *Guidelines for Lure Coursing Practice*. Rockford, IL: ASFA. (free)

———. *Guidelines for Course Design*. Rockford, IL: ASFA.

Arnold, Terri. *Steppin' Up to Success: Book 1—Theory, Footwork, Handling and Attention*. Freetown, Mass.: Steppin' Up, 1996.

———. *Steppin' Up to Success: Book 2—Novice*. Freetown, Mass.: Steppin' Up, 1996.

————. *Steppin' Up to Success: Book 3—Open and Utility*. Freetown, Mass.: Steppin' Up, 1996.

Baer, Ted. *How to Teach Your Old Dog New Tricks*. Hauppauge, N.Y.: Barron's Educational Series, Inc., 1991.

Bailey, Joan. *How to Help Gun Dogs Train Themselves: Taking Advantage of Early Training*. Hillsboro, Oreg.: Swan Valley Press, 1992.

Barish, Eileen. *Vacationing with Your Pet*. Scottsdale, Ariz.: Pet Friendly Productions, 1997.

Barwig, Susan, and Stewart Hilliard. *Schutzhund: Theory and Training Methods*. New York: Howell Books, 1991.

Bauman, Diane L. *Beyond Basic Dog Training*. New York: Howell Book House, 1991.

Bayley, Lesley, and Caroline Davis. *The Less-Than-Perfect Rider: Overcoming Common Riding Problems*. New York: Howell Book House, 1994.

Beaman, Arthur S. *Lure Coursing: Field Trialing for Sighthounds and How to Take Part*. New York: Howell Book House, 1994.

Benjamin, Carol Lea. *Mother Knows Best: The Natural Way to Train Your Dog*. New York: Howell Book House, 1985.

————. *The Second-Hand Dog: How to Turn Yours into a First-Rate Pet*. New York: Howell Book House, 1988.

————. *Surviving Your Dog's Adolescence: A Positive Training Program*. New York: Howell Book House, 1993.

Bennet, Bill. *Beagle Training Basics: The Care, Training and Hunting of the Beagle*. Wilsonville, Oreg.: Doral Publishing, 1995.

Bloeme, Peter. *Frisbee Dog: How to Raise, Train and Compete*. Atlanta, Ga.: PRB & Associates, 1994.

Boggs, Bernard. *Succeeding with Pointing Dogs, Field Trials and Hunting Tests*. Dogs Unlimited, 1989.

Booth, Shiela. *Schutzhund Obedience: Training in Drive with Gottfied Dildei*. Ridgefield, Conn.: Podium Publications, 1995.

Branigan, Cynthia. *Adopting the Racing Greyhound*. New York: Howell Book House, 1992.

Brown, Curtis M. *Dog Locomotion and Gait Analysis*. Wheat Ridge, Colo.: Donald R. Hoflin, 1986.

Bryson, Sandy. *Search Dog Training*. Pacific Grove, Calif.: Boxwood Press, 1991.

Buechting, LaVerne. *Beginning Conformation Training*. St. Louis: Kennelwood Village, 1989.

Bulanda. *Ready! Training the Search and Rescue Dog*. Wilsonville, Oreg.: Doral Publishing, 1994.

Burnham, Patricia Gail. *Playtraining Your Dog*. New York: St. Martin's Press, 1980.

Button, Lue. *Practical Scent Dog Training*. Loveland, Colo.: Alpine Publications, 1990.

Clean Run Productions. *Introductory Agility Workbook*. Turners Falls, Mass.: Clean Run Productions, 1996.

———. *Intermediate Agility Workbook* Turners Falls, Mass.: Clean Run Productions, 1996.

———. *Advanced Agility Workbook*. Turners Falls, Mass.: Clean Run Productions, 1997.

Clothier, Suzanne. *The Clothier Natural Jumping Method*. Stanton, N.J.: Flying Dog Press.

Coile, Caroline D. *Show Me! A Dog Show Primer*. Hauppauge, N.Y.: Barron's Educational Series, 1997.

Collins, Miki, and Julie Collins. *Dog Driver: A Guide for the Serious Musher*. Loveland, Colo.: Alpine Publications, 1991.

Daniels, Julie. *Enjoying Dog Agility from Backyard to Competition.* Wilsonville, Oreg.: Doral Publishing, 1991.

Davis, Kathy Diamond. *Therapy Dogs.* New York: Howell Book House, 1992.

Davis, L. Wilson. *Go Find! Training Your Dog to Track.* New York: Howell Book House, Inc., 1984.

DeBitetto, James, D.V.M., and Sarah Hodgson. *You & Your Puppy: Training and Health Care for Puppy's First Year.* New York: Howell Book House, 1995.

Donaldson, Jean. *Culture Clash: A Revolutionary New Way of Understanding the Relationship Between Humans and Domestic Dogs.* Berkeley, Calif.: James & Kenneth Publishers, 1996.

Elliot, Rachel Page. *The New Dogsteps.* New York: Howell Book House, 1988.

Evans, Job Michael. *Training and Explaining: How to Be the Dog Trainer You Want to Be.* New York: Howell Book House, 1995.

Falk, John R. *Gun Dogs: Master Training Series.* Stillwater, Minn.: Voyageur Press, 1997.

Feineman, Neil. *Wheel Excitement! The Official Rollerblade® Guide to In-Line Skating.* New York: Hearst Books, 1991.

Fishback, Lee. *Training Lead Dogs.* Tun-Dra.

Fishback, Lee, and Mel Fishback. *Novice Sled Dog Training.* Lynwood, Wash.: Raymond Thomson Company, 1989.

Fisher, John. *Dogwise: The Natural Way to Train Your Dog.* London: Souvenir Press, Ltd., 1992.

Flanders, Noel K. *The Joy of Running Sled Dogs.* Loveland, Colo.: Alpine Publications, 1989.

Fox, Michael. *The Healing Touch.* New York: Newmarket Press, 1990.

Fraser, Jacqueline, and Amy Ammen. *Dual Ring Dog: Successful Training for Both Conformation & Obedience Competition.* New York: Howell Book House, 1991.

Friskies. *Ashley Whippet® Catch a Flying Disc Dog Training System®.* Send a self-addressed, stamped envelope to Friskies Training Manual, P.O. Box 2092, Young America, MN. 55553-2902 for this free booklet.

Gallup, Davia Anne. *Running with Man's Best Friend.* Loveland, Colo.: Alpine Publications, 1986.

Ganz, Sandy, and Susan Boyd. *Tracking from the Ground Up.* Show-Me Publications.

Gorman, Stephen. *The AMC Guide to Winter Camping, Backcountry Tenting and Travel in the Cold-Weather Months.* Martinsville, Ind.: AMC Books, 1991.

Haggerty, Arthur J. *How to Get Your Pet into Show Business.* New York: Howell Book House, 1994.

Hall, Lynn. *Dog Showing for Beginners.* New York: Howell Book House, 1994.

Hatley, George. *Horse Camping.* Moscow, Idaho: The Appaloosa Museum, 1992.

Hawcroft, Tim. *First Aid for Dogs: The Essential Quick-Reference Guide.* New York: Howell Book House, 1994.

Hill, Cherry. *Becoming an Effective Rider: Developing Your Mind and Body for Balance and Unity.* Pownal, Vt.: Garden Way Publishing, 1991.

Hobday, Ruth. *Agility Is Fun!* Manchester, England: "Our Dogs" Publishing Co., 1989.

Hoe-Raitto, Mari, and Carol Kaynor. *Skijor with Your Dog.* Fairbanks, AK: OK Publishing, 1991.

Hogan, Julie, and Donna Thompson. *Practical Tracking for Practically Everyone.*

Holland, Vergil S. *Herding Dogs—Progressive Training.* New York: Howell Book House, 1994.

Holmes, John. *The Farmer's Dog.* London: Popular Dogs Publishing Co.

Hunter, Roy. *Fun Nosework for Dogs.* Eliot, Maine: Howlin' Moon Press, 1995.

Johnson, Glen. *Tracking Dog: Theory and Methods.* Arner Publications, 1975.

Kaynor, Carol, and Mari Hoe-Raitto. *Skijoring: An Introduction to the Sport.* Fairbanks, AK: OK Publishing, 1992.

Kita, Joe, ed. *Bicycling Magazine's New Bike Owner's Guide.* Emmaus, Penn.: Rodale Press, 1990.

LaBelle, Charlene. *A Guide to Backpacking with Your Dog.* Loveland, Colo.: Alpine Publications, 1993.

Lerner, Richard, D.V.M. *The Nuts 'n' Bolts Guide: Backpacking with Your Dog.* Birmingham, Ala.: Menasha Ridge Press, 1994.

Levorsen, Bella, ed. *Mush! A Beginner's Manual of Sled Dog Training.* Sierra Nevada Dog Drivers, Inc. Canastota, N.Y.: Arner Publications, 1976.

Lithgow, Scott. *Training and Working Dogs for Quiet, Confident Control of Stock.* Manchester, N.H.: University of Queensland Press, 1991.

Ludwig, Gerd. *Fun and Games with Your Dog.* Hauppauge, N.Y.: Barron's Educational Series, 1996.

Marlewski-Probert, Bonnie. *The Animal Lovers Guide to the Internet.* Red Bluff, Calif.: K&B Products, 1997.

Mason, Robert L. *The Ultimate Beagle: The Natural Born Rabbit Dog.* Centreville, Ala.: OTR Publications, 1997.

Bibliography

Masson, Jeffrey Moussaieff. *Dogs Never Lie about Love: Reflections on the Emotional World of Dogs*. New York: Crown Publishers, Inc., 1997.

Migliorini, Mario. *Dig In! Earthdog Training Made Easy*. New York: Howell Book House, 1997.

Milani, Myrna M., D.V.M. *The Body Language and Emotion of Dogs*. New York: William Morrow, 1986.

Mulak, Steven J. *Pointing Dogs Made Easy: How to Train, Nurture, and Appreciate Your Bird Dog*. Country Sport Press, 1995.

Nealy, William. *Mountain Bike! A Manual of Beginning to Advanced Techniques*. Boulder, Colo.: VeloNews Books, 1992.

Noakes, Timothy D. *Lore of Running*. Champaign, Ill.: Human Kinetics Publishing, 1991.

Parkin, Jacqueline. *Flyball Training . . . Start to Finish*.

Payne, Joan. *Flying High: The Complete Book of Flyball*.

Pearsall, Milo D., and Hugo Vergruggen, M.D. *Scent: Training to Track, Search and Rescue*. Loveland, Colo.: Alpine Publications, 1982.

Pitcairn, Richard H., D.V.M., Ph.D., and Susan Hubble Pitcairn. *Dr. Pitcairn's Natural Health for Dogs and Cats*. Emmaus, Pa.: Rodale Press, 1982.

Powell, Consie. *Newfoundland Draft Work*.

Powell, Mark. *Qualify! A Guide to Successful Handling in AKC Pointing Breed Hunting Tests*. Houston, Tex.: Attwater Publishing, 1995.

Powell, Roger. *The Draft Equipment Guide*. Newfoundland Club of America Working Dog Committee.

Pryor, Karen. *Don't Shoot the Dog: The New Art of Teaching and Training*. New York: Bantam Books, 1994.

———. *How to Teach Your Dog to Play Frisbee*. New York: Simon & Schuster, 1985.

Reed, John Avalon. *The Whole Dog Catalog*. New York: Three Rivers Press, 1997.

Reid, Pamela J., *Excel-erated Learning*. Oakland, Calif.: James & Kenneth Publishers, 1996.

Rooks, Robert L., D.V.M., and Connie Jankowski. *Canine Orthopedics*. New York: Howell Book House, 1997.

Savoie, Jane. *That Winning Feeling!* North Pomfret, Vt.: Trafalgar Square Publishing, 1992.

Shearer, Tamara S., and Stanford Apseloff. *Emergency First Aid for Your Dog*. Columbus, Ohio: Ohio Distinctive Publishing, 1996.

Simmons-Moake, Jane. *Agility Training: The Fun Sport for All Dogs*. New York: Howell Book House, 1991.

Smith, Cheryl S. *On the Trail with Your Canine Companion: Getting the Most Out of Hiking and Camping with Your Dog*. New York: Howell Book House, 1996.

Taggart, Mari. *Sheepdog Training—An All Breed Approach*. Loveland, Colo.: Alpine Publications, 1991.

Tarrant, Bill. *Gun Dog Training: New Strategies from Today's Top Trainers*. Stillwater, Minn.: Voyageur Press, 1996.

———. *Gun Dogs: Humane Way to Get Top Results*. Stockpole Books, 1989.

Tatsch, Kenneth A. *Construction Plans for Dog Agility Obstacles*. 1995.

Tellington-Jones, Linda. *TTouch for Dogs and Puppies*. La Quinta, Calif.: Thane Marketing International, 1994.

Templeton, John, with Matt Mundell. *Working Sheepdogs Management and Training*. New York: Howell Book House.

Volhard, Wendy. *Canine Good Citizen*. New York: Howell Book House, 1984.

Bibliography

Volhard, Wendy, and Kerry Brown, D.V.M. *The Holistic Guide for a Healthy Dog*. New York: Howell Book House, 1995.

Walters, Heather MacLean. *Take Your Pet Too!* MCE, 1997.

Weston, David. *Dog Training: The Gentle Modern Method*. New York: Howell Book House, 1990.

Wycoff, Joyce. *Mind Mapping: Your Personal Guide to Exploring Creativity and Problem-Solving*. New York: Berkeley, 1991.

Zeigenfuse and Walker. *Dog Tricks: Step by Step*. 1997.

Zink, M. Christine, D.V.M., Ph.D., and Julie Daniels. *Jumping from A to Z: Teach Your Dog to Soar*. Luterville, Md.: Canine Sports Productions, 1996.

———. *Peak Performance: Coaching the Canine Athlete*. New York: Howell Book House, 1992.

Index

Index

Index